Good Morning!! How Are My College Buddies?

By Rev. LaVon Post

Copyright © 2008 by Rev. LaVon Post

Good Morning!! How Are My College Buddies?
by Rev. LaVon Post

Printed in the United States of America

ISBN 978-1-60477-641-6

All rights reserved solely by the author. The author guarantees all contents are original and do not infringe upon the legal rights of any other person or work. No part of this book may be reproduced in any form without the permission of the author. The views expressed in this book are not necessarily those of the publisher.

Unless otherwise indicated, Bible quotations are taken from The New International Version (NIV) of the Bible. Copyright © 1984 by Zondervan Publishing House.

www.xulonpress.com

To Bently,
   Best Wishes and Congratulations. May you all your dreams come truth.
   Love You,
   Aunt Mim
   July 27, 2010

Dedication

To the world's greatest daughters, Shelley and Amber......and to Crystal, Tiffany and Brittany......and to Ami, who lit up a room with her smile.

Preface

In 1997, I learned that an empty nest is incredibly miserable! Shelley, my oldest daughter, had already left for college and my youngest daughter, Amber, had just left for Duke University. I missed both of them terribly. I would send them a Bible verse each day and a short note.

At the same time, I was appointed as the pastor of the First United Methodist Church in DeWitt, Arkansas. There were 17 college students in that church and over the next few months, I got to know them. I was amazed at the quality of these young adults, they were excellent Christians and their lives displayed a character of class.

I didn't think it would work, but I decided to send them a short note and a Bible verse. I would send one note to Amber, then forward it 17 times to the other college students. I had no idea that you could send them all at once! :-)

Good Morning!! How Are My College Buddies?

I was amazed at the response! Not only did they read them, they forwarded it to their friends at college. I started getting requests to add names from fraternities and sororities, college kids whom I knew only as an e-mail address. Soon the Arkansas statewide newspaper and some radio stations did interviews with me regarding this new ministry, and the mailing list continued to grow. Today, a conservative guess is that the devotional goes out to 6,000 people around the country.

The Lord gave me an assurance in my heart in 1998. He assured me that if I would give my heart to these college kids, He would take care of my daughters. And He has done just that, Shelley is a nurse working in a facility for people with special needs and Amber just graduated a year ago with her PhD in physics from Princeton University.

I hope you enjoy the devotionals. It's practical stuff, not lofty theological principles. I hope the devotionals give you hope in your tough times. Mostly, I hope it helps you understand how deeply and intensely our Father adores all of His kids.

Rev. LaVon Post
January, 2008

Table of Contents

"Don't let your dreams become dusty and
  tarnished." 21
"I'll lean on you and you lean on me and we'll be
  okay." 22
"Move your Dr. Pepper can today." 23
"Shine a bright, glaring spotlight on your fear." 24
"Your Sermon is in Your Storm." 26
Maybe you're praying for the wrong thing." 28
"Sometimes We Should Be Angry…Just Like
  Jesus." 29
"Ticked Off Under a Shade Tree." 31
"Keep water in your basin and a towel handy." 33
"Divine Brakes" 35
"Singing in a Wasteland" 37
"It's hard being human." 39
"Sleeping With Hubert On My Pillow" 41
"Divine TLC.'" 43
"I want my warm nest back!!" 45
"In God's mind, the problem is already solved." ...47

Good Morning!! How Are My College Buddies?

"A North Carolina Life Sermon" 48
"Unfair Expectations"..49
"An Expert in Agape Love." 50
"Lord, help me to be an eagle. Lord stop me from
    being a crow." 52
"I'm tired of waiting, I can fix this." 54
"I'll turn the water into wine, you just
    fill the pots." 56
"Three Crucial Questions" 57
"Our Father is an Expert Orthopedist." 58
"I know you're tired…I know you're rattled…
    Let's rest a while." 60
"Turning on a Dime?" 62
"Soaring…….Running……..Trudging" 64
"A Trapped Angel" 66
"I feel so helpless!! I wish I could
    do something!!" 68
"A Cleansed Conscience" 70
"I Don't Have Any Problems." 71
"When someone loves you, your name is safe in
    their mouth." 73
"Blessing a Doubter" 74
"The Disaster of Partial Forgiveness" 76
"There is no limit to what God will do,
    if we refuse to take the credit." 78
"We never disappoint God by asking too much,
    we disappoint Him by asking too little." 80
"The nets did not break…they were stretched
    to the limit, but they did NOT break."
    (John 11:13) 82
'The Ministry of the Magnifying Glass' 84

Good Morning!! How Are My College Buddies?

"Totally irrelevant, it doesn't matter, it changes nothing." 86
"Fiercely Protective." 88
"Give her a call.' 90
"Break Open Your Bottle" 91
"Walking Wet" 92
"Counting to Ten with God." 93
"Inventing a Terrifying Monster." 94
"Up to your neck." 95
"Ministering in the Background" 96
"As Christians, someday we will have to answer to God for every sin that we have committed, either in our thoughts or by our actions." 97
"I believe that friends are quiet angels who lift us to our feet when our wings have trouble remembering how to fly." 99
"Thanks for the Sermon" 100
"I know what it feels like; I will help you." 102
"Amazing Potential" 104
"Lord, calm me down on the inside because I can't slow down on the outside!" 106
"Meltdown Recovery." 108
"A Temporary Separation…Not a Permanent Loss." 110
"Spiritual Friendship" 112
"Take off the Judicial robes, God doesn't need your help." 113
"Super Sensitive Days" 115
"The weight of another person will make your steps secure." 117
"Put your sword away. I will take care of this." .. 119
"A blessing delayed is not a blessing denied." 121

"Walking Blind" 123
"That's not what I said! You're twisting everything!" 125
"Sometimes God's love is a gentle whisper...
...Other times, His love is a loud shout from heaven." 126
"Father, make them a walking visual aid to your power." 128
"Roadblock Ahead" 130
"Wounds and Scars" 131
"The Pitfalls of Fatigue" 133
"Waiting Without a Clue." 134
"Agape love is not myopic." 136
"Don't throw in the towel." 138
"Monday Morning Praying." 140
"He's concerned about His reputation." 141
"How dare you try to harm my child!" 143
"Lighten up, ok?" 145
"God doesn't scare His kids.'" 147
"Jumping Scared" 148
"Spiritual Magnets" 149
"A terrifying but harmless roar." 150
"Resentment...Separation...Retaliation...
Recruitment" 151
"Relish it...Revel in it...Remember it." 153
"You Are a Masterpiece" 154
"Pray.......Keep Praying.......Even when you're faith is weak and battered." 155
"Doubt Your Doubt" 157
"The God of a Second Chance" 159
A message from your Father: "Your worst nightmare? It's not going to happen." 160

"A Step by Step Blessing" 162
"Scary stuff on the outside…anxious dread
   on the inside." 163
"I do not want to do this." 164
"Agape love causes us to climb down from the
   pedestal." 166
"Feasting in the Dining Hall…….or……Working
   on the Deck." 168
"Oil on a Rusty Hinge" 170
"Weeping and Venting" 171
"Verbal Junk - Letting It Go" 173
"Don't trust in a raven…trust in the God of the
   raven." 175
"Don't be ashamed of your 'soul scars'" 176
"A Strong Faith…….A Churning Heart." 177
"Let God be God." 179
"Praying Without a Clue." 180
"Relax my Child, have I ever let you down?" 182
"Be Careful - Thin Ice" 184
"Not Me!! I Can't!!" 185
"A Blessing in the 'Blah Months.'" 187
"God's Circle of Rescue" 189
"Lord, help me to clap and cheer." 191
"Stumbling or Straying." 193
"The lousier the day, the sweeter
   the blessing." 195
'Mountaintop Experiences' are great!!" 196
"When Life Becomes a Dry, Dusty Desert." 197
"Transfer Frustration" 199
"A Hug From the Heart." 200
"He remembers how weak we are, He knows
   how tough it is." 202

"How Weak We Are" 204
"Love Them Stubbornly." 205
"Maybe It's Right Under Your Nose.' 206
"Stewing." 208
"Pre-Blessing, Imagined Disasters." 209
"Thinking is also spiritual." 210
"Get apart or fall apart." 211
"Divine Coincidences." 212
"There is no way He would lie about it." 213
"God...Money." 215
"Give Them a Verbal Vitamin." 217
"It really DOES matter." 218
"The crocodiles may have circled the basket,
 but the crocodiles were not allowed to
 touch the basket." 220
"Stop Being So Full of Yourself." 222
"How well do you 'duck and hide?'" 224
"Don't contribute to fracturing your family." 225
"Maximizing the Trivial." 226
"You don't have to say EXACTLY what is
 on your mind!" 227
"If you live your life without compassion,
 your life will become a dry, barren desert." ...228
"The Agony of Waiting." 229
"Abandoning the Ship" 231
"God nudges more than He pushes." 233
"Caught Between Two Ticked Off People" 234
"A Travel Agent for Guilt Trips." 235
"FORGIVEN...REMOVED......
 FORGOTTEN" 237
"Reshape, Not Ruin" 239
"She was an 'Expert at Rejoicing.'" 241

'Rushing Away From an Opportunity.' 243
"Spiritual Crosswinds" 245
"Thinking vs. Doing" 247
"Leo, Could You Hurry Up?" 249
"Lord Jesus, you can have my sack lunch." 250
"The Swirling Vat of Discontentment" 252
"You're not important so it doesn't matter how
    I speak to you or treat you." 253
"How Well Do You Smell?" :-) 255
"You'll be fine; God will take care of you." 257
"Just because we don't know what He is
    doing does not mean that HE does not know
    what He is doing!" 259
"Nagging' 'Stewing' 'Terror" 260
"Maybe you're wearing the wrong yoke." 262
"Know where you're weak, know who
    can help." 263
"Levels of Thanksgiving" 264
"Like a mother humming a lullaby, God
    whispers gently to His children. Listen for the
    whispers of God - let them give you rest and
    peace." 265
"Praying doesn't help much, praying mixed
    with believing does wonders." 266
"Lose the word 'lucky.'" 267
"Ruining a Good Funeral" 269
"Trust In His Heart" 270
"You're trying to serve the Lord, but look at your
    problems! It seems like God promised you
    blessings, but He has only given you
    burdens. Is it really worth it?" 272
"Come back to Me…Come as you are." 274

"The Boring Habit of Praying Safely." 275
"Brutally Honest." 277
"Let Your Nets Down…Today" 279
"A Spiritual Tug of War." 280
"Father, I ask you this for your Name's sake." 281
"God does not scare His kids." 283
"Highlight The Strength!" 285
"Pain and a Pearl" 286
"Borrowing Tomorrow's Trouble." 287
"The First Step" 288
"Open up the faucet." 289
"I don't want to, but I have to." 290
"Stop badmouthing yourself…you're talking about my child." 291
'Tear down the Facade of Perfection.' 293
"God doesn't miss the runway." 295
"Having trouble forgiving someone?" 296
"Join the Club!" 298
"As Pure as Jesus." 299
"Could have happened…Should have happened …Didn't happen." 301
"The Sour Suspicion of a Cynical Person." 302
"Dear Lord, please help me to be more stubborn." 304
"A Foul Weather Faith." 306
"Falls are not Fatal…Failures are not Permanent" 308
"Walk Toward the Blessing" 310
Fulfillment: "I can do this. I enjoy doing this. This is what I'm supposed to do, what God wants me to do." 311
"Function in the Fire." 313

Good Morning!! How Are My College Buddies?

"Flying Without Fear"..315
"Dream Monsters" 316
"Misreading the Mirror." 317
"The School of Lingering Burdens" 319
"Walk this way, I know it's scary, but it's
    perfectly safe. God will soon bless you." 321
"God's power is not limited by the lack of fair
    play." 323
"Intensely Loved." 325
"Job's Comforters." 327
"Love just won't let go." 329
"The Miserable Interval." 330
"On a Need to Know Basis" 332
"Their life plans were ruined, their hopes were
    dashed, and their future was scary!" 333
"To be a burden bearer, you have to have a
    burden of your own." 335
"It's better to light your candle than to curse the
    darkness." 337
"Looking into the eyes of someone you have
    helped." 339
"If you try to do God's work on the outside
    without having God's love on the inside,
    you do a lot more damage than good!" 341
"'From' and 'Out Of.'" 343
"I'll keep reminding you…and I won't stop." 344
"A Blessing in Installments." 346
"Hope and Compassion." 347
"Walk, Not Drown" 349
"What goes around, comes around. I can't
    wait to see them get it!" 351
"Be gentle…Be gentle…Be gentle." 352

"FEAR. DREAD. PRESSURE…" 353
"A Simmering Burn." 355
"Behind every Former Failure is a God-sent
    Barnabus." 356
"Look for a Love Token" 358
"The Take It Back Test." 359
"Sometimes we can't see the forest for
    the trees." 361
"He was standing to show His concern, His
    compassion and His power." 362
"The mountain is not as high as you thought,
    once you start climbing it." 363
"God rarely fixes things in fifteen minutes." 364
"God, save me from myself…especially on a day
    like today!" 366
"Crossroads of Faith." 367
"Praise the Master, not the brushes." 369
"Scaring the Heck Out of Ourselves'" 370
"Lord, help me to back off." 372
"Who Do You Think You Are?!" 373
"Faith, not Feelings." 374
"You lean on me and I'll lean on you and we
    will be ok." 375
"Pre-Blessing, Imagined Disasters." 377
"911 Christians" 378
"Please try again." 380
"Pray yourself to sleep." 381
Always remember this: "Sometimes, it's not what
    you're saying, it's how you're saying it." 382
"Lord, help me stop this RIGHT NOW." 383
"I have a right to this!!" 384
"Naive to believe it, foolish to pass it on." 385

"Unseen Protectors"..386
"The Room of Unanswered Questions."..............387
"Repair Specialist"..388
"A Transfusion of Hope" 390
"All of us occasionally get a case of
   the 'Frenzies'."...391
"Think About It Carefully…You're Making
   a Huge Mistake" 392
"As Low As It Gets." 394
"Speak kind words and you will hear
   kind echoes."..396
"Hold their head up." 397
"Through a Lover's Kind and Gentle Eyes."........398
"A Dad Thing" 400
"<u>Confused</u> is Good. <u>Bewildered</u> is very Good.
   <u>Helpless</u> is excellent." 402
"You can hide, but the Lord will find you.".........403
"What's Behind the Door?!"................................404
"Look at the Big Picture."....................................405
"You can't live your life without getting hurt."...406
"The Ghost of Past Sins" 407
"'It Never Fluctuates"..408
"A Grace Encounter" 409
"To the world you might be one person, but
   to one person you might be the world.".........411
"Go ahead and peek, you'll be pleased." 412
"You First." 413
"The clinging hand of His child makes a
   desperate situation a delight to Him.".............415
"Human sweat never made a rainbow. When you
   think about it, it makes little sense to try to
   impress God." 417

"Don't give up on your day, the Lord can salvage it." 419
"You can't love someone on an empty tank." 421
"DECISIONS! WHAT TO DO AT THE CROSSROADS OF LIFE " 422
"Breakable!! - Handle With Care" 429

"Don't let your dreams become dusty and tarnished."

Many times, before the Lord sends a special blessing, He gives you an inner desire or longing for that blessing. This is God's way of leading you, nudging you to trust Him and believe that He will send it. Now the Lord could just drop the blessing immediately, but He rarely does that. He 'nudges' us, He encourages us and then He sends the blessing step be step.

The risk is that we may look at the obstacles and cringe, then we store away the dream, rationalize that it may happen some day, but not now. That's when our dream becomes dusty and tarnished. Imagine your Heavenly Father in front of you, encouraging you: "Trust me, my child, use your faith, you will see that I will not let you down." At His perfect time, the full blessing will come and you will be amazed at your Father's goodness:

"Commit your way to the Lord, trust also in him and he WILL BRING IT TO PASS."
Psalm 37:5

Love You!!   Praying for You!!   Proud of You!!   Bro. Post
✶✶✶✶✶✶✶✶✶✶✶✶✶✶✶✶✶✶✶✶

Good Morning!! How Are My College Buddies?

"I'll lean on you and you lean on me and we'll be okay."

College Buddies, there is one American cultural tendency that will cost you dearly: "Individualism." You know, "I am the Captain of my fate"…Ridiculous. God never intended for Christians to 'go it alone' in life. Individualism will leave you alone in times of deep distress because you won't share your burden with others. 'Going it alone' gets old when you don't have friends to share your happiness. Individualism will keep you out of church because you will deceive yourself into believing that all you need is just you and God.

The Family of God is not a chain of individual islands; it is a close knit continent with each member linked together, dependent upon each other. The older I get, the more I realize the truth of this statement: "Friends are God's way of taking care of us."

"And let us consider how to provoke one another to love and good deeds, not neglecting to meet together, as is the habit of some, but encouraging one another…" Hebrews 10:24-25

Love You!!   Praying for You!!   Proud of You!!   Bro. Post

✶✶✶✶✶✶✶✶✶✶✶✶✶✶✶✶✶✶✶✶✶

Good Morning!! How Are My College Buddies?

"Move your Dr. Pepper can today."

When my youngest daughter wanted to learn to ride her new bike, she announced that she would learn and then ride it around the house, all in one day. (Typical Type A! :-) She tried about 20 times, I would start her and then it would end in a spectacular crash! After each try, I noticed she was riding a little further. She was about to quit in discouragement, so I placed a Dr. Pepper can in the yard, then encouraged her to try only riding past it, to forget about riding around the house. She rode her bike shakily past the can, lost control, then crashed. But this time she pops back up, looks excitedly at me, "Daddy, did I move the Dr. Pepper can?!" In a couple of days, she had reached her goal.

The difference was that she was now looking at her PROGRESS instead of the FRUSTRATION of not yet reaching her goal. College Buddies, there are a lot of goals you are striving to achieve, you will achieve them, but you won't reach them today. HOWEVER, you can move your Dr. Pepper can! Ask God to help you rejoice as you get nearer a goal, don't wait until you have totally reached the goal to be happy:

> "Our steps are made firm by the Lord and he delights in our way; though we stumble, we shall not fall headlong, for the Lord holds us by the hand." Psalm 37:23-24 (Really great promise!!)

Love You!!   Praying for You!!   Proud of You!!   Bro. Post

✶✶✶✶✶✶✶✶✶✶✶✶✶✶✶✶✶✶✶✶✶

"Shine a bright, glaring spotlight on your fear."

When we are troubled by something, it never really goes away. It's like the fearful thought lurks in the shadows of our mind, waiting for a perfect time to return, to scare us and rattle us. The fearful thought works its misery - we mull over the fear, we exaggerate it and we enhance it. We then pray and the fear fades, the thought retreats and hides. However, a little while later, it usually returns with a vengeance and ruins our day.

Maybe we should be more aggressive......maybe we should expose the fear, not let it lurk and hide. Maybe we should expose it to the bright light of God's promises.

Ok, God gave us His 'protection promises' for a reason. It's nice to frame one on the wall, but the real reason that He gave them is to help us in the everyday battles of the Christian life. Every Christian I have ever met has one or two areas of battle - areas which our enemy uses to scare us, to rattle us, to shake our faith.

Turn the spotlight on your fears. Be completely honest with your Father. "Father, you know this scares me to death. You also know that I sometimes have a hard time believing You, so when I worry about this, I make it bigger and I make myself miserable. Father, I claim this promise. I believe what You said WILL happen and I believe what the enemy says will NOT happen. I give this fear to you."

Good Morning!! How Are My College Buddies?

Use God's 'protection promises' as a bright spotlight on your fears. Here's a delightful protection promise, it will shine a glaring spotlight on our fears:

> "Those who love me, I will deliver; I will protect those who know my name. When they call to me, I will answer them; I will rescue them and honor them." Psalm 91:14-15

Love You!!   Praying for You!!   Proud of You!!   Bro. Post
✷✷✷✷✷✷✷✷✷✷✷✷✷✷✷✷✷✷✷✷✷✷

"Your Sermon is in Your Storm."

It's always good to tell people about Christ. But it's always better to SHOW them your faith in Christ. You can either preach a sermon with words or live a sermon with your life. The latter is always more effective.

Paul had been through a horrific two weeks. He cared about the sailors in the ship in which he was sailing, so he had told them about God. The result? They ignored him: "Yeah, yeah,……thanks for the advice, we will do what we want to do."

Now the Lord knew that these sailors wouldn't listen to a spoken sermon, so the Lord arranged it where Paul could LIVE a sermon. So the ship sailed into a horrible storm, for two weeks, and the men were terrified. But they were watching Paul, and he lived a sermon for them. In Paul's exhaustion, in the middle of mortal danger, Paul had confidence in God.

College Buddies, you may be living in a storm of problems that have left you exhausted. You may see danger to you or to your friend or family member. You may have ragged, panic times in which you are afraid, but then you refocus your faith in God. It may be a outside trial or an inside battle, but you're tired, haggard… but you're still trusting. You may end your day just thinking that with God's help, at least I have survived.

You've done a lot more than survived! You have done a powerful work for God! You have actually lived a powerful sermon for your Father! You may not have spoken a word, but you have witnessed for Him in a powerful way.

You see, your sermon is in the middle of your storm. That's where your witness is the most powerful......without saying a word. Of course, you will have periodic ragged times, but never forget the testimony that you're giving.

God will gently guard you and protect you as you live your sermon in your storm. This is very likely the best work that you will ever do for God. Please read carefully the verses below. David lived his sermon in the storm...look at the result:

> "I waited patiently for the Lord...He drew me up from the desolate pit, out of the miry bog and set my feet upon a rock......many shall see it and fear, and put their trust in the Lord." Psalm 40:1&3

Love You!!   Praying for You!!   Proud of You!!   Bro. Post
✶✶✶✶✶✶✶✶✶✶✶✶✶✶✶✶✶✶✶✶✶✶

Good Morning!! How Are My College Buddies?

Maybe you're praying for the wrong thing."

When you pray about your progress in your Christian life, remember this: "Start praying for the positives, stop praying about the negatives."

Here's what I mean. Many Christians pray about their negative faults and sins, they grit their teeth and ask God to help them stop. This rarely works. Instead, the Bible teaches us to pray for positive, spiritual traits in our lives. When we have these, it will eliminate the negative ones.

If you tend to gossip or criticize harshly, instead of praying that you will stop, instead pray that God will use your tongue to encourage and compliment. Guess what? The gossip and criticism stops because it has been REPLACED by a godly attitude. Discontented and complaining? Pray for a thankful heart. Worried about the future? Praise God by faith that He is in control. Nurturing unforgiveness? Ask God to remind you how much He has forgiven you.

God doesn't just take away evil altitudes, He has the ability to replace them with godly attitudes. Please think about the following verse:

"Do not be overcome by evil, but overcome evil with good." Romans 12:21

Love You!!   Praying for You!!   Proud of You!!   Bro. Post
✶✶✶✶✶✶✶✶✶✶✶✶✶✶✶✶✶✶✶✶✶✶✶

"Sometimes We Should Be Angry...Just Like Jesus."

Ok, I want to make myself very clear here! :-) I'm not talking about selfish anger, I am referring to godly anger, that emotion that Jesus felt when He crashed into a temple, upturned tables and used a whip! There are times when we should feel this emotion. When you see civilians slaughtered by a political uprising? When you see someone harming children? What about using God's name for a selfish motive? (This is what angered Jesus.) What about one person using and dominating another person for their own selfish interests? God gives us this emotion to rally us to pray and do anything that we can to alleviate the wrong.

Actually, in the history of our country, there have been many social evils that have been removed because of the anger of God's people - this anger motivated them to work and insist that this must stop. (More specifically, the godly anger of godly women. Perfect Example: Child Labor Protection Laws enacted.) This godly anger is directed against the evil act - it also holds out the opportunity of forgiveness to the person. (John Newton was converted when he was a slave merchant, an incredibly vile practice... He repented of this evil and later wrote 'Amazing Grace.') Ask God to stir your lethargy and fill you with His holy, appropriate anger...AND, ask God to help you offer Christ to the people involved:

Good Morning!! How Are My College Buddies?

"Jesus entered the temple and drove out all who sold and bought in the temple, and he overturned the tables of the moneychangers and the seats of those who sold pigeons. He said to them, 'My house shall be called a house of prayer'; but you have made it a den of robbers." Matthew 21:12-13

Love You!!   Praying for You!!   Proud of You!!   Bro. Post
✳✳✳✳✳✳✳✳✳✳✳✳✳✳✳✳✳✳✳✳✳✳

"Ticked Off Under a Shade Tree."

Jonah was struggling. He expected things to turn out a certain way, and they didn't. Haven't we all at times been bitterly disappointed about dashed hopes?

Jonah was struggling. He didn't want to admit it, but he was actually furious at God - you see, God was the one had who caused the disappointing circumstances that made Jonah so mad!

Jonah didn't want to say anything against God, so he just sat under a shade tree...furious, disappointed, wallowing in thoughts about how things would so much better if his plans had actually happened.

Haven't we all been there at times? Let's be honest here, all of us have unfulfilled dreams that leave us frustrated and unhappy. Now these dreams are not bad...actually they are blessings that we wish we had, but God hasn't allowed them.

I've been thinking about the verse below. "No good thing." Yet sometimes, like Jonah, we imagine a wonderful blessing and then we wonder why God will not allow it!

In God's plans, timing is crucial. An unfulfilled blessing does not mean a denied blessing. He may very well allow that very blessing later. God restored Jonah and He will restore us. He will command His perfectly tailored blessings for us IN HIS PERFECT TIMING! However, in the ticked off days that we occasionally experience, here is a promise that we can claim.

"No good thing will He withhold from him who walks uprightly." Psalm 84:11

Love You!!   Praying for You!!   Proud of You!!   Bro. Post
✷✷✷✷✷✷✷✷✷✷✷✷✷✷✷✷✷✷✷✷

"Keep water in your basin and a towel handy."

She could have easily retired, she was 70 years old. She could have lived comfortably, she had received about $400,000 by winning the Nobel Peace Prize. But instead, she gave the money away and went back to Calcutta, to care for the homeless and destitute.

A prominent business man was walking down a Calcutta street and saw a homeless man who had vomited all over himself, obviously it was the last hour of his life. There beside him, holding the dying man was Mother Teresa, gently speaking to him about the love of God as his life slipped away. The business man was so impressed, he told Mother Teresa, "I respect you so much, I wouldn't do what you are doing now for a million dollars."

Mother Teresa gently replied to the business man: "Neither would I."

College Buddies, when Jesus is in our hearts, He changes us. We develop a servant's heart - after all, Jesus took the dirtiest job of a servant when he washed the disciples' feet. If we are stuck on ourselves, or we are only concerned about ourselves, our problems or our own possessions, then we will walk right by opportunities to serve others - after all, it's all about me.

But when we allow Jesus to change us, we then have a servant's heart... now it's all about others, serving them in the name of Christ.

That was a powerful witness on the streets of Calcutta. But guess what, God wants to do the same

Good Morning!! How Are My College Buddies?

for you this week. Keep water in your basin, keep a towel handy, ask God to use you this week to serve others...you will be doing Jesus' work:

> "If I then your Lord and Teacher have washed your feet, you also ought to wash one another's feet. For I have given you an example, that you should do as I have done for you." John 13:14

Love You!! Praying for You!! Proud of You!! Bro. Post

✳✳✳✳✳✳✳✳✳✳✳✳✳✳✳✳✳✳✳✳✳

"Divine Brakes"

Sometimes in life, we are convinced that we are making the right decision, the correct choice that God wants us to make.

And we would be totally wrong.

If someone were to ask us, we would offer several reasons why we think we are right, we might even resist or ignore any evidence to the contrary.

And guess what? We would still be totally wrong.

It's at these times that the Lord uses His 'Divine Brakes.' He knows how committed we are to our choice, so He works circumstances to change our mind. We may feel an unease about our decision, a nagging doubt about it. This could be a 'Divine Brake.' We may read a Bible verse and the Lord speak to us, or we may pray and feel unsettled... again, a 'Divine Brake.' We may ask advice from a mature Christian and then reconsider. This advice can be an excellent 'Divine Brake.'

When you drive through Tennessee, you will occasionally see runaway truck ramps on the right side of the road. These are built to save truckers' lives when their brakes fail. The truck crashes into mounds of sand, often with quite a bit of damage. However, the trucker's life is almost always saved.

College Buddies, be sensitive to God's brakes in your life. Don't stubbornly barrel ahead in life, convinced you are always right. Let God guide you on the right path - stubbornness has caused many a wreck:

Good Morning!! How Are My College Buddies?

"Be not wise in your own eyes; fear the Lord and turn away from evil. It will be healing to your flesh and refreshment to your bones." Proverbs 3:7

Love You!!   Praying for You!!   Proud of You!!   Bro. Post
✼✼✼✼✼✼✼✼✼✼✼✼✼✼✼✼✼✼✼✼✼

"Singing in a Wasteland"

It sounded weird but the Lord had a point to make. The city of Jerusalem was a wasteland, most of it was left in rubble after an invasion. A few people lived among the ruins, the majority had been carried off as slaves. Now God's people longed and prayed for the city to be rebuilt and God had promised that He would send that blessing - the rebuilding of Jerusalem. Isaiah was the prophet during this time and he had a message from God to His people: Walk among the rubble, sing a song of rejoicing and praise me now for the coming blessing in the future!

Amazing. Would you do that?

College Buddies, it's easy to praise God AFTER the blessing comes, but God wants us to have a higher faith - to praise Him BEFORE the blessing comes. Do you have any dreams or hopes that are 'rubble' today? Are there parts of your life that seem like a vast wasteland? I know, we all have them. Our Father knows this, and He has plans to change these tough circumstances, to send us wonderful blessings in these areas. Why not take a walk through the wastelands of your life and praise Him NOW that He will bless these areas in the future? Sounds weird? No not really, if you do this, you will be truly living a life of faith:

> "Break forth into shouts of joy together, you ruins of Jerusalem, for the Lord has comforted his people, he has freed Jerusalem." Isaiah 52:9

Good Morning!! How Are My College Buddies?

Love You!!   Praying for You!!   Proud of You!!   Bro. Post

✶✶✶✶✶✶✶✶✶✶✶✶✶✶✶✶✶✶✶✶

"It's hard being human."

And that is exactly the reason why we need our Father's forgiveness and help.

On this side of heaven, we are totally forgiven when we come to Christ. In our hearts, we truly want to live for Him and please Him. But we stumble often, don't we?

We decide that we will love other people - then we allow bitterness and anger to poison our words. We decide to be thankful - then we whine and complain about little stuff. We decide not to worry - then we stew and fret and scare ourselves to death! We decide to be humble - then we catch ourselves thinking that we're a cut above another person. We decide to be content - then we become agitated and bitter because we have not received that one thing that we really want.

Isn't it amazing that our Father doesn't give up on us? Throw up His hands in exasperation and decide never to deal with us again?

HE JUST CANNOT DO THAT. Our Father knows how hard it is to be human, how difficult it is, how often we stumble. That is why He gives us His grace, His undeserved kindness in forgiving our sins. That is why He gives us His help, to pick us up, cleanse us and help us to start walking with Him again.

Maybe today you are painfully aware of your humanness - you have stumbled and failed and you are wondering of your Father still loves you. Please read and claim the beautiful promise below - trust me, all of us Christians need our Father's forgiveness, often:

> "If we confess our sins, he is faithful and just and will forgive us our sins and purify us from all unrighteousness." I John 1:9

Love You!! Praying for You!! Proud of You!! Bro. Post
✶✶✶✶✶✶✶✶✶✶✶✶✶✶✶✶✶✶✶✶✶

"Sleeping With Hubert On My Pillow"

Hubert is an adorable stuffed puppy with big, floppy ears. He was given to me 23 years ago. It seems that my youngest daughter, then 4, felt that Hubert would feel safer sleeping with me. She placed the stuffed puppy on my pillow each night and then checked every morning to make sure he was still there. Soooo, I slept with Hubert on my pillow. :-)

Now why would a grown man sleep with a stuffed puppy on his pillow?

BECAUSE OF THE PERSON WHO ASKED ME.

College Buddies, please remember this when you pray and ask your Father for His help. You are NOT a stranger, begging and pleading, hoping God will somehow, just maybe, answer your prayer. Remember, you are His SON......you are His DAUGHTER.

This simple truth means that our Father's heart is bursting with intense affection and love for you - just thinking about you is delightful to Him. A dad takes delight when a child needs his help and your Father is thrilled when you call to Him. Dads do not make a child beg, dads feel happiness when they can give something to a child. Dads experience a quiet, inner happiness when their kids are safe and protected....... our Father feels the same way.

Today, remember who you are! When you pray, remember how your Father adores you. When you stumble, remember how quickly your Father will forgive you. Remember who you are - remember who He is - then you're ready to pray:

> "How great is the love the Father has lavished upon, that we should be called children of God! And that is what we are!" I John 3:1

Love You!! Praying for You!! Proud of You!! Bro. Post
****

"Divine TLC."

We all need it at times, an extra amount of God's gentle, tender care.

When a shepherd is moving his sheep, he is watching closely two particular types of sheep in his flock. He knows that these are the ones who need his gentle protection and nurture, so he gently pays more attention to them. The first group is the ewes who are near child birth. These sheep have to be moved gently, so the shepherd slows the pace and walks close to them, finding an easier path for them. The reason? Because of the present condition of the ewes, they struggle, the path is much harder for them. Therefore the shepherd gives them plenty of TLC.

The little lambs belong to the second group of special care. These lambs are easily spooked, they get jumpy and rattled. Amazingly, the shepherd will pick one up and hold it close to his heart. When the little lamb senses the heartbeat, the lamb relaxes, the terror is gone.

Jesus is the perfect shepherd. He knows when our path in life becomes difficult, when we walk in exhaustion because of the present burdens that we are bearing. He then gives you His 'Divine TLC' - that special care for you. Like the little lambs, He also knows when we become rattled and jumpy, afraid of what's around the bend. He then gives you a special sense of His presence and soon the dread and fear eases.

Maybe today you are like one of these groups, your path is exhausting and your heart is frightened. Why not pray a simple prayer - "Jesus, be my Shepherd today." :

> "He tends his flock like a shepherd: He gathers the lambs in his arms and carries them close to his heart; he gently leads those with young." Isaiah 40:

Love You!!   Praying for You!!   Proud of You!!   Bro. Post
✶✶✶✶✶✶✶✶✶✶✶✶✶✶✶✶✶✶✶✶

Good Morning!! How Are My College Buddies?

"I want my warm nest back!!"

The mother eagle knows when it's the right time to teach her eaglets to fly. She knows she can't convince them to leave their warm nest that she has made, the eaglets are too comfortable. Left alone, the eaglets would live out their lives in the warm nest, they would never soar the skies.

So she does something that appears very cruel to the eaglets, she puts the eaglets on a limb and then rips and shreds the nest. Their cozy home is now gone, the eaglets are shocked and scared on the limb. Then the mother eagle 'hovers' in front of the eaglets, trying to coax them to fly. This rarely works, the eaglets are thinking, "I want my warm nest back!!" She then takes an eaglet high in the sky and drops it and at the last moment she catches the eaglet on her wings....... and then she takes the eaglet up and drops it again. Eventually the eaglet learns to fly.

We love our warm nests just as well, don't we? Left to ourselves, we would never leave one, it's too comfortable. So our Father allows our warm nest to be shredded and it is always a painful shock. Our Father then gently encourages us to use our faith, to learn to fly.

College Buddies, have you recently lost a warm nest? Our Father knows it is very difficult, but He wants us to trust Him, He has everything in control. He will never allow something to destroy you, He will always be there to catch you and protect you.

Here is a beautiful prayer I read recently about losing a 'warm nest.' I hope it encourages you:

"Father, You have shown me that it is time to fly by faith, with small but growing wings. It is exhausting to try to repair the nest that you have scattered, even with the broken pieces patched together, it is not the warm haven that it once was, You do not want it to be. Turn my eyes away from yearning for the past, turn my eyes toward the sky, where you want me to soar. Take away my yearning exhaustion and please replace it with Your settled acceptance of this new chapter in my life. And I thank You for your gentleness as You help me. In Jesus' name, Amen."

Love You!!   Praying for You!!   Proud of You!!   Bro. Post

✶✶✶✶✶✶✶✶✶✶✶✶✶✶✶✶✶✶✶✶✶

"In God's mind, the problem is already solved."

This simple truth can change our prayer life. You see, we think in linear time...we see events as they unfold. However, God sees everything all at once... He sees things right now that will happen two weeks, two years, two centuries from now. Ok, let's keep this in mind when we pray!

The very problem that we are praying about, God knows the very solution that He has planned. The very issue we are 'stewing' about, He has the perfect resolution. Let's try praying this way: "Lord I thank you that this problem I am praying about is already solved in your mind, you know exactly what you will do. Now help me to be patient as I watch you work out the details." If we pray this way we don't end up begging God, we end up thanking Him in advance. Praying this way gives us confidence in the waiting period – that time between when the problem arrives and the time when He solves it:

> "I waited patiently for the Lord; He leaned over to me and heard my cry. He drew me up from a desolate pit, out of the miry bog, and set my feet upon a rock, making my steps secure." Psalm 40:1-2

Love You!!   Praying for You!!   Proud of You!!   Bro. Post

✸✸✸✸✸✸✸✸✸✸✸✸✸✸✸✸✸✸✸✸✸

Good Morning!! How Are My College Buddies?

"A North Carolina Life Sermon"

The sunset was spectacular. I was watching the sunset in Kitty Hawk, NC, looking west across Pamlico Sound. The late afternoon sky was an explosion of orange, pink and bright blue, the sinking orange ball reflected across the water. It's interesting that 4 hours earlier, the scenery was definitely not pretty! Heavy thundershowers and high winds had been the weather all day. But after the storm, the sky seemed more beautiful, more appreciated, more awesome.

One thing that I have noticed in life is that God sometimes allows some storms just before sending one of His beautiful blessings. After the blessing has come, it even more appreciated because of the storms that preceded it. God has the power to calm your storms of rough circumstances, often in a dramatic way. So if your life has been a little stormy lately, PLEASE don't despair and PLEASE don't beat yourself up, wondering why God is mad at you. He's not mad at you, He's just getting ready to send you a spectacularly beautiful blessing:

> "I believe that I SHALL see the goodness of the Lord in the land of the living! Wait for the Lord; be strong and let your heart take courage; yes, wait for the Lord!" Psalm 27:13-14

Love You!!   Praying for You!!   Proud of You!!   Bro. Post
✶✶✶✶✶✶✶✶✶✶✶✶✶✶✶✶✶✶✶✶✶✶✶✶

"Unfair Expectations"

We end up disappointed and we have no one to blame but ourselves.

The problem is our own expectations - we mentally create the exact way that we expect someone to act or react. When that person doesn't, our expectations are crushed by reality, we are disappointed. Often our expectations are so high that a person rarely can meet them and a friendship is strained.

College Buddies, everyone deserves a little space and room, don't try to squeeze them into what you want, which often is unfair and unrealistic. This will do wonders for your friendships, your coworkers and your future mate. We need to burn our list of expectations and allow people to occasionally fail, to be imperfect...all without a lecture from us. When we truly love with God's love, we don't limit them to reacting just like we want, we love them regardless. It seems to me that Jesus loves us the exact way, He doesn't cast us away when we disappoint Him:

> "Thou shalt love your neighbor as yourself. But if you are continually wounding and tearing one another to pieces, be careful that you do not destroy your fellowship altogether." Galatians 5:14-15

Love You!!   Praying for You!!   Proud of You!!   Bro. Post
✳✳✳✳✳✳✳✳✳✳✳✳✳✳✳✳✳✳✳✳✳✳✳

"An Expert in Agape Love."

Have you ever been around a Christian who is an 'Agape Expert?' These Christians are a tremendous witness for the Lord and are used by God to accomplish an unbelievable amount of good. They seem to have similar qualities, here are a few of them.

- They will walk beside you, through the hot fires of tough times, they will not blink nor leave you by yourself.
- They have a gentleness in word and manner, this gentleness opens up the hearts of other people to experience God's love.
- They truly are thrilled when you experience a happy event!
- When a Christian stumbles in a sin, they are there beside the person, gently leading the person back to God.
- They 'experience' other people's misery by carrying their pain in their hearts. When you are around this Christian and you are struggling, you just know that this person REALLY cares. They are expert 'Burden Bearers.'
- They are practical - they see practical ways to show God's love to others. (In Wyoming, I met a woman who walks with her puppy in a nursing home, letting the patients play with her puppy. As you can imagine, it is by FAR the most favorite event of the week.)
- They tend to want to know about YOU - your fears, hopes, joys and dreams. They downplay

their own problems, they are reluctant to talk about their own successes.
- You just get this feeling when you around them: "Jesus spoke like this, Jesus acted like this, Jesus cared like this."

Why not make this a life goal? To be so filled with God's love that it naturally flows though us to other people:

"Dear friends, let us love one another, for love comes from God. Everyone who loves has been born of God and knows God. Whoever does not love does not know God, for God is love." I John 4:7-8

Love You!!   Praying for You!!   Proud of You!!   Bro. Post
✳✳✳✳✳✳✳✳✳✳✳✳✳✳✳✳✳✳✳✳

"Lord, help me to be an eagle. Lord stop me from being a crow."

Crows fight all the time. The look for an opportunity and then try to knock another crow down. They caw loudly and are quick to take advantage of another's weaknesses.

If an eagle flies at the altitude of a crow, the eagle is in trouble. The crows quickly attack the eagle. Now the eagle doesn't stay at the altitude of the crows, the eagle has the power to escape. The eagle simply soars to an higher altitude where the eagle is free from the harassment of the crows.

College Buddies, some people in life are like 'spiritual crows', their tendency is to verbally attack others. It doesn't matter whether if it's gossip, insinuation, ridicule or harsh criticism, their nature is to try to bring others down.

'Spiritual crows' can't help it - it's their nature - they do not know God.

God can help us to be a 'spiritual eagle.' We can choose, by God's power in us, to refuse to fly at the level of the crows. Our role to build people up, not to tear them down. We can refuse to be a part of other people's quarrels, like Jesus, we can just take a pass. We can refuse to be a part of gossip……actually we can help squelch the gossip by complimenting the person who is a victim of gossip! We can use our tongues to be a spiritual healer, not a character destroyer.

Good Morning!! How Are My College Buddies?

Let's ask God to help us today to soar far above the altitude of the bickering crows and fly at the altitude of the eagles:

"Love is not rude, it is not self-seeking." I Corinthians 13:5

Love You!!   Praying for You!!   Proud of You!!   Bro. Post
✳✳✳✳✳✳✳✳✳✳✳✳✳✳✳✳✳✳✳✳✳

"I'm tired of waiting, I can fix this."

And that is a perfect way to screw things up, big time.

God had promised a beautiful promise to Abraham and Abraham was excited! He rejoiced and then he waited for God to keep His promise. Abraham waited and waited and waited......months turned into years......... years into decades.......and it just didn't happen. So Abraham took things into His own hands and a ton of heartache and misery was the result. Later, God did send His blessing, but it just wasn't on Abraham's timetable, so he became antsy, and he made a bone-headed mistake.

College Buddies, our Father loves us so much that He DOES have the solution to those unresolved concerns, trials and burdens that all of us endure. But it is so easy to be a 'fixer', isn't it? We think we see a solution and we jump in and do our best to solve the problem or ease the misery.

It helps to remember that our Father is working in the background, preparing the solution or blessing that He will send to each of us. But He does ask us to wait for His perfect timing. God had the power to rescue Daniel immediately from the lion's den...... but He made Daniel wait all night. God had the power to help Joseph after he was sold as a slave......but He made Joseph wait 13 years. Now when these blessings did come, and they did, they were awesome!! But let's be careful and wait for our Father to work, let's not make a huge mess by acting like Abraham:

"Commit your way to the Lord; trust in him and he will act……..be still before the Lord and wait patiently for him.." Psalm 37:5, 7

Love You!! Praying for You!! Proud of You!! Bro. Post
✳✳✳✳✳✳✳✳✳✳✳✳✳✳✳✳✳✳✳✳✳

"I'll turn the water into wine, you just fill the pots."

Sometimes we Christians try to do Jesus' job, to perform a miracle, create a blessing.

We forget that only God can do this, we cannot bless anyone. But we try and try...and we end up frustrated. Remember Jesus' first miracle? He was the one who would make the blessing, nobody else could. HOWEVER, the servants at the banquet had the privilege of delivering the blessing that Jesus had created. So they filled the water pots up, put their heart into the work, they then waited and Jesus did His miracle.

The servants did their part, then Jesus did His part.

Today, God doesn't expect you to create a blessing for anyone - but very likely He wants you to DELIVER a blessing to someone. A person discouraged, a person who has sinned, someone grieving, someone frightened...God wants to bless these people. And He wants to use you to deliver the blessing – He wants to use your voice, your compassion, your encouragement. So let's get this one right, let's pray this morning: "Lord, I'll fill the pots, You make the wine."

> "He who abides in me, and I in him, he it is that bears much fruit, for apart from me you can do nothing." John 15:5

Love You!!   Praying for You!!   Proud of You!!   Bro. Post
✶✶✶✶✶✶✶✶✶✶✶✶✶✶✶✶✶✶✶✶✶✶

Good Morning!! How Are My College Buddies?

"Three Crucial Questions"

When a little child takes a fall and badly scrapes a knee, the child will run with the pain to see a parent. Sometimes in a child's mind, he will have three questions as he cries out in pain. Will my dad/mom still love me? Does my dad/mom know how much this hurts? Will my dad/mom help me?

All of us take bad falls in life, and we cry to our Father in heaven. It's interesting how we sometimes ask the very same questions regarding Him. Does my Father still love and accept me, even though I am struggling? I know I'm supposed to be strong. Is He disappointed in me when I'm weak? Does my Father knows how much I hurt? Does He know what this feels like? Will my Father help me? Will He ease the pain and make me okay again?

A hurting child doesn't try to deny the scraped knee. The child points to it as he cries to his dad. Here is a beautiful verse from the Bible to assure us how our Father reacts to our hurt.

> "In all their distress he too was distressed, and the angel of his presence saved them. In his love and mercy he redeemed them; he lifted them up and carried them all the days of old."
> Isaiah 63:9

Love You!!   Praying for You!!   Proud of You!!   Bro. Post
✸✸✸✸✸✸✸✸✸✸✸✸✸✸✸✸✸✸✸✸✸

"Our Father is an Expert Orthopedist."

A broken bone is an intensely painful experience. Often the person, when seeking medical help, only wants the doctor to remove the pain by medicine.

But to only ease the pain would be a mistake, wouldn't it? The doctor knows that the bone must be set correctly. It may cause more pain, but the orthopedist carefully sets the broken bone so that it will heal correctly.

Amazingly, a few months later, the bone is stronger at the point where it was broken than before the fracture!

Our Father knows that in a lifetime, we have many breaks and fractures. He knows how painful they are - the list of fractures is long, and the intense pain is very real for God's children. Your Father knows how to gently 'set the bone' - to work in our lives where we can heal and mend. This does not happen overnight, it always takes time. We always want the pain to be removed immediately! But our Lord begins the healing process, mending our wounds and healing our broken hearts.

What part of your life is broken today? All of us have them and all of us need the touch of the Great Physician. You may not even want the help of the Lord; you may be engulfed by bitterness. Trust me, the Lord will help you there also. Take your broken areas to God, allow Him to start the healing process. Notice the beautiful verse below. Notice the word that is capitalized. Guess what that word means in the original Greek? It means to 'set a broken bone.'

Good Morning!! How Are My College Buddies?

"Now the God of all grace, who called you to his eternal glory in Christ, after you have suffered a little while, will himself RESTORE you and make you strong, firm and steadfast."
I Peter 5:10

Love You!!   Praying for You!!   Proud of You!!   Bro. Post
✴✴✴✴✴✴✴✴✴✴✴✴✴✴✴✴✴✴✴✴

"I know you're tired...I know you're rattled...Let's rest a while."

College Buddies, a shepherd always cares intensely for his sheep. The shepherd knows the nature of sheep; he knows their strengths, and he knows their weaknesses. One danger for sheep is the time immediately after a tiring or stressful journey. Okay, the shepherd got them through the dangerous pass, none of the sheep were lost, now the sheep are okay, right?

Actually the sheep are NOT okay. Sheep have a tendency to be rattled after a stressful time. They can't rest, they nervously pace back and forth, and they won't eat or drink. The shepherd knows that the sheep will stress themselves to exhaustion, so he forces them to stop, to 'decompress' and to recuperate.

Lately you may have experienced high stress circumstances. The problem has eased now, but you're still jumpy and rattled. You find yourself running back and forth, assured that the near future holds another exhausting burden. This is perfectly normal; you're reacting as all Christians do immediately after a storm.

The Lord, the good Shepherd, is looking for you. He wants to settle you, to take away the unsettling dreads, and to give you some spiritual rehab and recuperation. He knows the best way for each of us, and since He loves you, His sheep.......He will slow you down and He will calm you down.

Good Morning!! How Are My College Buddies?

"He makes me lie down in green pastures, he leads me beside the still waters, he restores my soul." Psalm 23:2-3

Love You!! Praying for You!! Proud of You!! Bro. Post
✸✸✸✸✸✸✸✸✸✸✸✸✸✸✸✸✸✸✸✸✸

Good Morning!! How Are My College Buddies?

"Turning on a Dime?"

You can't turn the Queen Elizabeth II on a dime; it takes a while. It would be nice if the captain could turn this massive ocean liner quickly, but he can't. He uses the left rudder, adds power to the right props, and reduces power in the left props. Eventually, the liner is turned around...and the whole process takes about eleven nautical miles. Now the captain knows what he is doing, and he patiently waits until the ship is turned.

College Buddies, when our Father changes the tough circumstances in your life, He rarely does it instantaneously. He does it in steps, and these steps do take a while. It's easy to become frustrated and wish all the misery was gone......now!! But our Father knows the exact course of your life, and He knows exactly the calmer seas where He is taking you. The fact that it takes time does not mean that God is off course - He knows EXACTLY when and what to do. If you have been sailing through some rough seas lately, and you've pleaded with your Father to ease the storms......He will, He always does. He is at the helm of your life, and He has already started steering you to calmer seas...just give Him time; He has your course perfectly planned.

> "Though you have made me see troubles, many and bitter, you will restore my life again; from the depths of the earth you will again bring me up. You will increase my

honor and comfort me once again." Psalm 71:20-21

Love You!!   Praying for You!!   Proud of You!!   Bro. Post
✼✼✼✼✼✼✼✼✼✼✼✼✼✼✼✼✼✼✼✼

"Soaring.......Running........Trudging"

We have days like these, and our Father makes some wonderful promises in the middle of them.

Maybe you're 'soaring' spiritually today - the circumstances are wonderful, the Bible is a delight, and it seems like your Father is so close that you can touch Him. Enjoy this day, relish it... it is a love-gift from your Father to remind you that you are His and that He adores you.

Or maybe you're 'running' today - the schedule is brutal, the demands are heavy, and the day will be very long. Our Father, in these days, infuses us with His energy and strength, He helps us to manage an exhausting day and still be gentle and kind. He also helps us to control ourselves so that we do not use a tough day as an excuse to unload on someone.

Maybe you are 'trudging' today - the burdens are so heavy or the heartaches are so deep that you don't think you can take another step. You are convinced that these problems will break you. Our Father is VERY gentle with His children in these days. He gently helps us to get up, get dressed, and meet the responsibilities of the day without collapsing. He holds us up, and He helps us to take one step...then another......then another.

Regardless of what our day is like, our Father is right beside us, and He gives us this delightful promise:

> "Those who hope in the Lord will renew their strength. They will soar on wings like eagles;

Good Morning!! How Are My College Buddies?

they will run and not grow weary, they will walk (trudge) and not be faint. (collapse)" Isaiah 40:31

Love You!!   Praying for You!!   Proud of You!!   Bro. Post
✳✳✳✳✳✳✳✳✳✳✳✳✳✳✳✳✳✳✳✳

"A Trapped Angel"

His students were confused.

They knew that their master, Michelangelo, was a brilliant and talented artist. What they couldn't understand was why he would spend so much money and go to such effort to find a jagged, dirty piece of marble. Finally, one student mustered the courage to ask, why so much trouble and why so much expense for such an unattractive and imperfect piece of rock?

Michelangelo's eyes twinkled as he said, "I see an angel trapped inside, I want to set it free."

And that's exactly what he did...he chiseled, he chipped, and he smoothed out the edges until he sculptured a spectacular angel, still admired today.

And that's exactly what our Father does for us...that's what grace is all about. We had absolutely nothing of spiritual worth or beauty, we could have easily been ignored or cast aside. But Jesus came and gave himself for us. You see, Jesus could see the type of person we would become after we were converted. Therefore, He paid a tremendous price to purchase us, all the time smiling at what He would make of us.

God is still forming that beautiful person in you today. He is still chipping away at the selfishness and imperfections that we Christians still have. He is patiently removing these flaws and replacing them with the love, gentleness, and compassion of Christ.

Good Morning!! How Are My College Buddies?

It takes time and the process is painful, but our Father is the Master Sculptor, and He is truly sculpting a beautiful spiritual masterpiece...you.

"If anyone is in Christ, they are a new creation, old things are passing away, new things are coming." I Corinthians 10:13

Love You!!   Praying for You!!   Proud of You!!   Bro. Post
✼✼✼✼✼✼✼✼✼✼✼✼✼✼✼✼✼✼✼✼✼

"I feel so helpless!! I wish I could do something!!"

College Buddies, when the Lord brings you in contact with a person who has severe problems, this is almost always our reaction. We feel helpless and we would give anything if we could help, to remove their distress. Interestingly, I have learned that we are not helpless, we are doing a lot more good than we could possibly imagine! God is using that inner tenderness to encourage and support the person who is suffering. They do not expect us to solve the problem, but they can see the soft eyes, they can hear our gentle words, they appreciate our hug of concern. College Buddies, always remember this motto when sharing godly compassion: "People do not care how much you know until first they know how much you care."

Your gentle compassion lifts them to a level where they start to see some glimmer of hope in God - when you are gentle, they understand that God is gentle. They often feel guilty that their faith is shaken, when you embrace them with their battered faith, they understand how God embraces them, He hasn't cast them away. We should care about rescuing a person who doesn't know Christ, so that their life would be saved. How about a Christian who is on the brink of giving up? Ask God to send you to them, give them God's compassion and love...now you are no longer helpless, you are doing a ton of good:

Good Morning!! How Are My College Buddies?

"Blessed be the God and Father of our Lord Jesus Christ...who comforts us in ALL our afflictions, so that we may be able to comfort those who are in ANY affliction, with the comfort which we ourselves are comforted by God." II Corinthians 1:3-4 (emphasis mine)

Love You!!　Praying for You!!　Proud of You!!　Bro. Post
✶✶✶✶✶✶✶✶✶✶✶✶✶✶✶✶✶✶✶✶

Good Morning!! How Are My College Buddies?

"A Cleansed Conscience"

Have you ever asked God to cleanse your conscience? When we stumble and sin, it's only natural to ask God to forgive us and cleanse our soul. But have you ever gone another step, and asked Him to take away the guilty conscience?

Some Christians struggle here, they beat themselves up with guilt, assuming that God doesn't love them anymore. This is an old trick of the Enemy, if he can load us up with guilt he knows that we will be ineffective in serving God. God has the power to help us stop doing this!

If God only loved perfect Christians, there would be no Christians for Him to love. If He only used perfect Christians for His work, no work would ever get done! Tonight, if you are struggling with guilt, take your sins and give them to your Father. ALSO, give Him your guilt feelings. Ask Him and He will help you with both of these problems:

> "Let us draw near to God with a sincere heart in full assurance of faith, having our hearts sprinkled to cleanse us from a guilty conscience and having our bodies washed with pure water." Hebrews 10:22

Love You!! Praying for You!! Proud of You!! Bro. Post

✳✳✳✳✳✳✳✳✳✳✳✳✳✳✳✳✳✳✳✳✳

"I Don't Have Any Problems."

Godly perspective is a huge blessing. It helps us to see more clearly and to reset our emotions.

Last December, I received a phone call asking me to go visit a young mom in the hospital. I entered the room and her shy, adorable 8 yr. old daughter was peeking from behind the door as she whispered, "Hi Preacher." I didn't know this family so I took the mom's hand and asked her if she wanted me to pray for anything specific. She replied, "Please pray that I can live until Christmas, I want one last Christmas with my daughter." This young mom was fighting a fierce battle with pancreatic cancer and the pain was becoming more intense as I visited her each day.

I learned some perspective in that hospital room. Before I met this lady for the first time, I was tired, I was thinking about some of my own problems…….. ok, I was feeling sorry for myself. But day after day, visiting this classy, brave lady and seeing her adorable daughter, I kept thinking to myself, "You don't have any problems……compared to this lady, your problems don't even appear on the radar screen."

Godly perspective does that for us, it helps us see our own problems realistically, not the huge mountains that we tend to make them. Godly perspective makes us more patient in our tough times because we know that there are other Christians with a lot tougher times! Godly perspective moves us away from constantly thinking about our own problems and it helps us to pray and to care about another Christian's problem.

Good Morning!! How Are My College Buddies?

Isn't it wonderful how our Father deals gently with us when we need a new perspective? He could scold us, but He doesn't - He could berate us for our selfishness, but He doesn't do that either. What He often does is bring us in contact with a wonderful Christian with intense problems, like this excellent Christian mom. The result is that we are less selfish, less egocentric and more willing to carry the burdens of others:

> "This is how we know what love is: Jesus Christ laid down his life for us. And we ought to lay down our lives for our brothers." I John 3:16

Love You!!   Praying for You!!   Proud of You!!   Bro. Post
✶✶✶✶✶✶✶✶✶✶✶✶✶✶✶✶✶✶✶✶✶

Good Morning!! How Are My College Buddies?

"When someone loves you, your name is safe in their mouth."

If you want to speak evil of someone, your possibilities are endless. Even the best person you know is still human, prone to imperfections and flaws. If it takes a perfect person to cease gossip, then this evil will always flourish. Speaking evil of someone usually comes from pride, that inner drive to feel superior to others.

Why not try something different? When you're around others, look for something excellent about that person, some area where the person has done well. Then look for an opportunity to mention that good trait, to that person and to others. Make a habit of this and others will NOT gossip around you, they will feel hesitant. In addition, when you're tempted, you will feel very uneasy on the inside. "Another person's name is safe in your mouth" - what an excellent witness for the Lord:

"Do not speak evil against one another, brothers and sisters." James 4:11

Love You!!   Praying for You!!   Proud of You!!   Bro. Post
✳✳✳✳✳✳✳✳✳✳✳✳✳✳✳✳✳✳✳✳

"Blessing a Doubter"

"If God is with us, why is all of this bad stuff happening? I know He helped people in the past, why is He not helping us today?! I guess God has forsaken us and forgotten about us!"

When a person's faith is that shaken, God isn't pleased and He certainly is not going to answer, right? Actually, that is not true. Our Father is looking for Christians like this. The man who said these words was Gideon, an O.T. hero of faith…He said these words in a tough time, right before God sent a huge blessing to His people. God actually used Gideon to bring the blessing, the very man who's faith was badly shaken, the man who fought many doubts. (Judges 6) When you read the story, God moves Gideon to an impossible position, where it would be clear to all that GOD had sent the blessing, not Gideon.

College Buddies, God is not upset with us because we occasionally struggle, we have times in which our faith is weak. God delights in working in situations like these, He does it over and over. The God of Gideon is your Father and He knows you perfectly, nothing catches Him by surprise. He will help you, He will use you, He will protect and bless you:

> "Fear not, for you will not be ashamed; be not confounded, for you will not be put to shame…….with everlasting love I will have compassion on you, says the Lord, your Redeemer." Isaiah 54:4,8

Good Morning!! How Are My College Buddies?

Love You!!   Praying for You!!   Proud of You!!   Bro. Post
✶✶✶✶✶✶✶✶✶✶✶✶✶✶✶✶✶✶✶✶✶

"The Disaster of Partial Forgiveness"

King David's son, Absalom, had done some terrible things. They were inexcusable, wrong and awful. Absalom was afraid for his life, so he ran away to another city and lived away from his father. As time passed, Absalom wanted to return home, to live in his father's home, to experience his forgiveness. However, there was one big problem...his father, King David.

King David never made any overtures to Absalom while his son was away, he probably reasoned that he knew that he son was alive, but if he stays away, I don't have to deal with one big headache. Or maybe David was embarrassed by what Absalom had done. Or maybe David felt guilty, in many ways Absalom was acting like David acted when he was that age!

So instead of acting like the Prodigal Son's dad in the New Testament, David offered Absalom partial forgiveness. He allowed Absalom to return to his home city, Jerusalem, but David banned him from his home and said that he didn't want to see his face......a classic example of partial forgiveness. By doing this, David set the stage for another disaster, just down the road. Absalom, hurt and embittered, actually led a rebellion against his father, and as a result, Absalom was killed.

Partial forgiveness always leads to a greater disaster down the road.

College Buddies, in your lifetime you will be involved in many roles - son/daughter, husband/wife, dad/mom, friend, coworker, church member. Ask

Good Morning!! How Are My College Buddies?

God to help you remember that there is no such thing as 47% forgiveness - when a person wrongs you and regrets it, ask God to help you forgive them. Ask God to help you act like the Prodigal Son's dad, do NOT act like King David:

> "Bear with each other and forgive whatever grievances you may have against one another. Forgive as the Lord forgave you." Colossians 3:13

Love You!!   Praying for You!!   Proud of You!!   Bro. Post
✸✸✸✸✸✸✸✸✸✸✸✸✸✸✸✸✸✸✸✸✸

"There is no limit to what God will do, if we refuse to take the credit."

College Buddies, do you have a vital, energized prayer life? How often do have a spiritual 'wow' moment, when you see God answer in an awesome way?

Here's some crucial ingredients to a prayer life that is wonderful. 'FAITH' - do you really believe that God is powerful enough to answer, even if the majority are doubting? 'PATIENCE' - do you really believe that God has a reason when He doesn't answer immediately, that He has perfect timing?

Will you continue trusting? 'LASER FOCUS' - do you make your prayer specific? Do you refuse to get mired in vague requests? ("Lord, bless everybody.") 'PARTNER PRAYING' - will you share your requests with some prayer partners, where all of you can believe and trust? 'PRAISE RESPONSE' - do you love to give credit to your Father, to make sure that He gets ALL of the credit?

If you feel that you're prayer life has been anemic and mundane, try mixing these ingredients together -there will be times when the Lord will leave you speechless:

> "And whatsoever you shall ask in my name, that will I do, that the Father may be glorified in the Son. If you shall ask anything in my name, I will do it." John 14:13-14

Good Morning!! How Are My College Buddies?

Love You!!   Praying for You!!   Proud of You!!   Bro. Post
✼✼✼✼✼✼✼✼✼✼✼✼✼✼✼✼✼✼✼✼

"We never disappoint God by asking too much, we disappoint Him by asking too little."

It's interesting how many Christians struggle here, it's like we assign God a 'difficulty gauge'. On prayers of lesser difficulty, we believe that He will probably answer - on prayers for a greater difficulty, we waver in our faith - maybe, hopefully He will answer. It's helpful to remember two things here: First, there is no difference in God's eyes is answering a 'small' request' or a 'large request', He is all-powerful. Secondly, He has ALREADY given us His biggest miracle when He saved us from sin. All of our other requests are MUCH lesser in difficulty.

Sooo, why don't you just ask? Does He answer every prayer exactly as we ask? Of course not, He answers every prayer perfectly. But His disappointment comes when we don't ask, or, when we ask tentatively, doubting, only as a last resort. God is not strained or pressured when we offer Him our requests, so go ahead, ask, and then thank Him that He will answer. Check out this promise, maybe it will help us to stop 'asking too little.'

> "Now to him who by the power at work within us is able to do far more abundantly than all we ask or imagine, to him be glory in the church and in Christ Jesus unto all generations........." Ephesians 3:20

Good Morning!! How Are My College Buddies?

Love You!!   Praying for You!!   Proud of You!!   Bro. Post

✶✶✶✶✶✶✶✶✶✶✶✶✶✶✶✶✶✶✶✶✶

"The nets did not break...they were stretched to the limit, but they did NOT break." (John 11:13)

After Jesus' resurrection, He appeared to His disciples who had been fishing with nets. They hadn't caught one fish, they were tired and weary and they didn't recognize Jesus standing on the shore. Jesus told them to cast their nets on the other side of the boat and they did. Wow...the nets were immediately filled to the breaking point, a massive blessing.

That's nice, but what if the nets had broken? They would have experienced the blessing and then they would have lost it. Do you think God deals with His kids that way?

It's interesting how at times we think the nets of God's blessings and goodness will break. We stew, we worry, we even panic......will my life unravel, will the pressures be too much? Will God promise His love and blessing and then withdraw them?

ALL Christians occasionally have doubts and questions like these. Life sometimes gets so rough that it is easy to wonder if our lives will unravel in the heat of fiery trials. But our Father does not get angry at us for these times, He gently reminds us: "I am here beside you to protect you and to bless you."

The answer to our doubts is no, your nets will not break, your life will not be ruined, God's goodness and blessings will continue until you are safely home with your Father:

Good Morning!! How Are My College Buddies?

"Surely goodness and mercy shall follow me ALL the days of my life……" Psalm 23:6

Love You!!   Praying for You!!   Proud of You!!   Bro. Post
✵✵✵✵✵✵✵✵✵✵✵✵✵✵✵✵✵✵✵✵✵

'The Ministry of the Magnifying Glass'

When you enter this ministry, God will use you to do some incredible good for others. Some will receive your ministry and feel a huge relief...others will be renewed to face a brutal day...even others will believe again that God cares for them...some will be so moved that tears will well up in their eyes.

It's really simple, imagine that you have a magnifying glass in your heart - now use it to find points of excellence in other Christians, then TELL THEM ABOUT IT!! If Jesus could compliment a man who wasn't even a Christian, (Nathaniel), and if Paul could sincerely give a compliment to the worst church in the Bible, (Corinth), then why are we so silent? This ministry can be used by God to uplift someone in the present and to encourage them to excel even more in the future.

When someone is beginning to serve God or when they are experiencing tough times, they need to hear from God. Often, God speaks to them through you, when you use your magnifying glass. The sincere compliment that you gave them will refresh them, lighten their load and assure them that God is still in control.

Notice below how the Apostle Paul uses a magnifying glass. Today, ask God to give you an opportunity today to highlight excellence in another Christian. Then tell them about it, ok?

> "We always thank God for you, brothers, and rightly so, because your faith is growing,

and your love for each other is increasing. Therefore, among God's churches, we boast about your perseverance and faith..." I Thessalonians 1:3-4

Love You!!   Praying for You!!   Proud of You!!   Bro. Post
✳✳✳✳✳✳✳✳✳✳✳✳✳✳✳✳✳✳✳✳✳✳

"Totally irrelevant, it doesn't matter, it changes nothing."

College Buddies, all of us have days in which we are run over by an exhausting schedule. These days leave us weary, stressed and feeling bummed out. In the middle of these days, we face a sneaky temptation. When our body is dragging and our emotions are ragged, it's easy to doubt that our Father still loves us, it's easy to think that He's upset with us and it's tempting to think our prayers are ignored.

Think about who you are! You are a son or a daughter! A parent adores a child even when the child is having a bad day. A parent protects a child constantly. A parent is always eager to help a child who struggles. The parent is bonded and linked to the heart of a child.

The fact that you are having a rough day changes nothing in the way your Father adores you…how He protects you…how He cares for you…how He helps you. His heart is actually MORE tender toward you on your rough days, He loves to help a struggling child.

Pray honestly on your rough days, open your heart and tell your Father all about it, He's listening carefully. How about this - "Father, it's noon and this day is awful! I'm tired, irritated and I feel like you are a million miles away and I have to keep going until late tonight. Father I don't feel like you're close to me and I feel vulnerable. I really need your help."

In the middle of your exhausting day, your Father is sending you a special love note: "I'm right here beside you, you're perfectly safe, I will answer your prayer and I totally adore you." The fact that we don't feel like this is true? "My child, trust in me, not in your feelings. When it comes to my love, your ragged feelings are totally irrelevant and your doubts change nothing."

"As a father has compassion on his children, so the LORD has compassion on those who fear him; for he knows how we are formed, he remembers that we are dust." Psalm 103:13-14

Love You!!　Praying for You!!　Proud of You!!　Bro. Post
✶✶✶✶✶✶✶✶✶✶✶✶✶✶✶✶✶✶✶✶

"Fiercely Protective."

It was the most terrifying experience in my nephew's life. He and a friend were walking a Wyoming mountain trail and came upon a grizzly bear protecting her young cub, less than 100 yards away. Very quickly the mother bear rushed them, roaring, bristling and intimidating them. Thankfully, Jim and his friend had the courage to freeze and not move, (run and you die), they were eventually able to back away, definitely shaken but thankful to be alive. As Jim told me this story, two questions popped into my mind. Where did this bear learn to be so fiercely protective? The mother bear was not doing anything abnormal, she was reacting quickly and ferociously to a threat to her cub.

Secondly, College Buddies, how safe do you feel? The same God who created the grizzly bear has a fiercely protective nature toward all of His kids - He can and will react quickly, forcefully and even miraculously, if needed, to protect you. He would never allow His son to die for you, then wring His hands in despair and allow circumstances to destroy you. You are so precious to Him that He even knows the number of hairs on your head. I hope you feel His protective presence today, for you, your family, your friends:

"In the reverence of the Lord is strong security: and his children shall have a place of safety." Proverbs 14:26

Good Morning!! How Are My College Buddies?

Love You!!   Praying for You!!   Proud of You!!   Bro. Post
✶✶✶✶✶✶✶✶✶✶✶✶✶✶✶✶✶✶✶✶

Good Morning!! How Are My College Buddies?

"Give her a call.'

A godly mom is God's best way of introducing you to His love. Think about it, who shows the quality of God's love better than a godly mom? A mom is the gentle nurturer who allows you to thrive and grow in your infancy. A mom is the one who gently teaches you right from wrong, she then allows you to meet the consequences of your wrong choice. A mom is an excellent encourager, who stretches you and then praises you for trying. A godly mom is a healer, whose gentle words turns your imagined disaster into a manageable, temporary setback. A mom loves unconditionally, she forgives freely...the similarities goes on and on. College Buddies, read carefully the following verse and then do your mom a favor. Give her a call today, ok?

> "Her children arise and call her blessed; her husband also, and he praises her: 'Many women do noble things but you surpass them all.'" Proverbs 31:28-29

Love You!!   Praying for You!!   Proud of You!!   Bro. Post

✳✳✳✳✳✳✳✳✳✳✳✳✳✳✳✳✳✳✳✳✳

Good Morning!! How Are My College Buddies?

"Break Open Your Bottle"

What bottle does the Lord want you to break this week?

The woman was simply overwhelmed at the kindness of Jesus. A former prostitute, she now was amazed that ALL of her sins were forgiven! Unashamed, she broke a bottle of expensive perfume as an act of worship, then she poured the perfume over Jesus' head. (The perfume would be worth a YEAR'S wages today - tens of thousands of dollars!) She loved the Savior, so she gave Him the gift dearest to her heart. (Mark 14)

College Buddies, what gift should you open and give to the Savior this week? What gift of value to express your deep gratitude for His goodness? It may be the gift of time - taking the time in your busy schedule to help someone else. It may be a gift of possessions - sharing a gift of money with someone who needs it desperately. It may the gift of your heart – to share your compassion with a person with a deep hurt.

The value of the gift is linked to the value of our blessing. Ok, let's think about this: a million years from now, you will be in heaven, living in your Father's house. All of this because of Jesus. So when He gives you an opportunity to serve Him this week, break open the bottle, ok?

"Serve the Lord with gladness." Psalm 100:2

Love You!!   Praying for You!!   Proud of You!!   Bro. Post
✶✶✶✶✶✶✶✶✶✶✶✶✶✶✶✶✶✶✶✶✶✶

"Walking Wet"

Peter walked on the water, became afraid and he sank! But wait a minute, don't forget the rest of the story. Jesus reached out, pulled him up, and then what? Well Jesus didn't pick him up and carry him back to the boat, Peter again walked on the water, back to the boat! Even though he was wet with failure, Jesus picked him up and he started living the miracle again.

College Buddies, ALL of us 'sink' occasionally in our walk with God, it's not a question of 'if', it's a question of 'when'. Jesus is always there to rescue us and He is so kind, He doesn't berate us or scold us. He forgives us and THEN He puts us back in His will, experiencing His love and power. So if you're ready to give up, you feel like you're sinking, or maybe you're ashamed that you have failed, very soon Jesus will reach down and pick you up. It's not His nature to let us drown…very soon you will walk again with renewed faith and confidence:

"When the righteous cry for help, the Lord hears them and delivers them out of all their troubles." Psalm 34:17

Love You!!   Praying for You!!   Proud of You!!   Bro. Post
****

"Counting to Ten with God."

College Buddies, God's love is very practical. This love has many facets, like the petals in a beautiful rose. One practical expression of love is to give someone else patience. Patience means that we give them kind words and a kind spirit - we are not demanding, critical nor harsh. We do not withhold our love until they meet our lofty expectations; we meet them where they are and we let God change them, as He wants them to be. We are not quick to lecture and correct, we do not nitpick over trivialities, we are not overbearing and rude. This type of love can work wonders in our home and in our churches.

For us to be sharply critical of other's shortcomings is the epitome of arrogance - after all, we have plenty of flaws ourselves. Many a friend and many a family member has been alienated because we fail to practice patience. It's like in a track meet, we set the High Jump bar so high that others cannot possibly jump over it - than we our scowl our disapproval at their failure.

We are certainly not everything God wants us to be on this day, we fail frequently - so let's give God the time to work in someone else's life also:

"Love is very patient, very kind." I Corinthians 13:4a

Love You!! Praying for You!! Proud of You!! Bro. Post
✶✶✶✶✶✶✶✶✶✶✶✶✶✶✶✶✶✶✶✶✶

"Inventing a Terrifying Monster."

Our imagination is very powerful and sometimes, it can be our worst enemy. It can be used by the enemy to invent a terrifying monster, something that we have invented in our minds that scares us to death!

Jesus once told the disciples to get into a boat and to cross over to the other side of a lake and he would meet them there. That's exactly what they did, but then they ran into a howling storm. They had forgotten Jesus' words that he would meet them on the other side, that they would cross safely. So they sat in the boat, inventing 'terrifying monsters.' In life, when we are experiencing a rough storm of circumstances, we tend to 'invent monsters.' The disciples did just this, they were exhausted and they had given up all hope. Into this scary scenario enters Jesus and He calms the storm.

It helps when we recognize that we are inventing monsters. It helps to ask the Lord to help us stop, it helps to remember that God is bigger than our fears, our weariness and our hurt. I keep this quote on my wall, I hope you enjoy the wisdom of it:

> "When we frighten ourselves with an apprehension of trouble to come, we put ourselves upon the stretch of anxiety how to avoid it, when after all perhaps it is the creature of our own imagination." Matthew Henry

Love You!! Praying for You!! Proud of You!! Bro. Post

✶✶✶✶✶✶✶✶✶✶✶✶✶✶✶✶✶✶✶✶✶✶✶

Good Morning!! How Are My College Buddies?

"Up to your neck."

In the Bible, 'waters' is sometimes a symbol of deep distress. It can be used to describe difficulty and it can be used to describe danger.

Imagine crossing a raging creek and the water is about to sweep you away....... a picture of danger. Imagine being in a basement and the water is up to your neck and you have to carefully walk out of the basement.......a picture of difficulty.

You may feel endangered or vulnerable today. You may wondering if the raging creek will sweep you away, or sweep away a friend or loved one. And the threat is very real! Or maybe you feel a rising surge of sadness, or grief or separation, and you have to function today in your world of difficulty.

Will the waters of danger destroy you? Will the flood of sadness suffocate you? All Christians face times like these and ask these questions.

Notice God's promise...you may want to tape it on your mirror. Remember, Your Father made this promise and He doesn't lie to His kids:

> "When you pass through the waters, I will be with you; and when you pass through the rivers, they will not sweep over you. When you walk through the fire, you will not be burned; the flames will not set you ablaze. Isaiah 43:2

Love You!!   Praying for You!!   Proud of You!!   Bro. Post
✶✶✶✶✶✶✶✶✶✶✶✶✶✶✶✶✶✶✶✶✶

Good Morning!! How Are My College Buddies?

"Ministering in the Background"

Dorcas never healed anyone, she never started a great church, she loved being in the background. She never preached a sermon, (she would have fainted! :-), but her life was incredibly worthwhile!! She watched her friends and neighbors carefully, she developed a spiritual antenna for someone who had a need. She would then quietly, in the background, sew coats and knit sweaters for the needy around her. She did this constantly, she served Jesus by 'ministering in the background.'

College Buddies, you may be the type of Christian who freezes with terror at the thought of serving Jesus in a public, conspicuous way. You may feel a little guilty because you can't give a testimony or pray in public. Stop worrying about it! It is very likely that God has called you to be one of His 'background ministers' - to serve Him away from the limelight. You will experience intense joy when others benefit from your service, you'll receive even greater joy when others do not know that you did it! Terrified of the limelight? Embrace the Background Ministry. Ask God for an antenna for other's needs, decide on a way that you can help......and then get started!!:

"As we have opportunity, let us do good for everyone; and above all, to those who are of one family with us in the faith." Galatians 6:10

Love You!! Praying for You!! Proud of You!! Bro. Post

✶✶✶✶✶✶✶✶✶✶✶✶✶✶✶✶✶✶✶✶✶✶

"As Christians, someday we will have to answer to God for every sin that we have committed, either in our thoughts or by our actions."

Well, if that's true, we are in deep trouble. Very deep trouble.

I have no idea where this idea came from, but it has shackled many Christians with guilt and shame and dread. The result? Our Enemy has a easy task of causing us to doubt our Father's love and also, he causes us to feel too unworthy to do God's work.

It IS true that unbelievers will answer for their sins - this establishes their guilt for rejecting Christ. HOWEVER, for God's cleansed and forgiven children, there is one word that we should remember: IMPUTATION: This means that God actually places in your account the perfect righteousness of Christ. So when we see our failures, God sees us as perfect as Jesus. When we see our mistakes, God sees us as being pure from sin, just like His Son.

Maybe you've been bludgeoned lately with guilt...you feel like a failure in God's eyes and you feel like He thinks you are worthless. College Buddy, tell your Father how you feel and I believe that He will show you that you are as precious to Him as Jesus is. Notice how God sees you TODAY, now that you are His child:

> "Once you were alienated from God.......But now he has reconciled you by Christ's physical body through death to present you HOLY

in his sight, WITHOUT BLEMISH and FREE FROM ACCUSATION..." Colossians 1:21-22 (What a verse to relish!)

Love You!!   Praying for You!!   Proud of You!!   Bro. Post
✳✳✳✳✳✳✳✳✳✳✳✳✳✳✳✳✳✳✳✳

Good Morning!! How Are My College Buddies?

"I believe that friends are quiet angels who lift us to our feet when our wings have trouble remembering how to fly."

God's plan is simple and beautiful: our burdens in life are just too heavy for us to carry alone, He wants someone else to help carry it. It doesn't mean that you are a inferior Christian, it doesn't mean that your faith is weak. In God's plan, the load is halved and the joys are doubled when we allow a Christian friend to help us, to care for us, to pray for us. I believe that this is one of the main reasons why some Christians start living for the Lord and then quit...they quit from spiritual exhaustion, they have carried their burdens alone too long. Imagine an upstairs apartment and you are exhausted from trying to get a heavy box up the stairs - imagine the relief when a friend comes and carries half the load.

College Buddies, 'going it alone' in the Christian life is a tough, brutal road to trudge. "But when I pray, won't the Lord help me?" Of course He will. But most of the time, He will take the burden from you and then give part of it to another Christian, who becomes a 'quiet angel' to you:

"Two are better than one, because they have a good reward for their toil. For if they fall, one will lift up the other; but woe to one who is alone and falls and does not have another to help." Ecclesiastes 4:9-10

Love You!!   Praying for You!!   Proud of You!!   Bro. Post
✷✷✷✷✷✷✷✷✷✷✷✷✷✷✷✷✷✷✷✷✷✷

Good Morning!! How Are My College Buddies?

"Thanks for the Sermon"

Guess which word in the Bible this is: "Trudging up a steep hill...at times exhausted...with a heavy backpack...and still making progress."

Do you feel that way at times? There are times in life when the road is not smooth, it is steep and winding. In addition, a stiff wind of circumstances is blowing against us. We trudge wearily, making slow progress on the road that God has placed us on.

If that is true of your life right now, congratulations!! You are living one AWESOME sermon!!

The word is 'patience' - and the meaning of that word in the Bible is much more than just enduring rough stuff without losing our temper. It actually means trudging up a hill of rough circumstances, weary, with a heavy load, and STILL making progress!

And many of you are doing that right now, you are preaching a sermon without saying a word... you're living a life of patience, and you are honoring your Father more than you can ever imagine. Your life is not a cakewalk, it is a life of daily burdens and tiring treks. Although not a cakewalk, your life is definitely a pulpit - your faithfulness to our Father is being watched and noticed by other people.

Some may tell you that your present circumstances means that your faith is weak, or even that you're being punished. Don't listen to that stuff, ok?

Instead, you are a shining light for God, you are showing your strong faith each time you take another

Good Morning!! How Are My College Buddies?

weary step...against the wind...uphill...with a heavy load:

> "Now for a little while, you have had to suffer grief in all kinds of trials. These have come so that your faith.........may be proved genuine and may result in the praise, glory and honor when Jesus Christ is revealed." I Peter 1:6-7

Love You!! Praying for You!! Proud of You!! Bro. Post
✶✶✶✶✶✶✶✶✶✶✶✶✶✶✶✶✶✶✶✶

"I know what it feels like; I will help you."

College Buddies, when you are struggling and you pray for help, Jesus doesn't frown at your weakness. He knows how it feels to be tempted and tested. Okay, here's a short list. Exhausted, but still have to keep going? Someone has spoken lies about you, twisted your words? Friends have disappointed you big-time? People think you're a nobody, not worth much? You are so dreading a future event that you are burdened down with dread and agitation? You feel like God has deserted you in your tough times? People judge you, write you off as a failure? ALL of these tests Jesus faced. Actually, there isn't a struggle that He HASN'T experienced!

We have this terrible tendency to think that our Father is disappointed with us when we struggle. Actually, just the opposite is true - He is eager and anxious to comfort us and help us. Read the verse below and then pray...I bet you'll hear, "My child, I know EXACTLY what this feels like; I know it's miserable, but I want to help you."

> "Our High Priest is not one unable to be touched by the feelings of our weaknesses, but we have one who has been tested in all points as we have been tested, without committing any sin. Then let us come near the throne of grace without fear, to obtain his mercy and to find his strength when we need it." Hebrews 4:15-16

Good Morning!! How Are My College Buddies?

Love You!!　　Praying for You!!　　Proud of You!!　　Bro. Post

✭✭✭✭✭✭✭✭✭✭✭✭✭✭✭✭✭✭✭✭✭

"Amazing Potential"

"Too often we underestimate the power of a touch, a smile, a kind word, a listening ear, an honest compliment, or the smallest act of caring, all of which have the potential to turn a life around." Leo Buscaglia

These acts of kindness originate from God, and He sends them through us!! College Buddies, think back to a time when you were REALLY thirsty. I bet you didn't want a coke; I bet you longed for water. When we allow God to send to others these acts of kindness, it is like a long drink of cool water. A hurting person is thirsty to know that someone KNOWS about their hurt and someone CARES about their hurt. When you allow God to show kindness through you, you are almost always triggering a spiritual reaction in their lives. It allows them to open their hearts a little and there is where God can enter and work. When you read the Bible, you see little toddlers and infants always near Jesus - He picked them up; He spent time with them. For children to enjoy being around an adult proves at least one thing to me about Jesus- He was gentle and kind. Let's ask God to help us be the same way.

> "Therefore, as God's chosen people, holy and dearly beloved, clothe yourselves with compassion, kindness, humility, gentleness and patience." Colossians 3:12

Good Morning!! How Are My College Buddies?

Love You!!   Praying for You!!   Proud of You!!   Bro. Post

✷✷✷✷✷✷✷✷✷✷✷✷✷✷✷✷✷✷✷✷✷

"Lord, calm me down on the inside because I can't slow down on the outside!"

All of us have days that I call 'Burners' - days in which you are running and gunning, you're flush with adrenaline and your day's schedule is BRUTAL! I have learned, from my own mistakes, that there are two particular temptations on 'Burner Days'. The first is a peculiar tendency that we have to be short, even rude to others. It's almost like we feel somewhat justified, since we are loaded down. Interruptions become much more aggravating, it's like, don't these people know I'm running my tail off?! Sound familiar? :-) The other big temptation is more sneaky. College Buddies, when you are running on fumes, the Enemy can whisper a worry or concern into your ear. When this happens in the middle of a 'Burner' day, it always frightens us much more than on a normal day! Sound familiar? :-)

I am no expert here, but here are two tips. First, commit EACH day to the Lord the night before... before you go to sleep, pray for the next day. Secondly, take a verse with you through a rough day, think about it, meditate on it in the middle of the madness. Sounds crazy? I dare you to try it... Start with this one:

> "Fear thou not, for I am with you; be not dismayed, for I am your God. I will strengthen you, I will help you, I will uphold you with my victorious right hand." Isaiah 41:10

Good Morning!! How Are My College Buddies?

Love You!!   Praying for You!!   Proud of You!!   Bro. Post
✷✷✷✷✷✷✷✷✷✷✷✷✷✷✷✷✷✷✷✷

"Meltdown Recovery."

Whoa, we all need this occasionally, don't we?!

A meltdown is a time when our attitude is rotten, our joy has been replaced by disgust, the flames of anger are rising, and we are mired in the mud of discontent.

Guess what? Every Christian occasionally has them.......and we are much better off when we realize that we will occasionally have one.

A perfect snapshot of a meltdown can be seen in two prophets of God, Elijah and Jonah. Their meltdowns were rather ugly. Elijah: "I have had enough, I can't take anymore." Jonah: "I am very angry at you God, angry enough to die!" Jonah: "It's your fault God!"

Immediately after a meltdown, our Father begins working on our 'meltdown recovery.' It's fascinating how He dealt with Elijah and Jonah. Amazingly, He doesn't scold them; He looks beyond their present complaints and gently tends to them. Amazingly, He doesn't discard them - He knows the reasons why they are struggling. Like a gentle shepherd leading a wounded and weakened sheep, He nurses and cares for us until the present despair has passed.

Meltdowns aren't pretty, are they? I really don't like myself when I have one. But when meltdowns happen, our Father quickly and effectively starts tending to us......He could never discard us; Jesus' very life is invested in us.

Good Morning!! How Are My College Buddies?

"All my longings lie open before you, O Lord; my sighing is not hidden from you. O Lord, do not forsake me,......come quickly to help me." Psalm 38:9, 22

Love You!!   Praying for You!!   Proud of You!!   Bro. Post
****

"A Temporary Separation...Not a Permanent Loss."

The father of the Prodigal Son was an amazing person. He recognized the present rebellion in his son and he prayed for a future conversion. He endured and he waited. The father endured the insults of his son, the stubbornness of his son and the destructive sins of his son. How long did he wait? We really don't know......at least months, possibly years. This father prayed for his son, this father cared for his son and this father waited for his son.

College Buddy, you may have a friend, a relative or a classmate who has walked away from God and is now walking the road of rebellion. You may be amazed because they are not the same person! At one time, you both were close, but now that person has left you. You have the same heartache that the Prodigal Son's father had, a deep ache, a heart longing for them to come to God.

Notice and copy the dad's example - pray for them daily, God has the ability to bring them to Christ. Care for them, let them see your aching heart for them, be careful about trite sermons. Wait for them, this may take time for God's to change a rebel's heart.

However, some day you will celebrate!! Just as the Prodigal Son's dad looked up one day and saw his son returning, some day you will see your friend come to Christ. Throw a party! Celebrate!! On that future day, you will have witnessed the greatest miracle on earth - the salvation of a soul:

Good Morning!! How Are My College Buddies?

"Quick! Bring the best robe and put it on him. Put a ring on his finger and sandals on his feet……..Let's have a feast and celebrate. For this son of mine was dead and is alive again; he was lost and is found. And they began to celebrate." Luke 15:22-24

Love You!!   Praying for You!!   Proud of You!!   Bro. Post
✷✷✷✷✷✷✷✷✷✷✷✷✷✷✷✷✷✷✷✷✷

Good Morning!! How Are My College Buddies?

"Spiritual Friendship"

Jonathan knew what to do, he knew his friend David desperately needed him. David was exhausted, he had been hiding from King Saul, who jealously wanted to kill him. Now David's faith was rattled, and he was at the lowest point of his life. (I Samuel 23)

Jonathan was a spiritual friend. He cared deeply for David so he went and found David. He didn't try to love David 'long-distance' - he was right beside David in his darkness hour. Jonathan knew what was frightening David so Jonathan spoke to him about his fears. By faith, Jonathan told David that the thing that he was worrying about was not going to happen. "King Saul will not even lay a hand on you." Then Jonathan, by faith, encouraged David to believe that blessings, not disasters, were coming to him from God. The result was that David's faith was renewed.

College Buddies, you will meet someone this week who needs a Jonathan, a true spiritual friend. There have been many times when we have needed a true spiritual friend, ask God to make you a Jonathan to someone else:

> "And we urge you, encourage the timid, help the weak, be patient with everyone….always try to be kind to each other and everyone else." I Thessalonians 5:14-15

Love You!!   Praying for You!!   Proud of You!!   Bro. Post

✶✶✶✶✶✶✶✶✶✶✶✶✶✶✶✶✶✶✶✶✶✶✶✶

"Take off the Judicial robes, God doesn't need your help."

Jesus made it very clear, He really did not leave us any 'wiggle room.'

"Stop judging." (Matthew 7)

It's really risky business, it's like walking on thin ice...eventually, we will crash through the shaky foundation of our wrong assumptions. It's really sneaky, isn't it? We tend to judge another Christian in two areas - their MOTIVES and their CHARACTER. Amazingly, we tend to do this with very few facts!! We know 10% of what is true, but we judge like we know 90% of the truth.

All Christians stumble at times and all Christians have tough days and all Christians have times in which we are certainly not a good witness for our Father. Ok, do you want to spiritually demote them when you see this happen? Throw them out of God's family? Question if they are truly saved? Assume that their faith is weak? Voice disappointment in them? Use a Bible verse as a spiritual hammer? Wow, no wonder Jesus ordered us to take off our Judicial robes. Can you imagine the damage done, in God's family, by judging?

Let's get off the thin ice, ok? If we are going to make a mistake, let's err on the side of love. God's love is very practical how it shows itself......one very loving act is verbal silence, refusing to judge:

"Do not judge, or you too will be judged. For in the same way you judge others, you will be judged, and with the measure you use, it will be measured to you." Matthew 7:1-2 (No Wiggle Room)

Love You!! Praying for You!! Proud of You!! Bro. Post
✶✶✶✶✶✶✶✶✶✶✶✶✶✶✶✶✶✶✶✶✶

"Super Sensitive Days"

Ok, let's be honest here, ok? We all have them occasionally, men and women. (Although men are often experts at trying to hide them.)

A 'Super Sensitive Day' is a day when we wear our feelings on our sleeve, we are a little touchy, our feelings are easily hurt and we read into or misread other people's words and actions. We are easily disappointed and a little frustrated with others' insensitivity. A 'Super Sensitive Day' can be triggered by a lot of things......fatigue, stress, dashed or unfulfilled hopes or an 'anomaly in previously consistent biorhythms.' (I'm not sure what that means, but it sounds good. :-)

Elijah once had a 'Super Sensitive Day' and he is a classic example. He felt unappreciated by others. He was exhausted beyond words. He magnified his burdens and he wished his life was a lot different.

Now this was a man who loved God totally...... and if he had a SS Day, maybe we shouldn't beat ourselves up when we have one.

It is so wonderful how our Father helped Elijah in this tough time. He did not lecture or scold Elijah...The Lord did not try to show how Elijah's complaints were wrong...it seems that the Lord knew the reasons for the complaints and just ignored them. Then our Father shows His gentle nurturing...He tends perfectly to his struggling child.

And that's exactly what our Father does for us when we have a SS Day. Think about how kind and gentle your Father is, and think about How He

Good Morning!! How Are My College Buddies?

perfectly helps you through a rough day. Think about this verse, it's a beautiful word picture of our Father gently nurturing us:

> "He tends his flock like a shepherd: He gathers the lambs in His arms and carries them close to His heart; He gently leads those who have young." Isaiah 40:11

Love You!! Praying for You!! Proud of You!! Bro. Post
✶✶✶✶✶✶✶✶✶✶✶✶✶✶✶✶✶✶✶✶

"The weight of another person will make your steps secure."

Two hundred years ago, there was an Indian tribe camping in northern Mississippi. They had camped beside a shallow river that had a raging current. Although the river was only waist deep, the fierce current would cause a person to lose their footing and drown. The tribe was attacked by another tribe and the braves retreated to the village and consulted with their chief. The decision was a brutal choice - stay in the village and all be slaughtered or flee with the healthy, leaving the elderly and children. The chief considered and then made his decision. "We live or we die together. Each brave will pick up an elderly person or pick up two children in his arms. Walk across the river with them to safety." The braves obeyed, but inside they felt that they were doomed to drown. But as they carried the weight of another person across their shoulders, an amazing thing happened. The extra weight made their steps secure in the treacherous current, they easily crossed the river and the tribe was saved.

College Buddies, we are at our best as Christians when we carry the burdens of another Christian. We walk closer to God, our prayer life is energized, our spiritual footing is secure. We are at our worst when we live the life of "it's all about me." And like the chief said, we are all in this together, the burdens of another Christian are automatically our burdens. We may feel that we lack time, ability or the assets to

Good Morning!! How Are My College Buddies?

help, but carrying the extra burden is the unlikely road of Christian maturity and incredible joy.

Do you know someone struggling today? Threatened by circumstances that are difficult and brutal? Don't bolt and run, stand beside them. Hoist their burden on your spiritual shoulders, love them, encourage them and pray for them:

"Carry each other's burdens, and in this way you will fulfill the law of Christ." Galatians 6:2

Love You!!   Praying for You!!   Proud of You!!   Bro. Post
✶✶✶✶✶✶✶✶✶✶✶✶✶✶✶✶✶✶✶✶✶✶

"Put your sword away. I will take care of this."

Peter loved Jesus very much and he couldn't stand it when Jesus was threatened. Some guards came to arrest Jesus and Peter took things into his own hands. Peter didn't understand the big picture that Jesus was more powerful than any puny army in the world. So Peter drew his sword and whacked off the guard's ear. Jesus healed the man's ear and then rebuked Peter.

Sometimes we draw a sword, don't we? We try to handle everything ourselves and we squeeze God out of the solution. We jump to swing a verbal sword, thinking that our words will cause immediate changes. When this sword doesn't work, we draw the mental sword, hashing and rehashing ways that we plan to correct the situation. We recruit others, we plan, scheme, fret and stew. We draw a sword to solve the problem and like Peter, we only make things worse!

"PUT YOUR SWORD AWAY, I WILL TAKE CARE OF THIS!!"

Jehoshaphat knew what it was like to be still and trust. Three massive armies were marching to wipe out Jerusalem. All Jehoshaphat had was a tiny ragtag army. He told God that the situation was impossible and asked God to work a miracle. God told Him to just watch quietly, praise Him and He will deliver. And that is exactly what God did. When Jehoshaphat waited quietly, God worked mightily. Notice the wonderful promise that God gives us when we 'put our sword away.':

> He said: "Listen, King Jehoshaphat and all who live in Judah and Jerusalem! This is what the LORD says to you: 'Do not be afraid or discouraged because of this vast army. For the battle is not yours, but God's." II Chronicles 20:15

Love You!!   Praying for You!!   Proud of You!!   Bro. Post

✶✶✶✶✶✶✶✶✶✶✶✶✶✶✶✶✶✶✶✶✶

"A blessing delayed is not a blessing denied."

Thirteen years is a very long time, especially if that 13 years is filled with misery, hardships and bewildering questions. It's tough when your very own family turns against you viciously - harsh words and cruel actions, born out of jealousy and hate. It's very rough to be uprooted from your dreams, living in a foreign land where you know no one. It's brutal to be imprisoned for years, KNOWING that you are totally innocent. But the roughest part is when you cry out to God, and it seems like He is doing NOTHING.

Hmm, I wonder why this man didn't quit...leave God...bitterly blame God.

Actually, God WAS working in the background, perfectly crafting a huge, future blessing where the Lord's name only would be praised! I wonder if this man ever got discouraged. Probably. I wonder if he was tempted by the enemy to forget about God. Most definitely. I wonder if there were times when he thought things would never get better. Very likely. From the time Joseph was sold as a slave to the time he got out of prison was 13 years, 4748 days of unanswered questions.

God was not idle - God blessed Joseph beyond his wildest hopes. College Buddies, having tough times? Will you have to wait thirteen years? Maybe, but not likely. Your Father is working but He will likely not tell you His plans until He unveils His blessing...... and it is coming:

"Let the name of the Lord be praised, both now and forevermore……..He raises the poor from the dust and lifts the needy from the ash heap." Psalm 113:2, 7

Love You!! Praying for You!! Proud of You!! Bro. Post
✸✸✸✸✸✸✸✸✸✸✸✸✸✸✸✸✸✸✸✸

"Walking Blind"

It is unsettling enough to have a walk a path in life that is totally unfamiliar to us, we do not know the risks nor the demands of the trail. All of us like to have details - we want to know what we are facing so that we can adequately prepare. Surely God wouldn't lead us to walk a path where, alas, we had no strategic plan to face it! Horrors!! :-)

Imagine a worse scenario, we have to walk down an unfamiliar path and we cannot see anything. Imagine that we're hiking that path at midnight with cloudy skies and we can't see our hand in front of our face. It would be VERY helpful if another person was with us, guiding us and guarding us as we were 'walking blind.'

College Buddies, God will see to it that there are times in your life when you have to 'walk blind.' You have to walk a path in life where you feel totally unprepared - you know little about that new path and you know there are risks and pitfalls - and yet, you have to walk it.

Guess who is waiting to walk with you?

'Walking Blind' down a new and risky path is not a bad thing at all when it's God's will, but we sure don't like it, do we?! In these periodic times when we have to walk a new path, our Father is doing a beautiful but painful thing for us: He is stripping away our 'safety nets.' Our Father is gently placing us in a position where we will depend upon Him only - our well laid plans, our own opinions and wisdom, our knowledge of similar, past experiences...these

Good Morning!! How Are My College Buddies?

'safety nets' are gone! Now walking blind down a risky path, we are very grateful to feel His hand as He leads us safely.

College Buddies, you may be bewildered and rattled about a new path in life and you're frustrated. You do not want to walk this path because you know there are pitfalls but you just can't adequately prepare! Your Father is waiting for you, after all, it's His plan for you to take this path. He will take your hand and guide you safely, step by step. At the end of the journey, you will feel a deeper love for your Father who is a Expert at helping His kids when they have to 'walk blind.'

> "I will lead the blind by ways they have not known, along unfamiliar paths I will guide them; I will turn the darkness into light before them and make the rough places smooth. These are the things I will do; I will not forsake them." Isaiah 42:16

Love You!!   Praying for You!!   Proud of You!!   Bro. Post
✼✼✼✼✼✼✼✼✼✼✼✼✼✼✼✼✼✼✼✼

Good Morning!! How Are My College Buddies?

"That's not what I said! You're twisting everything!"

College Buddies, it is VERY tough when people distort what you have said or done. It's also rough when they criticize your actions, often accusing you of an ulterior motive. Our first inclination is to 'set the record straight', to defend ourselves against this unfairness. Ok, College Buddies, go ahead and try, but angry and vindictive people are not interested in facts, they're only interested in their agenda of tearing someone down.

Jesus faced this problem constantly, His critics distorted almost everything He did or said. If He had tried to defend Himself, He wouldn't have had time to do anything else! In your lifetime, you will walk by a lot of 'verbal garbage dumps', situations that you will be tempted to 'clean up'. When it comes to this type of a verbal 'garbage dump', it's best to keep walking. If someone is unkind enough to spread distortions about someone, don't be naïve enough to believe the facts will stop them.

> "Never return injury for injury…If you can, so far as it depends on you, be at peace with everyone. Never take vengeance into your own hands, my dear friends…for it is written, 'Vengeance is mine, I will repay', says the Lord." Romans 12:18,19

Love You!!   Praying for You!!   Proud of You!!   Bro. Post

✶✶✶✶✶✶✶✶✶✶✶✶✶✶✶✶✶✶✶✶✶✶

"Sometimes God's love is a gentle whisper......Other times, His love is a loud shout from heaven."

College Buddies, have you learned to relax in God's love? To let go, to stop trying to impress God, to relax, to accept that God loves you deeply, intensely and eternally. He is a forever doting Father, His eyes are soft when He looks at you.

It's tiring to try to earn this love, that will wear you out emotionally and spiritually drain you. Let go, ok? We are people of grace and it is totally impossible to earn God's love...we just can't.

Now be assured, you have to use your faith to enjoy this love! Ok, you hear a moving testimony or you listen to a beautiful song - now it's easy to enjoy God's love, isn't it? Ok, you're dead tired, you're pushed with a tough day and all that you have to do in the next week makes you cringe. Now you don't feel God's love too much, do you? Hey, that's perfectly normal! In these times, you need to use your faith. Grab yourself by the collar, say to yourself: "I am a son/daughter of my Father. He loves me more than I could possibly imagine. He is crazy about me. The fact that I do not feel like He loves me this much is totally irrelevant. I will enjoy His love today, not because I feel it but because I believe it."

College Buddies, enjoy your Father's love today, ok? As you remember the cross of Jesus, you won't have to listen for His soft whisper. It will be loud shout from heaven: "I love YOU!"

Good Morning!! How Are My College Buddies?

"How great is the love the Father has lavished upon _____, that_____ should be called a child of God!" I John 3:1 (Put your name in the blank)

Love You!!   Praying for You!!   Proud of You!!   Bro. Post
✳✳✳✳✳✳✳✳✳✳✳✳✳✳✳✳✳✳✳✳✳✳✳

"Father, make them a walking visual aid to your power."

College Buddies, when the Lord wants to show His power, He does it in the life of a person. He works in a powerful and wonderful way, to show the world that HE is God......that HE has power to work. When this happens, the person whom God has blessed and changed becomes a 'walking visual aid', someone who shows and tells others about our Father's goodness.

Why not pray for someone this way? There are people around us, both Christians and non-Christians who have tremendous needs. Sometimes we are tempted to give up praying, to throw in the towel, to accept the inevitable.

Why not pray and ask God to work so that others can see HIS power? Pray that the Lord will save that person without Christ, change their life and make them a walking visual aid.

Pray that the Lord would restore health to a person to whom the doctors have given no hope and make that person a walking visual aid.

Pray that the Lord would ease the intense burdens of a Christian living in a daily fiery furnace and make that person a walking visual aid.

You see, when we pray this way, we are recognizing that God works to show His power and to glorify His name. Others will be converted and Christians will be encouraged when He works this way.

Good Morning!! How Are My College Buddies?

Have you been praying for someone who desperately needs God's help? Imagine, using your faith, how wonderful it would be if God worked in their life. Imagine how much glory it would bring to God! Then pray, "Father, make them a walking visual aid to your power."

"Now to him who is able to do immeasurably MORE THAN ALL WE ASK OR IMAGINE, according to the power that is at work within us, to him be glory in the church and in Christ Jesus throughout all generations, for ever and ever! Amen." Ephesians 3:20-21

Love You!! Praying for You!! Proud of You!! Bro. Post
✳✳✳✳✳✳✳✳✳✳✳✳✳✳✳✳✳✳✳✳

Good Morning!! How Are My College Buddies?

"Roadblock Ahead"

Sometimes God blocks the road that HE allowed you to travel on! Here's what I mean, we Americans are touchy about our own plans...we make them, we love them and we stubbornly stick to them! So we're cruising down the interstate of our lives, everything is planned out, no worries. Then we come around a curve and there is a roadblock - and it's quite obvious that we have to get off this road and travel another one.

I believe with all of my heart that roadblocks are from God. Now we can get mad at a roadblock, or sit down and cry......it won't matter, we are not going any further. It's not that the road you've chosen is always bad, but the truth is, God's road is ALWAYS better!

If you've made plans for marriage, vocation, future and today you're facing a roadblock, I know you're frustrated. But if you pray and look around, you will discover the new road that God wants you to travel and I promise you, that road is far better. :

"NO good THING does the Lord withhold from those who walk uprightly. O Lord of Hosts, HAPPY is the man who trusts in thee!" Psalm 84:11,12 (emphasis mine)

Love You!!   Praying for You!!   Proud of You!!   Bro. Post
✴✴✴✴✴✴✴✴✴✴✴✴✴✴✴✴✴✴✴✴

"Wounds and Scars"

"Tucked away in a quiet corner of every life are wounds and scars. If they were not there, we would need no Physician. Nor would we need each other." (Chuck Swindoll)

College Buddies, these wounds and scars are real, everyone has them and they ARE painful. These are the areas in our lives where God meets us and shows His tender care, in the part of our soul where we hurt the most.

Sometimes we practice 'spiritual make believe' - you know, "I shouldn't hurt like this"..."If I were a strong Christian, this wouldn't bother me." Have you ever thought that your Father longs for you to tell Him when you are hurting? He longs to soothe your fears and start healing your hurts...He longs to gently encourage and help you. Imagine a frightened child, weeping and scared...now imagine a dad who scoops the child up in his arms and comforts the child. Now we can go it alone...grit our teeth... ignore the hurts, leave the wounds untended. OR we can be honest with our Father, allow Him to comfort us, allow Him to show us how much He loves us. College Buddies, go to the part of your life where the wounds and scars are, your Father is waiting for you there. Tell Him how much it hurts, be perfectly honest...let Him scoop you up in His arms:

"Be merciful to me. Lord, for I am faint; O Lord heal me." Psalm 6:2

Good Morning!! How Are My College Buddies?

Love You!!   Praying for You!!   Proud of You!!   Bro. Post

✶✶✶✶✶✶✶✶✶✶✶✶✶✶✶✶✶✶✶✶✶

"The Pitfalls of Fatigue"

Have you ever noticed how tough it is to live for the Lord on days when you are bone-tired? College Buddies, you are WAY ahead if you are very cautious and careful in days of deep weariness. When we begin a day already dragging, we all fight the same tough battles.

Imagine a huge magnifying glass and that is exactly what happens! We 'enlarge' our troubles - in our weary mind, we magnify them and dwell on them. We enlarge a small offense - on weary days, we are much more 'touchy.' Often our joy in the Lord is gone, our confidence for the future is shaken. ALL Christians fight these battles on weary days, our Father knows this and He is always there to help us. He helps us rein in our runaway thoughts and face the day with a determined faith while enduring the 'fog of fatigue.'

College Buddies, I hope you having a wonderful day today!! But if you're not, your Father is not frowning at you. He's right beside you, He has His arm around you and He will gently help you, one weary hour at a time:

"He gives power to the exhausted and to him
who has no might, he increases strength.......
they who wait upon the Lord shall renew their
strength... ' Isaiah 40:29, 31

Love You!!   Praying for You!!   Proud of You!!   Bro. Post
✶✶✶✶✶✶✶✶✶✶✶✶✶✶✶✶✶✶✶✶✶✶

"Waiting Without a Clue."

College Buddies, you will have great times of blessings and joys in your lifetime - the Lord will see to it that you do.

However, there will be other times, difficult but necessary, when you will endure tough times...and you will have no idea what God is doing or why. We cry out for God to deliver us and He doesn't. We ask God why this happened, and God does not answer. God is very gentle with His children in these times, He does not scold us and He is not disappointed in us - really, He isn't. Think of this: the dark hours you are going through are like the darkest hours of the night, just prior to sunrise. The Lord is preparing the beauty of the sunrise, but it very tough to believe that at 4 in the morning!! God will allow the sun to shine again and He will ease the pressure, but He does not do this instantaneously, He allows us to endure the dark hours.

If, in your life, it seems like 4 in the morning, and you're enveloped with tough times, God wants to assure you: "Give me time, I'm working in ways you cannot see." Notice how King David, beaten down by tough circumstances, still had hope - at '4 in the morning.':

> "Though you have made me see troubles, many and bitter, you will restore my life again; from the depths of the earth you will again bring me up. You will...comfort me once again." Psalm 71:20-21

Good Morning!! How Are My College Buddies?

Love You!!   Praying for You!!   Proud of You!!   Bro. Post

✹✹✹✹✹✹✹✹✹✹✹✹✹✹✹✹✹✹✹✹

"Agape love is not myopic."

If you have nearsightedness, you know that you can see very well any person or object that is close to you. However, the further a person is standing from you, the more fuzzy they appear.

Spiritual myopia means that I see and care about myself and everything that relates to me, but when it comes to other people, their needs become fuzzy and blurred, and I just don't worry about it.

Spiritual myopia is a metaphor for old fashioned selfishness.

Isn't it interesting how zealous we are to care about our own concerns? We jam our schedule with our own plans which we want to do. This leaves little time for ministry to others - but we plan to do ministry someday when things aren't so hectic. We crimp a budget for new stuff that we feel that we have to have. This leaves little money left over for sharing with the needy.

It's like God calls us to serve Him, but that call hits the brick wall of a undisciplined schedule. Or He leads us to share our goods and money, but those assets are already committed.

'Spiritual Myopia.'

Our Father is patient with us and He lovingly nudges us to our higher purpose as Christians. He causes our life to intersect with someone that the Lord wants us to serve. Or, He may remove some of our selfish trappings so we are free to serve Him. He definitely gives us an incredible joy when we serve others in the name of Jesus. This process takes time, but our Father will not allow us to be redeemed by Jesus and then spend a lifetime pursuing myopic goals.

When we ask God to fill us with agape love, it is astounding how well we see others whom we now want to serve, in Jesus' name:

"Love is not selfish." I Corinthians 13:5

Love You!!   Praying for You!!   Proud of You!!   Bro. Post
✳✳✳✳✳✳✳✳✳✳✳✳✳✳✳✳✳✳✳✳

"Don't throw in the towel."

When it comes to praying with faith, really believing that God will work, sometimes it's a battle not to concede, to throw in the towel. Don't throw in the towel if God takes His time – His timetable is perfect, He knows exactly when to answer. Don't throw in the towel if things look worse now than when you first started praying – often the night is the darkest, right before the sunrise. Don't throw in the towel if, on the inside, you really feel that the problem is impossible to solve. Don't throw in the towel if you can't figure out ANY way it could be solved - our Father loves to work in those situations.

There was a widow in the Bible who easily could have 'thrown in the towel' - she had asked and asked and received absolutely nothing. She didn't stop... she didn't quit in discouragement, she didn't 'water down' her prayer, thinking it would be easier for God to answer. She just kept asking, she just kept believing and finally the answer came.

College Buddy, in your life and in my life there are some unresolved issues that you and I have prayed about for a long time, and nothing has changed. Hey, it's easy to get discouraged over these issues, isn't it? Let's not quit, let's keep praying, let's keep trusting. If God lets us down, we will be the first ones He has ever failed:

"Keep on asking and it will be given to you; keep on seeking and you will find; keep on

Good Morning!! How Are My College Buddies?

knocking and the door will be opened to you."
Matthew 7:7

Love You!!   Praying for You!!   Proud of You!!   Bro. Post
✷✷✷✷✷✷✷✷✷✷✷✷✷✷✷✷✷✷✷✷✷

"Monday Morning Praying."

Actually, it's probably better to start the night before! If you struggle with Mondays, assume certain attitudes will pop up. "Lord, I wish I could do something else!" "That person really ticks me off!" "How come everybody dumps on me?!" The Lord is with us when life gets ragged, He doesn't cast us aside. HOWEVER, here is a great opportunity!

College Buddies, start making a 'memory bank' of certain situations where you struggle...situations that frighten you, anger you, make you discontented, whatever. I can't tell you how valuable this is. Then, when you know it's coming, you can pray and prepare in advance! And when you caught off-guard, imagine a blinking caution light - pray and ask God to help you to be very careful in your words and actions. It is true that God's wisdom can be obtained from the Bible, prayer, Godly advice......it's also true that God gives us wisdom when we learn from our past mistakes and struggles.

> "If any of you lacks wisdom, let him ask God who gives to all men GENEROUSLY and without scolding, and it WILL be given him."
> James 1:5 (emphasis mine)

Love You!!   Praying for You!!   Proud of You!!   Bro. Post

✶✶✶✶✶✶✶✶✶✶✶✶✶✶✶✶✶✶✶✶✶✶

"He's concerned about His reputation."

One of the big reasons that God will not fail you, that He WILL make something wonderful out of your life, is very simple: He is concerned about His reputation, He doesn't want that tarnished. Think about it, when you came to Christ, you became God's child. He promised to forgive you, (He did), and He promised to take care of you, (He has and He will). Now if He forgets about you and allows your life to become a miserable failure, then He literally has broken His promises.

One dangerous fault of sheep is that they are naively curious - they easily leave the safety of the flock and wander off to new 'exciting' sights, intrigued and curious. Almost always, they end up hopelessly lost, sometimes injured, bleating in fear. When this happens, the Good Shepherd immediately starts looking for His sheep. He knows that the sheep will NEVER find the way back to safety. Once He finds the sheep, He tends to the injuries, places the sheep on His shoulders and takes him safely back.

College Buddies, does any of this sound familiar? :-) Jesus is watching us and He is helping us stay on the right path. HOWEVER, He knows that ALL of us occasionally wander off…it's our very nature. Once He finds us, He forgives us and returns us to the safety of His flock and His care. He does this for two reasons: First, He does love us immensely, and secondly, He is very concerned about His reputation:

Good Morning!! How Are My College Buddies?

"The Lord is my shepherd.......He leads me in right paths for HIS name's sake." Psalm 23:1,3

Love You!!   Praying for You!!   Proud of You!!   Bro. Post
✶✶✶✶✶✶✶✶✶✶✶✶✶✶✶✶✶✶✶✶✶

"How dare you try to harm my child!"

I am fascinated, when reading the Bible, how intensely protective our Father is toward each of us. This makes perfect sense, as a perfect parent, He is totally filled with incredible love and tenderness toward you. Although human parents try to shield their kids from ALL problems, our Father does not always do that; He knows that our faith and confidence in Him grows more in the middle of a problem...so He occasionally allows the pressure to come. He is always watching us closely and helping us perfectly in the days that are rough.

However, at the PERFECT time, our Father steps into our situation and turns back the efforts of the enemy to ruin us...He actually uses YOU as a living visual aid, to display His protection and care. I think that is so awesome! (But it gets better!) Then He often sends you special blessings after the trial, to let the world know that you are indeed His kid, and that He will not allow anyone or anything to destroy you.

If things are rough today, try thanking your Father now for the day in the future when the seas are calmer and the pressure is eased. If you do this, you may never preach a sermon, but I promise that you will be living a sermon - the very best witness for Christ that I know:

> "I waited patiently for the Lord; he inclined
> to me and heard my cry. He drew me up from
> a horrible pit, out of the miry bog, and set my

feet upon a rock, making my steps secure."
Psalm 40:1-2

Love You!! Praying for You!! Proud of You!! Bro. Post
✳✳✳✳✳✳✳✳✳✳✳✳✳✳✳✳✳✳✳✳

"Lighten up, ok?"

It's amazing how we Christians can sometimes be so rough on each other - instead of acknowledging that we ALL struggle, we try to present an image of near perfection. Nowhere can this trait be seen clearer than how we treat Christians who are struggling. Often we feel compelled to give them canned advice, religious clichés or hollow pep talks.

Have you ever encouraged anyone with words only? It's impossible to do.

Words without love is a waste of breath. But if you allow God to fill you with His tender compassion, you will be amazed how people will open their heart to you.

God can actually make us as tenderhearted as Jesus Himself - we can show His love and forgiveness and gentleness. Then we are ready to truly encourage.

Know someone having a tough time today? Thought you might share a cliché with them? Stop! First get on your knees and ask God to make you compassionate - to sense some of their misery and to feel some of their hurt. THEN and only then are we ready to speak to them. I bet we will speak a lot less advice and give a lot more gentleness:

> "Therefore, as God's chosen people, holy and dearly beloved, clothe yourselves with compassion, kindness, humility, gentleness and patience." Colossians 3:12

Good Morning!! How Are My College Buddies?

Love You!! Praying for You!! Proud of You!! Bro. Post

✶✶✶✶✶✶✶✶✶✶✶✶✶✶✶✶✶✶✶✶✶

Good Morning!! How Are My College Buddies?

"God doesn't scare His kids.'"

Always remember, when you are facing something that is frightening, and you are struggling with panicky feelings of fear, this is NOT your Father! Think about it, would a Father who dearly loves and adores all of His children, would a Father like that deliberately fill your mind with scary thoughts?

When my daughters were little and couldn't sleep, I would sit beside them to comfort them...I would never tell them scary things that might happen! College Buddies, unfortunately, every Christian has a spiritual enemy and he loves to scare us! He is an expert at helping us imagine terrifying or disastrous scenarios - it happens all the time, all Christians have to fight this. After he scares us with these thoughts, he then tries to make us believe that our Father is speaking to us!! It's in these panic moments that we can cry out to our Father - we can actually ask and expect Him to comfort and assure us. He knows when we struggle and He has the ability to calm us and renew our hope. He might use a verse like this one, a delightful promise to you:

> "In my anguish I cried to the Lord, and he answered by setting me free. The Lord is with me; I will not be afraid." Psalm 118:5-6

Love You!!   Praying for You!!   Proud of You!!   Bro. Post

✶✶✶✶✶✶✶✶✶✶✶✶✶✶✶✶✶✶✶✶✶✶✶✶

Good Morning!! How Are My College Buddies?

"Jumping Scared"

Little Billy couldn't make himself do it. He was determined to jump off the high diving board, but now, looking below, he fidgeted and decided to climb back down the ladder to the ground. A little girl was waiting on the ladder, watching Billy. She whispered, "Billy, it's ok to jump scared."

College Buddies, as God leads us in life, we often have to use our faith and 'jump scared.' It would be nice if we didn't have reservations and fears, but most of the time, we have a peculiar mixture of confidence and second guessing. Actually, this is not a reason to be ashamed, Jesus Himself once had a time of dread and uncertainty about the future. The issue is not whether we're scared, the issue is whether we, by faith, will go ahead and 'jump scared.' God may have led you to a new chapter in your life…You may be enduring a rough time of scary events…You may be facing a new way of serving God that leaves you nervous..it's ok, use your faith. God is whispering to you, "Trust me, I'll help you, go ahead - it's ok to jump scared.":

> "Be strong and of good courage; stop being frightened, neither be dismayed; for the Lord your God is with you wherever you go."
> Joshua 1:9

Love You!!   Praying for You!!   Proud of You!!   Bro. Post
✶✶✶✶✶✶✶✶✶✶✶✶✶✶✶✶✶✶✶✶✶

Good Morning!! How Are My College Buddies?

"Spiritual Magnets"

Our Father knows how very easy it is for us to wander away from Him - it is especially easy in times when we have no problems, few concerns, minor worries. We tend to think that if our lives were totally happy, we would then serve the Lord more effectively.

That is sooo not true!! Just like a magnet draws pieces of metal to it's core, so the Lord allows us, in all times of our lives, to have some unresolved problems, some unanswered questions and some future concerns. He uses these problems to draw us closer to Him, the only One who can truly make our lives worthwhile.

College Buddies, you can wish for a carefree, easy life......but it's not going to happen...your Father loves you too much to allow you to squander your life. Instead, He knows the perfect 'magnets' for each of us - circumstances that keep us from leaving Him ......circumstances that cause us to trust. I bet some of your best times in spiritual growth came while enduring some of your roughest times in outside circumstances. Notice King David's short testimony below, it speaks volumes about God's 'magnets' in our lives:

"Before I was afflicted I went astray, but now I obey your word." Psalm 119:67

Love You!!   Praying for You!!   Proud of You!!   Bro. Post
✳✳✳✳✳✳✳✳✳✳✳✳✳✳✳✳✳✳✳✳✳

Good Morning!! How Are My College Buddies?

"A terrifying but harmless roar."

The Lord certainly protected Daniel when he was in the lions' den - actually, he was the safest person in the whole country! The reason that he was so safe was because God had sent an angel to keep the lions from attacking Daniel. However, the lions were still free to roam about the den, these terrifying creatures may have come close to Daniel, they probably occasionally roared. Here's my point: their roar was certainly frightening, but because of our Father, their roar was totally harmless.

College Buddies, we all occasionally feel like Daniel, we are terrified because we are surrounded by threatening circumstances, like the lions roaming in the den. The Enemy whispers into our ears and causes us to invent future scenarios that end in disaster. We hear the 'roar of the lions', we wonder if God is still protecting us. I wonder if Daniel had a few bouts with fear - after all, he did have to stay in the den the whole night, living in the middle of danger. The same God who protected Daniel is protecting you and your family and your friends. All of us occasionally hear the 'roar of a lion' - our Father reminds us that the roar is harmless:

> "Call upon me in the day of trouble; I will deliver you, and you shall glorify me." Psalm 50:15

Love You!!   Praying for You!!   Proud of You!!   Bro. Post
✳✳✳✳✳✳✳✳✳✳✳✳✳✳✳✳✳✳✳✳✳✳

"Resentment...Separation...Retaliation...Recruitment"

These are the four components to the Cycle of Bitterness. College Buddies, when you are angry at someone, the anger you feel does not stay the same, it grows and spreads. Resentment is that 'stewing anger', it causes us to mentally replay the offense and feed the anger. Separation occurs when we physically avoid the person or we emotionally lose feelings of fondness toward that person. Retaliation comes soon after, usually verbal...when we speak unfavorably about that person. The last step is Recruitment - we start telling others about the offense so that they will agree with us that we were wronged.

Hmm, not a very pretty picture is it?

God will help us out of this pit when we turn to Him. We start by asking God to forgive us...for the sin of bitterness. What if you did nothing wrong, the other person was totally in the wrong? I understand how tough this is, but welcome to the world of spiritual maturity. God can release us from bitterness regardless of the other person, whether they ask forgiveness or not. Jesus did that and only He can help us do the same. Take a piece of paper, date it and write: "Today, with God's help, I forgive _____ _____. I ask God to remove the bitterness." Our Father will then set us free from this vicious cycle:

> "Let all bitterness and wrath and anger and clamor be put away from you, with all malice, and be kind to one another, tender-

hearted, forgiving one another, as God in Christ forgave you." Ephesians 4:31-32

Love You!!   Praying for You!!   Proud of You!!   Bro. Post
✸✸✸✸✸✸✸✸✸✸✸✸✸✸✸✸✸✸✸✸

Good Morning!! How Are My College Buddies?

"Relish it...Revel in it...Remember it."

College Buddies, when God sends you a wonderful blessing, and He always will, remember these three verbs, the three R's of thanksgiving. Years ago, when I would receive a blessing, I would fire off a quick "Thank you!" and then start looking for the next one! Whoa! Slow down!

Ok, let me explain it this way. Almost every night, at 9 PM, there is something I relish. I take a scoop of vanilla bean ice cream, one can of Dr. Pepper and I put it in a blender. (Do NOT set the blender too high...it will blow out the top! :-) I sit down and thoroughly relish this, it is SO delicious! That's the exact attitude that we should have when our Father sends us a love gift, a wonderful blessing that has brightened our day and made our burdens a little less heavy. Make yourself sit down, think about the blessing, relish it, and thank Him from your heart. Here's a verse to help us do just that:

> "O my God, you are my God; I will exalt thee, I will praise your name, for you have done wonderful things." Isaiah 25:1

Love You!!   Praying for You!!   Proud of You!!   Bro. Post

✶✶✶✶✶✶✶✶✶✶✶✶✶✶✶✶✶✶✶✶✶

Good Morning!! How Are My College Buddies?

"You Are a Masterpiece"

"God's hand is in your heartache. If you were not important, do you think He would take this long, and work this hard on your life?"
-Chuck Swindoll

The masterpiece of the Mona Lisa was crafted by da Vinci away from the crowds, in the seclusion of his studio. He didn't rush it - he patiently painted the outline, then applied the background, then defined the lady with the finishing touches of brilliance. College Buddies, some of you are in the throes of rough times - instead of things getting better, things are worse, you see no hope on the horizon, you really do feel that God is either angry or has forgotten about you.

Have you ever thought that God is forging a masterpiece? That He is humbling you, that He is molding you into that beautiful person who thinks, speaks and acts like Jesus? Your heart will be tender, your words will be kind and loving, your gentle actions will be an imitation of Jesus. This doesn't happen overnight - God takes His time as He is patiently molding you. Your Father is not angry at you, He is perfectly creating a spiritual masterpiece…and that masterpiece is you:

"But now, O Lord, you are our Father. We are the clay, you are the potter; we are all the work of your hands." Isaiah 64:8

Love You!!   Praying for You!!   Proud of You!!   Bro. Post
✸✸✸✸✸✸✸✸✸✸✸✸✸✸✸✸✸✸✸✸✸

Good Morning!! How Are My College Buddies?

"Pray……Keep Praying……Even when you're faith is weak and battered."

"But it won't do any good! God will only answer my prayer when my faith is strong. He would never answer my prayers when I'm struggling, when I am filled a lot of doubt and a little faith!"

That is just not true.

There are three levels of faith in the New Testament. These were occasions in which someone asked Jesus to help in a drastic need. You can describe these examples of faith in this way: Level 1: "I'll ask, but I don't believe it will do any good." Level 2. "I'll pray, but a part of me believes and a part of me does not believe." Level 3: "I will ask and I know He will help."

Surely God waits until we get to Level 3 before He answers our prayers, correct? No, that is just not true. Jesus answered all three prayers - from the weakest in faith to the strongest in faith…He responded to all three levels. Amazing. (Mark 9, Matthew 8)

Remember, God meets us where we are in our lives - He knows when the circumstances of life has left us weary and battered…He doesn't scold us in the days when we struggle. He listens for the weak whisper of His exhausted child and then He acts. Also, remember what Jesus told us, it doesn't take a huge massive faith for God to answer, it only takes a tiny faith……like a mustard seed.

Where is your faith today? Is it on Level 2? Keep praying…Jesus will meet you there. Maybe you're at Level # 1, you really don't believe it will do any good. Pray anyway, ask Him to work. Look closely at the verse below, it has encouraged me many times when my faith was weak:

> Jesus said, "Everything is possible for him who believes." Immediately the boy's' father exclaimed, "I do believe, help me overcome my unbelief!" Mark 9:23-24 (Jesus then answered his prayer.)

Love You!!   Praying for You!!   Proud of You!!   Bro. Post
✶✶✶✶✶✶✶✶✶✶✶✶✶✶✶✶✶✶✶✶✶✶

"Doubt Your Doubt"

"Whenever you doubt God, ask God to help you doubt your doubt." (John Wesley)

College Buddies, we can be more aggressive here! All of us know what it's like to be walking in fellowship with God, rejoicing and trusting Him for that day. We are believing His promises and rejoicing. Then comes trouble - that unsettling feeling that comes when we start doubting what God has said. "Will He really take care of this problem?" "Does he really care about me?" "I wonder if He will let me down."

All of us stumble here but we don't have to stay here.

Turn the spotlight on your doubt - why would I think that God would let me down? Turn the spotlight on your past, all of the times when God has been so good to you. Turn the spotlight on God's promises, remind yourself that these promises include you! As you do this, this crippling doubt from our enemy will dissipate, you'll have your faith restored and you will once again rejoice. Ask God to help you 'doubt your doubt.'

"And you know in your hearts and souls, that not one thing has failed of all the good things which the Lord your God promised concerning you; all have come to pass for you, not one of them has failed." Joshua 23:14

Good Morning!! How Are My College Buddies?

Love You!!   Praying for You!!   Proud of You!!   Bro. Post
✲✲✲✲✲✲✲✲✲✲✲✲✲✲✲✲✲✲✲✲

"The God of a Second Chance"

God will always give you a second chance. And a third chance, and a fourth chance. God doesn't possess our human fault of writing someone off, giving up on them. We Christians often have a diminished view of how loving and kind God is to all of His children. Sometimes we ministers are to blame for this, sometimes we highlight someone's sin and minimize Jesus' forgiving grace.

To stumble and to fail is sad; but don't forget that God is especially seeking you at these times. He wants to cleanse you, forgive you, help you start all over again. Here's a sad tragedy: to refuse to ask for God's wonderful forgiveness because we secretly think that He is disgusted and finished with us. Notice this beautiful promise from the Bible:

> "He (God) does not deal with us according to our sins, nor repay us according to our iniquities…as far as the east is from the west, so far does He remove our transgressions from us." Psalm 103:10, 12

Love You!!   Praying for You!!   Proud of You!!   Bro. Post

✸✸✸✸✸✸✸✸✸✸✸✸✸✸✸✸✸✸✸✸

A message from your Father: "Your worst nightmare? It's not going to happen."

God's people were excited and then terrified. They had just experienced God's deliverance from slavery, a huge blessing!! As they walked across the wilderness, free at last, they glanced behind them, and to their horror, they saw the Egyptian army bearing down on them. They knew they had no chance -the army would kill some of them and drag the rest back into cruel and vicious slavery. They cried out and then gave up, resigned to death or slavery.

HOWEVER, God wanted to show His children that they were safe, so He did something awesome. He moved the pillar of fire and the angel who had delivered them from Egypt, He moved them BETWEEN the Egyptian army and the Israelites. The message was clear: "To harm my people, you have to come through me. It's not going to happen." (Exodus 14) College Buddies, you may feel like an army of tough circumstances is closing in on you - you may be rattled, shaken, even terrified. It's hard to believe, in the middle of the scary stuff, that God has set a barrier around you. But He has done just that and those terrifying scenarios that you imagine? They're not going to happen. God will deliver you, He will protect you - that disaster you imagine has to first come through God - and He has surrounded and protected you.

Rattled today? Worried about scary stuff? Notice the promise God gave to His people in this terrifying time:

Good Morning!! How Are My College Buddies?

"Do not be afraid. Stand firm and you will see the deliverance the Lord will bring to you today......The Lord will fight for you; you need only to be still." Exodus 14:13-14

Love You!!   Praying for You!!   Proud of You!!   Bro. Post
✶✶✶✶✶✶✶✶✶✶✶✶✶✶✶✶✶✶✶✶✶✶

Good Morning!! How Are My College Buddies?

"A Step by Step Blessing"

When God sends you a miracle or a blessing, He will either give it instantaneously or send it in increments. Younger Christians make a big deal about the 'quick' answers to prayer. But think about it, often the really beautiful blessings come in steps, and that takes time. When God encourages the discouraged, comforts the grieving, restores the Prodigal Son or Daughter...if you're looking, you will see the wonderful steps that He takes, each step building on the one before.

College Buddies, it is immature to ask God for something and then get discouraged a day later because the answer hasn't come yet! It IS coming, but on God's timetable, not ours. In the meantime, watch for your Father's handiwork as He sends the first part, then the second, then the whole blessing! It's great to enjoy the full blessing when it arrives, but it is really fun to recognize your Father's work in the process:

> "Elijah was a human being like us, and he prayed fervently that it might not rain......then he prayed again and the heaven gave rain and the earth yielded it's harvest." James 5:17-18 (Actually, he sent his servant several times to look for rain clouds as he was prayed. God was sending the blessing, but Elijah had to wait a while.)

Love You!!   Praying for You!!   Proud of You!!   Bro. Post

✶✶✶✶✶✶✶✶✶✶✶✶✶✶✶✶✶✶✶✶✶✶

Good Morning!! How Are My College Buddies?

"Scary stuff on the outside...anxious dread on the inside."

Hmm, the person who said that must be weak in faith, right? College Buddies, I love how the Christians in the Bible were so honest!! The man who made that statement was none other than the Apostle Paul. (II Corinthians 7:5) He was worn down, exhausted - he was facing real dangers and he was fighting fears and terrifying thoughts inside his soul. He was surrounded by pain and that's exactly where God displayed His power.

Some might say that if our faith is strong enough, we would be immune from inner fears and dread. Really? The list of those in the Bible who were filled with dread is very long...and it includes Jesus, our Savior. Our Father does allow circumstances that unsettle us at times, but He NEVER allows us to face them alone. Like a parent calming a frightened child, He is right beside us, holding us. He soothes our fears by gently speaking to us...He may remind us of a verse, or His past victories or an encouraging song. He holds us in His protective arms and He speaks to us: "I know you're frightened my child, but I am here beside you, I will protect you."

"For I am the Lord, your God, who takes hold of your right hand and says to you, Do not fear; I will help you." Isaiah 41:13

Love You!! Praying for You!! Proud of You!! Bro. Post
✷✷✷✷✷✷✷✷✷✷✷✷✷✷✷✷✷✷✷✷✷✷

"I do not want to do this."

College Buddies, that sentence came from Jesus, He was speaking to His Father in prayer. Think about it for a moment, could Jesus have been any more honest? Jesus teaches us a truth about prayer - open your heart up, be brutally honest, tell your Father EXACTLY how you feel.

David, in the Psalms, was perfectly honest, he didn't hide his true feelings, afraid that God would punish him. Let's see, there were times when David was scared silly, hot and angry, hurt by others, disappointed by dashed hopes, lonely, resentful, spiteful, disappointed in God......he was a human, like us, prone to stumble. The beautiful thing about David is that he actually 'unloaded' these emotions to God! Then God helped him. If we wear a 'holy facade' when we talk to God or to others, the burdens are heavier, the pain is intensified and the fears are multiplied. Jesus and David can teach us a valuable lesson about prayer: brutal honesty. Our Father has an incredible tender heart to all of us, He is watching and waiting until a hurting child cries out to Him. Notice how David 'unloads' when he prays to his Father:

> "I am bowed down and brought very low; all day long I go about mourning. My back is filled with searing pain...I am feeble and utterly crushed; I groan in anguish of heart. O Lord, do not forsake me; be not far from

me, O my God. Come quickly to help me, O Lord, my Savior." Psalm 38:6-8, 21-22

Love You!!   Praying for You!!   Proud of You!!   Bro. Post
✷✷✷✷✷✷✷✷✷✷✷✷✷✷✷✷✷✷✷✷✷✷

"Agape love causes us to climb down from the pedestal."

When we walk with God, and He fills our heart with His love, we discover we don't want to live on our self-made pedestal anymore. We don't like it up there, we feel uncomfortable, so we climb down. Immediately we place Jesus on that pedestal. Then we place Jesus' people on that pedestal, we truly believe that other Christians are more important than ourselves.

It's easy to place ourselves up there, isn't it? It's uncanny how we can subconsciously take credit for what our Father has done. It's unsettling how we play the 'I'm better' game, fracturing God's family. Or maybe we find it easy to forgive Christians who stumble in a 'nice' way…but then we turn around and hammer another Christian for an 'unacceptable' failure.

Living on a pedestal will exhaust you, it will wither you spiritually and it will leave you arrogant and self-righteous. Why not place Jesus on that pedestal? He is the ONLY reason we enjoy blessings in life, He certainly deserves to be there. Why not place other Christians up there? Why not live to serve them, hoping, praying and longing for blessings to come to them.

Let's come down from the pedestal, ok? There is a life of fulfillment and joy when we give credit to Jesus and refuse to take credit for anything:

"Love does not boast, it is not proud." I Corinthians 13:4

Love You!! Praying for You!! Proud of You!! Bro. Post
✶✶✶✶✶✶✶✶✶✶✶✶✶✶✶✶✶✶✶✶

"Feasting in the Dining Hall.......or...... Working on the Deck."

Bill and his wife were enjoying the cruise, watching the sunset over the ocean. Without warning, a freak wave tilted the ship suddenly. Bill, his wife, and 10 others slid and went overboard.

Whenever this happens, the ship's crew goes into a standard response. The captain slowed the ship, turning to allow the life boats to launch. The crew fought the waves, pressed for time as they moved the life boats closer. After the rescue, the people rescued are cold and shivering......they were given warm blankets, something warm to drink.

The rescue only took 30 minutes, Bill and his wife were safely back on the deck. They were deeply appreciative to the crew for their very lives. The crew re-launched the boat, pressed for time to rescue the others. They asked Bill and his wife if they would wait and help the other passengers when they were brought to the deck. Bill replied, "We would love to, but there is a formal dinner tonight in the Dining Room. We thank you so much for being good to us, but we need to get ready."

Sadly, Bill and his wife, an hour later. were enjoying themselves in the Dining Room. But the dinner was not too satisfying, and finally it dawned on them. "We should not be feasting in the Dining Room when we are needed up on the deck."

College Buddies, God has work for each of us to do 'up on the deck.' He didn't save us to make our lives a continual feast, we are saved to share God's love with others. If we spend our lives pursuing self-gratification, we will lose the very purpose that we exist as Christians.

For us, there's work up on the deck. Let's allow God to use us up there today, ok?

> "Always give yourselves FULLY to the work of the Lord, because know that your labor in the Lord is not in vain." I Corinthians 15:58

Love You!!   Praying for You!!   Proud of You!!   Bro. Post
✴✴✴✴✴✴✴✴✴✴✴✴✴✴✴✴✴✴✴✴✴

Good Morning!! How Are My College Buddies?

"Oil on a Rusty Hinge"

God can use your words to be 'oil on a rusty hinge.' Some people keep the door to their heart tightly closed, they remember past times of terrible hurt, pain and anguish. God wants them to open their heart and receive His love, but they are afraid to try and receive anyone's love. Sadly, their heart's door has been closed so long that even the hinges are rusty.

College Buddies, here is one of the more wonderful ways that you can serve God - let God use you and your words to minister to them. Show them and tell them how much they are worth......God gave His Son for them. Show and tell them that God loves them, more than they could possibly imagine. Show and tell them that God will forgive their past sins...assure them that you have also been forgiven. Tell them God has a wonderful plan for their lives, tell them you are praying for them. As God uses your gentle words to minister to them, the Holy Spirit will open the door of their heart and you will soon have a new brother or sister in Christ:

"'Everyone who calls on the name of the Lord shall be saved.' But how are they to believe in one whom they have never heard? And how are they to hear without someone to proclaim to them?" Romans 10:13-14

Love You!!   Praying for You!!   Proud of You!!   Bro. Post
✸✸✸✸✸✸✸✸✸✸✸✸✸✸✸✸✸✸✸✸✸✸✸

"Weeping and Venting"

When Christians go through times of deep distress, they very often respond in one or both of these ways, and Jeremiah was an expert at both!! He is called the 'Weeping Prophet', but he should also be called the 'Venting Prophet' - at times he really unloaded to God, he let his complaints fly very forcibly. Some Christians are comfortable with the weeping part but very uncomfortable with the venting part - it seems so unspiritual to complain to God!!

All through the Bible, spiritual men and women would occasionally 'let it fly' - they would vent their pain and misery to their Father. Actually, probably 30% of David's writings in the Psalms is venting, big time venting.

God didn't jump down Jeremiah's throat when he complained - God responded gently, He corrected and encouraged Jeremiah. My point? All of us occasionally have very rough days...we may try to force a cheery smile, but that's not real Christianity. In these rough days, yes, we will either shed tears or vent loudly to God! When you do this, you will be responding like many godly men and women in the Bible- DO NOT beat yourself up with guilt! Our Father knows us perfectly and He is waiting to gently help us:

> "I am a man who has seen affliction...He (God) has besieged and surrounded me with bitterness and hardship...He has walled me in so I cannot escape...Even when I call out

Good Morning!! How Are My College Buddies?

or cry for help, he shuts out my prayer...I became the laughingstock of all my people.. I have been deprived of peace...YET THIS I CALL TO MIND AND THEREFORE I HAVE HOPE: Because of the Lord's great love we are not consumed, for his compassions never fail...The Lord is good to those who wait for him...it is good to wait quietly for the salvation of the Lord." Lamentations 3:1-25 Notice how Jeremiah 'vents' and then God gently restores his faith.

Love You!!   Praying for You!!   Proud of You!!   Bro. Post
✸✸✸✸✸✸✸✸✸✸✸✸✸✸✸✸✸✸✸✸✸

"Verbal Junk - Letting It Go"

Jesus knew how to let verbal junk go. Martha was incensed with him, Jesus had not arrived on her timetable. "If you had been here, my brother would not have died!"

Jesus let that remark slide, He didn't defend himself, He didn't get into it. Even good people like Martha, (and all of us!), can occasionally let fly a verbal dart. Did He deserve it? No. Was the remark justified? Of course not. But amazingly, Jesus just let it go. When good people unload on you, there is usually a pool of unhappiness producing the remark. With Martha, it was numbing grief. With others, it is a dashed dream, disappointment, bitterness, health problems...the list is endless. Wise is the Christian who knows this, and like Jesus, decides to just let it go.

There is a part of us that wants to defend ourselves on these occasions. But what good would it do? The same pool of unhappiness that produced the remark is still there, and it will produce more remarks. It doesn't mean that the person is evil, it does mean that the person is struggling. It seems to me that Jesus understood the origin and decided to overlook the remark. It also seems to me that this is a wonderful expression of love for someone...after all, all of us, at times, have hurled verbal darts. College Buddies, JUST LET IT GO:

"It is good sense in a man to be forbearing, and it is his glory to pass over an offense."
Proverbs 19:11

Love You!! Praying for You!! Proud of You!! Bro. Post
✸✸✸✸✸✸✸✸✸✸✸✸✸✸✸✸✸✸✸✸✸

Good Morning!! How Are My College Buddies?

"Don't trust in a raven...trust in the God of the raven."

Here's what I mean. Elijah was a prophet who was hiding for his life. God led him to a remote area and then, amazingly, made the ravens of the air bring him bread and meat every morning. Each day, God blessed Elijah and provided for him. Guess what? One day the ravens didn't show up! Worse, the brook he depended on for water went dry.

You see, God wanted Elijah to realize that HE sent the blessings, the ravens were just the tools He used. We get in trouble when we trust more in the instruments of God's blessings and forget the Source of our blessings. God may use a lot of 'tools' to bless you - a good job, parents, friends, wonderful pastors...remember that these are just the 'tools' - God is the Blesser!

If your life has recently had some changes and some 'tools of blessing' are no longer there, don't panic, God will still be with you and He will still bless you - He will just use a different 'tool':

"If you then know how to give good gifts to your children, how much more will your Father who is in heaven give good things to those who ask Him!" Matthew 7:11

Love You!!   Praying for You!!   Proud of You!!   Bro. Post
✵✵✵✵✵✵✵✵✵✵✵✵✵✵✵✵✵✵✵✵✵

Good Morning!! How Are My College Buddies?

"Don't be ashamed of your 'soul scars'"
Chuck Swindoll

'Soul scars' are areas in your life where you have been hurt, where you have failed, where you feel inadequate, areas where you may even be ashamed. ALL Christians have 'soul scars' - few Christians admit it. We try to maintain a facade of perfection but inside, all of us have areas where we are hurting.

God is at work in your weaknesses, inadequacies and failure. It is in your weakness or failure that His grace and forgiveness is received and exhibited. He gently encourages us, strengthens us, even helps us to release past hurts. Only God can meet a soul in the pit of despair and gradually forgive and restore. The very 'soul scar' that you are trying to hide is God's arena of victory - where He can show others, not how good you are, but how wonderful He is. Then, after he has helped and restored you, everyone is positive that the power came from God, not from us. Notice how Paul praised the work of God in his 'soul scars':

> "I prefer to find my joy in the very things that are my weakness; and then the power of Christ will come and rest upon me. I am well content with these humiliations of mine, the hardships, the persecutions, the times of difficulty I undergo for Christ; for when I am weak, it is then that I am strong." II Corinthians 12:9-10

Love You!!   Praying for You!!   Proud of You!!   Bro. Post

✶✶✶✶✶✶✶✶✶✶✶✶✶✶✶✶✶✶✶✶✶✶

"A Strong Faith.......A Churning Heart."

Sometimes Christians face trials so severe, dangers so ominous and burdens so heavy that their emotions start churning. The trials are intense and the emotions accompanying these trials are just as intense.

The problem comes when we think that our churning emotions are a sign that we have a weak faith. Our spiritual enemy will whisper that if we really had enough faith, we would be totally relaxed, incredibly serene and smiling graciously.

Hmm.......not always.

Ok, remember Elisha in the Bible? He had a strong faith and prayed that a certain woman's son would be restored to health...he even went and prayed for the child. Now you would think, after he had prayed, that Elisha would announce that everything would be ok and then go his way.

That didn't happen. After Elisha prayed for the child, waiting for God to answer, Elisha "walked to and fro in the house." (II Kings 4) Elisha had strong faith but he also had churning emotions.

David was an expert at having a strong faith in God, but often, he had a churning heart. He would express his faith in God, but then he would vividly express the emotional whirlwind he was feeling.

If you are facing tough times and you find yourself dealing with intense and strong emotions, that's ok, that's perfectly normal. In the middle of these emotions, if you still choose to believe that God is in

Good Morning!! How Are My College Buddies?

control and He will work in the problem...congratulations, your faith is like David's and Elisha's.

Please read the following verses. Notice how David had both a strong faith...and a churning heart.

> "I am utterly bowed down and prostrate; all day long I go around mourning........I am utterly spent and crushed; I groan because of the tumult of my heart........But it is for you. O Lord, that I wait; it is you, O Lord my God, who will answer." Psalm 38:6,8,15

Love You!! Praying for You!! Proud of You!! Bro. Post
✻✻✻✻✻✻✻✻✻✻✻✻✻✻✻✻✻✻✻✻

Good Morning!! How Are My College Buddies?

"Let God be God."

We run ourselves to exhaustion trying to fix or ease the problems that we are enduring. Have you thought that your Father may not allow the problem to be eased until we cease striving... and let God be God. Our Father's heart is completely intertwined with our hearts - He feels the shock, the pain, the weariness and the hurt. We try to tell Him how much this hurts - He already knows, He has been weeping with you.

When we let God be God, there comes a release in the middle of the pain - the release is on the inside, we have given Him the hurt. Our Father's heart is so tender that He would never allow His child to hurt without time limits...He knows exactly WHEN the burden will be lifted. And never doubt that He CAN reverse the circumstances. He also restores a greater degree of joy in the future, when the burden is lifted. Actually, our Father's heart is so tender that He actually places your tears in a bottle, so He will always remember your present pain, your sleepless hours. (Psalm 56:8) College Buddies, today, are you struggling to 'trust through the tears?' Give your burden again to your Father...and let God be God:

"The Lord is near the brokenhearted and saves those who are crushed in spirit." Psalm 34:18

Love You!!   Praying for You!!   Proud of You!!   Bro. Post
✶✶✶✶✶✶✶✶✶✶✶✶✶✶✶✶✶✶✶✶✶✶

"Praying Without a Clue."

Sometimes when we pray, we 'laser pray' - we pray with confidence for a specific answer. We sense that He is about to work in the way that we are praying and we rejoice when He answers.

Other times we pray and we aren't quite as sure, we can see two or three ways that the Lord could answer and meet the need, so we pray and ask for His perfect answer.

Other times we pray and the need is so great, or the circumstances are so confusing that when we start to pray, we honestly have no idea how to pray. Every solution that we have does not work and we realize that we are praying with a lot of questions and no answers............'Praying Without a Clue.'

The Christian life so practical...God has designed it that way. Our Father knew that we would occasionally have times of confusion like this and He has designed a wonderful solution.

Every Christian has the Holy Spirit living within them. He lives in our hearts and helps us in our walk with God. The beautiful promise is that even we are totally bewildered and confused, He, the Holy Spirit, actually communicates with God the Father when we pray. And He knows exactly how to pray, the perfect answer......so He makes that request to your Father for you. Even though we have no idea how this works, it is a wonderful truth to know that the perfect request is being offered to God the Father on our behalf.

Good Morning!! How Are My College Buddies?

"Lord, I don't have a clue how to pray, but I pray anyway, expecting your perfect answer, in your perfect way, in your perfect time."

"In the same way, the Spirit helps us in our weakness. We do not how we ought to pray, but the Spirit himself intercedes for us in groans that words cannot express." Romans 8:26

Love You!!   Praying for You!!   Proud of You!!   Bro. Post
✶✶✶✶✶✶✶✶✶✶✶✶✶✶✶✶✶✶✶✶✶✶

"Relax my Child, have I ever let you down?"

The Ropes Course is fascinating. It helps people learn to TRUST......it is designed so that you cannot finish the course and you certainly can't enjoy the course unless you depend on someone else. You simply have to believe that the person controlling your rope will not let go. The result? You have a deeper friendship and higher respect for the other person – you trusted them, they didn't let you down.

Your friend could tell you all day long, "I won't fail you. I will hold your rope, you won't fall." But it truly sinks in when you're suspended on the course and you HAVE to trust them!

That is the biggest reason that God allows scary stuff to happen to us. He knows that we will grow and mature in our faith only when we HAVE to trust Him...times when we just can't fix the problem and we're scared half to death.

So He enrolls us in the 'Spiritual Ropes Course' - we feel like we are suspended high up and we long for the safety of the ground.

But our Father is the one controlling our rope, He is the One who causes us to avoid disaster. And He hangs on tightly, you are one of His kids and He adores you. In the middle of the course, it's easy to look around and think about how horrible it would be if you were to fall. Our Father then speaks gently to you, He wants you to hear His words: "Relax my Child, trust Me. Have I ever let you down?"

Good Morning!! How Are My College Buddies?

"As I was with Moses, so I will be you; I WILL NOT FAIL YOU OR FORSAKE YOU. Be strong and courageous..." Joshua 1:5-6

Love You!!   Praying for You!!   Proud of You!!   Bro. Post
✻✻✻✻✻✻✻✻✻✻✻✻✻✻✻✻✻✻✻✻✻

Good Morning!! How Are My College Buddies?

"Be Careful - Thin Ice"

One of the more dangerous places we can be is when we refuse to offer forgiveness from the heart…instead, we place ourselves in harsh judgement. We mull over the other person's offense, we tell others about it, we go through the process of convincing ourselves: "I'm better than that, I would never do that."

College Buddies, be careful………this is a very dangerous place to be!!

When we see a Christian stumble and sin, we should immediately pray for their repentance - that they would return to the Lord. And when they return and are forgiven, then we offer them spiritual restitution, we receive them back completely into God's family. Don't mentally demote them to second class saints. Learn a lesson from their stumble. We are not immune to temptation, we could stumble in a worse way tomorrow!! None of these spiritual steps are easy, sometimes it takes a while before we reach them completely. However, to sit in arrogant judgment and spotlight their failure…College Buddies, you're on thin ice……..don't be surprised if you fall through and sin yourself:

> "If a person is overtaken in a sin, you who are spiritual should restore the person in the spirit of gentleness; considering yourself, for you may be tempted too." Galatians 6:1

Love You!!   Praying for You!!   Proud of You!!   Bro. Post

✸✸✸✸✸✸✸✸✸✸✸✸✸✸✸✸✸✸✸✸✸✸

"Not Me!! I Can't!!"

When the Lord called someone in the Bible to serve Him, it's amazing how many had these two responses!! The first response, "Not me!" is linked to our feelings of imperfection - we sin so often, we feel so unworthy. The second response, "I can't!" is linked to our feelings of inadequacy –we can't do this, someone else can do this so much better. If you feel inadequate or unworthy when God leads you to serve Him......Congratulations!! You're in the perfect position for Him to use you in a wonderful way!!

Serving the Lord is about honoring God's name, not our own. God uses weak, imperfect Christians like ourselves so that others will see HIS power in us. Take an ordinary glove and it can do nothing.. it is lifeless and useless. However, allow a talented sculptor to place his hand inside the glove and the glove can be part of sculpting a beautiful masterpiece. Feel unworthy to serve the Lord? Feel inadequate, like you would do a poor job? Perfect! Please read carefully the verses below:

> "Think about what you were when you were called. Not many of you were wise by human standards; not many were influential; not many were of noble birth. But God chose the foolish things of the world to shame the wise; God chose the weak things of the world to shame the strong...so that no one may boast

before him......Let him who boasts, boast in the Lord." I Corinthians 1:26-31

Love You!! Praying for You!! Proud of You!! Bro. Post
✶✶✶✶✶✶✶✶✶✶✶✶✶✶✶✶✶✶✶✶✶✶

"A Blessing in the 'Blah Months.'"

For many people, January and February are tough months......and it easy to see why. The holiday excitement is over, the days are short and often dreary, and these two months just seem to carry an extra amount of troubles and trials.

No wonder a lot of us Christians struggle in these days.......I refer to them as the 'Blah Months.'

Our Father knows our struggles and He knows when and how to encourage us. He always knows the perfect time to refresh our soul and He often does it by sending a unique and unexpected blessing in the middle of a 'Blah Day.' It may not be an earth - shaking blessing, it may even be the joy of someone else's blessing...but it stills serves it's purpose when it comes: it lifts our soul, it refreshes us and it reminds us of a gentle Father who cares deeply about His kids.

When your Father sends you a blessing in the middle of the 'blahs', relish it. Spend time thinking about it, mentally think about the way that your Father crafted this blessing, just for you. You may want to have a 'Blessing Day' - a day in which you do not ask God for anything, the only prayers all day are prayers of thanksgiving.

The Lord is still faithful in the 'Blah Months', He is a doting Father who loves you so much. If today, you're experiencing the 'Fog of the Blahs', don't be surprised if your Father surprises you with a delightful love gift.

"By day the Lord commands his steadfast love, and at night his song is with me." Psalm 42:8

Love You!! Praying for You!! Proud of You!! Bro. Post
✼✼✼✼✼✼✼✼✼✼✼✼✼✼✼✼✼✼✼✼

"God's Circle of Rescue"

Everything was going great for the Apostle Paul... he was very successful, doing what God had wanted him to do in the city of Lystra. However, things went downhill in a hurry...Paul's plans seemed dashed, everything looked hopeless. Just after things were going so well, Paul was beaten senseless and drug outside of the city and left for dead. (Acts 14)

Interesting, but sometimes in life, we experience similar events...our plans are shot, our confidence gone, there is little or no hope for future blessings. Did God rescue Paul? Of course......but He didn't do it alone. When Paul awoke from this beating, he was circled by a group of Christians - they were there to encourage him, to tend to his injuries, to help Paul in his worst time. The result? Paul was able to continue serving the Lord in an even better way! You see, God used these Christians who were willing to help someone who desperately needed help - they didn't just wring their hands, they circled Paul and helped him get back up.

God may very well may want you to do the same today. He may want you and others to form a 'circle of rescue' for another Christian - go to them, encourage them, help them, pray for them and allow God to use you to rescue them:

"Then they stoned Paul and dragged him out of the city, supposing that he was dead. But when the disciples surrounded him, he got up and went back into the city...there they (Paul

Good Morning!! How Are My College Buddies?

& Barnabus) strengthened the souls of the disciples and encouraged them to continue in the faith......" Acts 14:19-22 (Thank God for the Christians who rescued Paul!!)

Love You!!   Praying for You!!   Proud of You!!   Bro. Post
✽✽✽✽✽✽✽✽✽✽✽✽✽✽✽✽✽✽✽✽

Good Morning!! How Are My College Buddies?

"Lord, help me to clap and cheer."

Little Johnny wanted badly to be in the 4th grade class play. His mother was worried, knowing he wasn't a very good actor. However, when she picked him up at school, Johnny was excited! "Mom, I got a part! I've been selected to sit in the audience and clap and cheer!"

College Buddies, how well do you 'clap and cheer' when something good happens to someone else? The same Father who blesses you is blessing them, so be happy with them! How well do you spotlight other Christians when they excel in something? Now remember, they very likely don't see the areas where they are doing well, they probably have blinders and just do not see these godly qualities.

Encouragement is like a spiritual B-12 shot, it lifts the burdens and helps others to strive even more to please God. Today, we will be around other Christians and we will notice an area that we admire, an area where they are honoring God. Now we can be silent or we can offer them two special gifts: RECOGNITION of their beautiful qualities and as a result of this, the ENCOURAGEMENT that they will feel when we speak to them.

Today, let's ask God to help us to 'clap and cheer.'

> "Not neglecting to meet together, as is the habit of some, but ENCOURAGING ONE ANOTHER, and all the more as you see

the day nearing." Hebrews 10:25 (emphasis mine)

Love You!!   Praying for You!!   Proud of You!!   Bro. Post
✳✳✳✳✳✳✳✳✳✳✳✳✳✳✳✳✳✳✳✳

"Stumbling or Straying."

These are two different ways that we can fail the Lord. The first is to STUMBLE - when we confront a temptation, give in, and fall flat on our faces. Explosive anger is a good example, when we're tempted by irritating events or irritating people, then we unload!

The second way that we can fail is to STRAY, and this one is tougher to stop! It usually starts with a minor attitude, but we nurture it, we feed it and over the course of time, that attitude can consume us. Think of stewing here, the type of anger that lingers for weeks or months. Stumbling is when we fall down in our walk with God, straying is when we wander off and stay on a wrong path.

Regardless of which way we have failed, the way back to God is the same – we recognize our mistake and we ask for God's forgiveness. College Buddies, everyone needs God's forgiveness, all of us fail God. However, when you notice that you have stumbled, ask for forgiveness, get back on your feet, and start walking with God again. When you notice that you have strayed down a wrong path, ask God's forgiveness, turn around, and go back to the correct path of walking with God.

> "Have mercy on me, O God, according to your abundant mercy blot out my transgressions. Wash me thoroughly from my iniquity, and cleanse me from my sin." Psalm 51:1-2

Good Morning!! How Are My College Buddies?

Love You!!   Praying for You!!   Proud of You!!   Bro. Post

✲✲✲✲✲✲✲✲✲✲✲✲✲✲✲✲✲✲✲✲

"The lousier the day, the sweeter the blessing."

It is fascinating to watch how God deals with His kids. All of us have days that 'run us over' - days in which our patience is shattered, our faith is shaken, our frustration level is off the charts...just a crappy day. I bet you sometimes think that God is disappointed with you on days like this. No, not really, He really isn't. He is the perfect Father to us and He actually hurts when we are struggling.

Because He adores us so much, He loves to do something very special for us on a day that is wearing us out. He sends a 'load lightener', a special blessing to reassure us, to lift us up, to restore our battered faith. This unexpected blessing comes straight from Him, it is a visual aid to you that He still loves you and He is in control. It's like He's saying, "I know you're irritated, I know you're feeling sorry for yourself. Here's a special blessing to let you know I am taking care of you." Do you need a 'load lightener' today? Hey, all of us do on this side of heaven. If you need one, your Father will certainly send one...watch for it today...I bet He's smiling when He sends it:

> "He who did not spare his own Son, but gave him up for us all, how shall he not with him freely give us all things?" Romans 8:32 (Take some time and think about this verse.)

Love You!! Praying for You!! Proud of You!! Bro. Post

****

Good Morning!! How Are My College Buddies?

'Mountaintop Experiences' are great!!"

All of us have times in which the Lord seems especially near, we strongly feel His love and care, and He sends some totally wonderful blessings. As much as we would love to do so, we cannot stay up on a mountaintop forever, eventually we return to our daily Christian walk. Ok, College Buddies, when we do come down from the mountain, guess who's waiting for us?

The Enemy of our faith is waiting, he especially wants to make things miserable for us immediately after a great blessing! Why? He doesn't want our thanksgiving to God to continue - so he tries to make things rough. He doesn't want us to remember how God protects us - so he tries to frighten us and make us dread the future. He doesn't want us to bask in our Father's love - so he tries to make things so miserable that we even wonder about God's love! College Buddies, this is so normal, this happens to all Christians!! (Been there, done that, many times!) But our Father knows what's going on and He is watching us carefully, He will help us and encourage us and lift us back up. Enjoy this beautiful verse about your Father's tender, gentle care for you:

> "He will feed his flock like a shepherd, he will gather the lambs in his arms, he will carry them in his bosom, and gently lead those that are with young." Isaiah 40:11

Love You!! Praying for You!! Proud of You!! Bro. Post

✸✸✸✸✸✸✸✸✸✸✸✸✸✸✸✸✸✸✸✸✸✸✸

"When Life Becomes a Dry, Dusty Desert."

It's interesting that every Christian seems to have an occasional period of the 'Spiritual Blahs' - those times when we know that we're Christians, but God seems a million miles away. There are certain symptoms that we all endure in these times and the result is that our life becomes tedious, our love for God seems to weaken, and our excitement in knowing Him and serving Him seems to slip away.

Instead, we care little about the Bible, pray half-heartedly and rejoice sporadically.

Life becomes a chore.......like trudging through a dry dusty desert.

Maybe it will encourage us to know that many of God's children in the Bible had times like these. There was a time when Jeremiah thought God had lied to him, he was filled with suspicion. Elijah threw a huge pity party, (haven't we all at times?!), and loudly insisted that God would kill him. Moses, overwhelmed and worn out from leading, in effect, told God to take this job and give it to someone else!

Yep, we all have been there, done that.......an occasional journey through a spiritual desert.

There is no way that our Father will leave us there, He will restore us and return the joy and fruitfulness. But there are wonderful truths that we can learn in the desert that we can learn no where else. He teaches us to trust in the withering heat of tough circumstances. He teaches to trust and to refuse to be guided by our emotions. He teaches us that although

Good Morning!! How Are My College Buddies?

---

we may be struggling, HE is still in control and He is the God of the desert.

Isaiah and David... they both struggled like we do. Notice what they said below about the dry desert times of life:

"He restores my soul." Psalm 23:2

"When the poor and needy search for water and there is none, and their tongue is parched with thirst, I, the Lord will answer them....... I will make rivers flow on barren heights...... I will turn the desert into pools of water." Isaiah 41:17-18

Love You!! Praying for You!! Proud of You!! Bro. Post
✶✶✶✶✶✶✶✶✶✶✶✶✶✶✶✶✶✶✶✶✶

"Transfer Frustration"

One of the more unfair things that we all occasionally practice is to 'transfer frustration.' You know, we're irritated at someone or something, and we 'unload' on someone who is totally uninvolved and innocent! College Buddies, fast-forward with me ten years, now you're settled in your job. One client comes in and explodes, totally dissatisfied with your company. You have another appointment in 15 minutes with a potential customer. See the problem? If you unload the frustration with the first client onto the potential customer……..not a pretty picture, is it? Here's a short list of people that sometimes catch it from us: mates, boy/girlfriends, roommates, parents, coworkers……the list goes on.

I believe the Christian life is PRACTICAL - that God helps us in the everyday stuff and He can help us here. He can help us bite our tongue…… He can help us cool down……..He can help refocus and He can help us gain control. No one likes to get hit with a dart that was thrown at someone else - God can help you calm down and not hurl the verbal dart in the first place:

> "The mind of the wise makes their speech judicious, (appropriate) ……Pleasant words are like a honeycomb, sweetness to the soul and health to the body." Proverbs 16:23, 24

Love You!!   Praying for You!!   Proud of You!!   Bro. Post

✽✽✽✽✽✽✽✽✽✽✽✽✽✽✽✽✽✽✽✽✽✽✽✽

"A Hug From the Heart."

It's fascinating to watch a parent gently help an upset or frightened child. This process of a dad or mom calming and assuring a child is identical to what the Lord does for us! The first stage is always venting…often the child cries even louder, making sure the parent knows how bad things are. Have you ever 'vented' to your Father, telling Him in detail how you're hurting? I hope that you have. Often the next stage is resisting – the child actually briefly resists the parent's attempt to soothe, the child continues to think and insist that no, things will not be ok because this is horrible! Hmm, I wonder if we have ever done this? Of course we have - the Lord has to tell us often He will help us, we're too busy cringing over the coming disaster! :-) The next stage is transference - the child's crying eases, the child starts calming down. This is almost always linked to transferring the fear or problem to mom or dad - unconsciously the child has a faith that mom/dad will take care of it, so they calm down. Lastly comes the 'resume' stage - the child resumes their life, eased from the burden.

College Buddies, when you are frightened and upset, your Heavenly Father is always waiting to be a perfect Father to you, He doesn't scold you or look down at you. Tell Him all about it - He loves to comfort and assure His upset kids:

> "Then you shall call, and the Lord shall answer; you shall cry and He shall say, Here I am." Isaiah 58:9

Good Morning!! How Are My College Buddies?

Love You!!   Praying for You!!   Proud of You!!   Bro. Post

✶✶✶✶✶✶✶✶✶✶✶✶✶✶✶✶✶✶✶✶

"He remembers how weak we are, He knows how tough it is."

College Buddies, read carefully the verses below. Our Father knows how easily we stumble, how often we fail, how difficult it is to always live by faith. He is a tenderhearted Father, He will always be the first to lift us up when we fall flat on our face. HOWEVER, we do have a spiritual enemy and he delights in heaping guilt upon us. Do you think your Father would forgive you and then turn around and tell you how horrible you are? Of course not. But Satan will gladly remind you of your sins, he will rehash past mistakes and he will try to shackle you spiritually...using his favorite weapon: guilt. He wants you to grow discouraged and leave the Lord because you don't feel worthy enough to be his child anymore.

Your Father just won't allow that - He will find you, forgive you and restore you. Remember the Prodigal Son when he returned to his father? He certainly felt guilty and ashamed - he didn't think his father would ever forgive him. Yet his father hugged him, kissed him, forgave him, even threw a party to celebrate his son's return!! Your Father in heaven feels the same way. Today, if you have failed God, simply ask for His forgiveness. You'll go to bed tonight amazed at His forgiving heart - and your Father will be thrilled that you are safely back with Him:

"The Lord is merciful and gracious, slow to anger and abounding in steadfast love...As a father pities his children, so the Lord pities those who fear him." Psalm 103:8, 13

Love You!!   Praying for You!!   Proud of You!!   Bro. Post
✶✶✶✶✶✶✶✶✶✶✶✶✶✶✶✶✶✶✶✶✶✶

Good Morning!! How Are My College Buddies?

"How Weak We Are"

Suppose a Mercedes dealership offered me the free use of a new car, the only requirement being that I tell others where the car is sold. Then suppose I looked at the Mercedes, and on the rear fender was a small scratch. Would I reject the beautiful car because of a minor imperfection? Of course not. I would ignore the scratch and enjoy the Mercedes! :-)

College Buddies, even the finest Christians you know are still human, they still have flaws. God can help us overlook their imperfections and enjoy the beauty of the person, a redeemed child of God. Yet some Christians never ENJOY other Christians, they are too busy magnifying their imperfections. To really love and enjoy other Christians, remember this:

> "Lose the magnifying glass. Enjoy the Mercedes. Overlook the scratch."

> "And be kind to one another, tenderhearted, forgiving one another, as God in Christ has forgiven you." Ephesians 4:32

Love You!!   Praying for You!!   Proud of You!!   Bro. Post
✻✻✻✻✻✻✻✻✻✻✻✻✻✻✻✻✻✻✻✻✻

"Love Them Stubbornly."

College Buddies, when it comes to showing God's love to others, always love them stubbornly.

Don't show God's kindness occasionally, don't give God's love conditionally. God loves us at our worst moments - show God's love to others when you see them struggling. God forgives us often and then puts away our sins – show God's love to someone else by forgiving them...and then refusing to remind them. When you are in contact with someone, embrace this as an opportunity to give them God's gentle love, regardless of how that person is doing. Also, don't stop loving someone even when they do not seem to respond to you - God is using you to soften their hearts and restore them. It's easy to watch someone wander off and then write them off, but remember, the good Shepherd searched for the lost sheep, He found the lost sheep and He rejoiced when He found the lost sheep. Want to love others like Jesus? Love them stubbornly:

"Love is always supportive, loyal, hopeful, and trusting. Love never fails." I Corinthians 13:7-8

Love You!!   Praying for You!!   Proud of You!!   Bro. Post
✶✶✶✶✶✶✶✶✶✶✶✶✶✶✶✶✶✶✶✶✶✶

"Maybe It's Right Under Your Nose."

College Buddies, if you're looking for a way to effectively serve God, maybe it's right under your nose.

What do you like to do? God gave you that interest, look closely there for a way to serve God. What can you do well? God gave you that ability, look there for a way. Do what you can do for God, don't worry about what you can't do.

No way would my dad ever speak in public, he would have fainted! But he did have a hobby - he loved to raise a LARGE, beautiful garden every year. Now he could have bemoaned the fact that he couldn't teach Sunday School or lead a Bible study. Instead, he worked hard in his huge garden. I'll always remember the times when I was home from college and there were cars lining the road in front of my house. My mom was handing out grocery bags, my dad met the folks in the garden. Previously, he had driven around town and invited needy people to come to his home. He met them at the garden and invited them to take all they wanted. I have never seen him any happier.

See my point? College Buddies, serving the Lord is not frightening, it's spiritual fun. Inventory your hobbies, your likes, your talents and your abilities. I bet you that God will lead you to a wonderful way to serve Him......it will be the happiest times of your life:

Good Morning!! How Are My College Buddies?

"Serve the Lord with gladness." Psalm 100:2

Love You!!   Praying for You!!   Proud of You!!   Bro. Post
✶✶✶✶✶✶✶✶✶✶✶✶✶✶✶✶✶✶✶✶

Good Morning!! How Are My College Buddies?

"Stewing."

When we become anxious and worried, we usually react one of two ways. The first is to become jumpy, rushing around, caught up in a flurry of nervous activity. However, some of us react the opposite, we suffer a internal, churning turmoil that I call 'stewing.' Gaining the victory over worry is a daily struggle - it would be nice if we could once turn over our worries to God and be done with them, but they tend to rear back up!

I am convinced that one great help in our struggle is to remind ourselves of the SECURITY that we enjoy as God's child. No problem, trial, struggle or hardship can touch us unless He has allowed it - He knows the breaking point of our faith. In other words, there is no such thing as the 'straw that breaks the camel's back'. The next time you catch yourself 'stewing', remind yourself of your Father's complete, protective care. Below is a wonderful promises to help us remember:

(I took out the pronouns in the verse below so you could insert your name.)

"Because ____ loves me, I will deliver ____; I will protect _____, because _____ knows my name. When _____ calls to me, I will answer _____; I will be with ____ in trouble, I will rescue _____ and honor _____."
Psalm 91:14-15

Love You!!   Praying for You!!   Proud of You!!   Bro. Post
✶✶✶✶✶✶✶✶✶✶✶✶✶✶✶✶✶✶✶✶✶✶

Good Morning!! How Are My College Buddies?

"Pre-Blessing, Imagined Disasters."

When it comes to God sending a blessing to His child, I have noticed an interesting trend. Sometimes, right before the blessing comes, the circumstances start to fall apart. It's almost as if we get our hopes up, then tough circumstances dash those hopes. And no, I don't believe that these discouraging circumstances are always from Satan.

I believe our Father is sometimes responsible, He allows the circumstances to look more and more impossible, just before He works the miracle. Why would He do this? If we prayed and everything went smoothly right up to our Father's answer, guess who we would be tempted to credit? Either ourselves or others. But our Father waits until there is NO DOUBT who sent the blessing, then He acts. So if things have gone to you know where in a hand-basket lately,.. God is still in control. Very likely, He is getting ready to send you a blessing so wonderful that you will be overwhelmed:

> "Blessed be the Lord, for he has wondrously shown his steadfast love to me. I had said in my alarm, 'I am cut off from God's sight.' But God heard my prayers, when I cried to him for help." Psalm 31:21-22 (Wonderful verses!!)

Love You!!   Praying for You!!   Proud of You!!   Bro. Post
✳✳✳✳✳✳✳✳✳✳✳✳✳✳✳✳✳✳✳✳

Good Morning!! How Are My College Buddies?

"Thinking is also spiritual."

College Buddies, God speaks to us in different ways, the Bible, prayer, wise advice. However, have you thought that God can lead you as you THINK about an issue? Ask Him to guide your thoughts and then you're ready to consider what is the best decision to make. While you're thinking, He will help you remember a Bible verse, or some Christian advice that you had heard earlier. Here's my point: some of the worst decisions I have made in my life occurred when I rushed into a choice and did not THINK ABOUT IT. I never gave God the chance to lead me. This is especially helpful when you're 'stumped', when you're trying to decide between two seemingly good choices.

Pray and then think…consider the decision, consider the consequences, apply the Bible. Sometimes God does lead us to make 'snap' decisions, but more often, He wants us to trust Him through the disciplines of prayer, Bible reading and spiritual thinking.

"Ponder (consider well) the path of your feet, then ALL your ways will be sure." Proverbs 4:26 (Spiritual Thinking)

Love You!!   Praying for You!!   Proud of You!!   Bro. Post
✸✸✸✸✸✸✸✸✸✸✸✸✸✸✸✸✸✸✸✸✸✸✸

"Get apart or fall apart."

God never intended for you to run through life at full acceleration. There comes a time when you have to ease up, let the batteries recharge. We know that Jesus gave long and grueling hours to His earthly work, but even He saw the need to get away, slow down, renew His physical strength.

How often do you, (especially the Type A's), schedule 'down time'? Notice I said 'schedule'. 'Down time' is a valuable investment in your spiritual and emotional health - it returns huge dividends to the ones who practice it. You would never get out of your car at night and leave the engine idling all night so that it would be ready to go in the morning! Yet some people live this way, always stressing about the things that have to be done, never turning the ignition off! Occasionally schedule a rest, schedule a recreation…turn the engine off, let your body wind down and cool down. Jesus did this, we should also:

> "He makes me lie down in green pastures, He leads me beside still waters; He restores my soul." Psalm 23:2-3

Love You!!   Praying for You!!   Proud of You!!   Bro. Post

✶✶✶✶✶✶✶✶✶✶✶✶✶✶✶✶✶✶✶✶✶✶

Good Morning!! How Are My College Buddies?

"Divine Coincidences."

College Buddies, our lives are not at the mercy of random events, our lives are in the hands of a loving Father. I want to challenge you to look for your Father's hand behind these 'coincidences', to appreciate how perfectly He takes care of you. I bet you can remember a time in the past when you were in danger and something happened to rescue you - that was your Father. Remember when you were really discouraged and you just happened to bump into a friend, or received a card in the mail, or read a perfect Bible passage…that was your Father helping you. Remember in church when your pastor preached a sermon that was PERFECT for you at that time? Again, that was your Father.

Our Father knows us completely and He knows when we need a spiritual boost - He knows the perfect circumstance or person who will bring you help and encouragement. Look for one of these 'Divine Coincidences' today, then thank Him for His perfect care for you:

> "A man was going down from Jerusalem to Jericho, and he fell among robbers, who stripped him and beat him, leaving him half dead…… But a Samaritan, as he journeyed, came to where he was; and when he saw him, he had compassion." Luke 15:29, 33 (Divine Coincidence)

Love You!!   Praying for You!!   Proud of You!!   Bro. Post
✶✶✶✶✶✶✶✶✶✶✶✶✶✶✶✶✶✶✶✶✶✶

"There is no way He would lie about it."

Do me a favor, please read the verse below. It is my favorite promise in the whole Bible.

This verse tells us about a past blessing, a present blessing and a future blessing. It is so simple but so precious. When we come to Christ and believe in Him, God gives us all three...and they belong to you.

The PRESENT blessing is everlasting life. You begin your eternal life when you are converted, not when you get to heaven. This gift is forever and forever.

The FUTURE blessing is a promise not to be condemned. How can that be? I know I have done things that deserves God's condemnation. Because of Jesus' death, we can be forgiven and cleansed.

The PAST blessing is that we are no longer spiritually dead, but we are spiritually alive. We can now be alive to God and to His service.

Now the enemy of our faith would love to convince you that these things are not true - that these promises are nice, but you can't count on them.

Have you put your faith in Christ? Are you trusting Him only for your salvation? Then please read the verse again - claim it, relish it, it applies to you.

And your Father would never lie to you.......it is true:

"I tell you the truth, whoever hears my word and believes him who sent me HAS eternal life and WILL NOT be condemned; he has CROSSED OVER from death to life." John 5:24

Love You!!   Praying for You!!   Proud of You!!   Bro. Post
✸✸✸✸✸✸✸✸✸✸✸✸✸✸✸✸✸✸✸✸

"God...Money."

Actually, they go together quite well. God gives us, as Christians, a Biblical road map to make the use of our money a blessing and a joy. First is the principle of OWNERSHIP...God is the owner of every dime that comes to you. You are the financial steward of what He owns. The second principle is the principle of APPRECIATION...we could not have anything without God giving us the health, the ability and the opportunity to hold a job. The third principle is the principle of SHARING...we are to return a portion back to God. Some Christians are able to give a lot, others not as much, but when you give some of your possessions away, you are worshipping God. Another principle is the principle of RECIPROCITY...when you give to the Lord, He returns financial blessings to you. ("Give and it shall be given unto you...") When you withhold from giving back to the Lord, you then have a wallet with holes in it! (The words of the Bible, not mine! :-)

A few years back, a college student in our group went to church in her college town. She didn't have much money, but she wrote a small check and in the lower left line wrote 'tithe.' The pastor of the church was so amazed that he mentioned this to her, how her gift was a witness. That college kid is still giving regularly to God today and I am so thrilled that she, at a young age, has the idea of Biblical giving in her heart:

Good Morning!! How Are My College Buddies?

"Each one must give as he has made up his mind, not reluctantly or under compulsion, for God loves a cheerful giver. And God is able to provide you with every blessing in abundance so that you may always have enough of everything and may provide in abundance for every good work." II Corinthians 9:7-8

Love You!!   Praying for You!!   Proud of You!!   Bro. Post
✷✷✷✷✷✷✷✷✷✷✷✷✷✷✷✷✷✷✷✷✷

"Give Them a Verbal Vitamin."

We hear a lot about the destructive power of words, and yes, a lot of damage can be done. However, God gave us the ability to speak and a lot of good can be done through speaking!! One beautiful way is to use kindly, encouraging words. Someone you will meet today is needing you to do just that - to speak kindly to them, to encourage them. This person has been beat up by tough circumstances and they need you, they need your hope-filled words. I promise you, some person needs you today! When you do this, your words can actually be spiritually therapeutic, a 'verbal vitamin.' It gives them a ray of hope, it helps adjust their vision to where everything is no longer gloom and doom. You will experience an inner joy also, you will have the thrill of knowing that God used YOU.

A lot of times we think God does His greatest work through preaching great sermons...not really, I doubt it. I think the really important stuff happens 'one on one' - when God sends a message to another person through you. Ok, get ready for today, God will bless someone through you.

> "Kindly words are like drops of honey, sweet to the soul and healing to the body." Proverbs 16:24

Love You!!   Praying for You!!   Proud of You!!   Bro. Post
*******************████

"It really DOES matter."

Sometimes, in our prayer times, we frankly are not very honest with our Father. We maintain a 'stiff upper lip', we do not open our hearts and tell Him how we are hurting. We practice a form of 'spiritual denial' – we minimize our hurts, downplay our disappointments, ignore our fears - it's like we think that our Father will be disappointed in us if we truly tell Him everything. The result is that we ignore our bleeding wounds of the past and the present, subconsciously thinking that as Christians, we should be above these hurts. I believe that when we do this, we hurt our Father's feelings. We also hurt ourselves - we continue to carry the burdens, whether we admit it or not.

King David, in the Psalms, was a very honest man. He threw open the door of his heart, he honestly and frankly admitted his fears, his hurts, his disappointments, even his complaints. Tonight, when we pray, let's try being totally honest with our Father. "Father, I want to tell you about my disappointment...anger...unfulfilled dream...terrifying fear...grief...past failure. Father, it really does matter to me, the pain is real. I now ask you to help me." Tell your Father the truth, whatever your wound may be. You'll be amazed how tender and kind He will be to you.

" I cry with my voice to the Lord...I pour out my complaint before him, I will tell my trouble before him......Give heed to my cry;

for I am brought very low!" Psalm 142:1-2,6 (Excellent example of David's honest praying!!)

Love You!!   Praying for You!!   Proud of You!!   Bro. Post
✶✶✶✶✶✶✶✶✶✶✶✶✶✶✶✶✶✶✶✶

"The crocodiles may have circled the basket, but the crocodiles were not allowed to touch the basket."

Jochebed was in a terrifying position - she had just given birth to her son and instead of being filled with joy, she lived with terror. The King of Egypt had just decreed that all Jewish male babies, including Jochebed's, were to be put to death at birth. So she lived in fear as she tended to her child and desperately tried to hide him at home. If the child cried out at the wrong time and was discovered, the child would be killed. Knowing that her baby would soon be discovered at home, she wove a basket, lined it with tar, placed her baby in the basket and floated it on the edge of the Nile River. However, now there are more dangers - the Nile is filled with crocodiles, water pythons and hippos. Think about this woman - she learned to trust, even in the terrifying days in which she had to wait. (This went on for 3 months!!)

College Buddies, what concerns have you 'placed in the basket?' Somebody or something that is precious to you and you feel threatened, frightened, and like Jochebed, you think about all of the things that CAN go wrong! Hey, this is normal, we all do this at times! God is the one who protected little Moses from the crocodiles and He will work perfectly in your life...give your fears to your Father, place your needs 'in the basket' and trust Him:

Good Morning!! How Are My College Buddies?

"Cast your burden upon the Lord and He will sustain you; He will never allow the righteous to fall." Psalm 55:22

Love You!!   Praying for You!!   Proud of You!!   Bro. Post
✷✷✷✷✷✷✷✷✷✷✷✷✷✷✷✷✷✷✷✷

"Stop Being So Full of Yourself."

Hmm, I wonder if the Lord is trying to tell us that sometimes.

Truth is, the good qualities that we possess are all gifts from Him – and make no mistake, you do have some beautiful qualities! God placed them there and He is the source, not us.

Trouble comes when we starting acting like we are 'resident authorities on everything.' :-) If this arrogance is allowed to grow, then we become a 'perpetual fountain of unsolicited advice.' :-)

Seriously, we miss out in joys and blessings when we do not accept the fact that we are not the best in what we do. And neither does God EXPECT us to be the best, He only asks us to give OUR best.

But sometimes we subconsciously think that we need to be ALWAYS right, ALWAYS do better than others and ALWAYS show others the best way to think and act.

And that my friends, is being 'full of yourself.'

Think of the human body, an incredible creation of God. Ok, think about the eye, a fascinating part of the body. The eye can guide you, inform you, protect you and please you. But can the eye do everything? Can the eye speak? Digest your food? Cleanse the blood like the kidneys? Of course not.

All of us Christians make up the Spiritual Body of Christ. You are one part, like the eye. Do your part well and give God the credit. However, let's not try to tell the hand or the liver or lungs how to do their job, Ok? :-) :

Good Morning!! How Are My College Buddies?

"The fruit of the Spirit is………humility…"
Galatians 5:23

Love You!!   Praying for You!!   Proud of You!!   Bro. Post
✶✶✶✶✶✶✶✶✶✶✶✶✶✶✶✶✶✶✶✶

"How well do you 'duck and hide?'"

As you read the Book of Proverbs, you read a lot about ducking and hiding. It seems that God first gives us His wisdom and then He gives us an inner feeling when there is trouble ahead - and then He helps us to avoid it. This is so awesome of our Father! As Christians, we don't have to always stand up and confront a bad situation 'face to face' - actually we have the inner power to avoid it and to let it pass on by. Think of different kinds of 'trouble' that we may face in the future: a temptation, an abrasive person, a touchy circumstance, future problems in a potential relationship...the list is endless.

College Buddies, a LOT of these potential headaches can be avoided if we just duck and hide and let the problem go right by us! Of course, some headaches and heartaches in life are unavoidable, but you know, a lot of my headaches in life were self-inflicted - I could have avoided them, but I didn't duck and hide!

Please read carefully the following verse and always remember that the Christian life is so practical!

"The wise person sees danger and hides; but the simple go on, and suffer for it." Proverbs 22:3

Love You!!   Praying for You!!   Proud of You!!   Bro. Post
✴✴✴✴✴✴✴✴✴✴✴✴✴✴✴✴✴✴✴✴✴

"Don't contribute to fracturing your family."

I guess that some of the fiercest battles are fought in the area of a family. I am amazed at the damage that the Enemy can do here, it's heartbreaking to watch. The closeness of family members does not give us the right to sin against them. As a family, we will occasionally see the unattractive side of a family member when they are struggling. One 'Fracturing Sin' is when we speak evil of another family member to cast ourselves in a better light, often to our parents. This jockeying for favor can do a lot of harm. Another "Fracturing Sin" is when we are irritated at one family member and we try to recruit the rest of the family to our side. Now add the volatile issue of money to a family dispute and wow, things can get ugly, big time!

I think when it comes to our families, one great rule is: "Don't start a fire, don't step in a fire." When you're tempted to tell something about a family member, whoa, don't start a verbal fire that will come back and burn you. When you see another family member using incendiary words against another, just don't step into their fire:

> "He who troubles his household will inherit wind, and the fool will serve the wise."
> Proverbs 11:29

Love You!!   Praying for You!!   Proud of You!!   Bro. Post
✳✳✳✳✳✳✳✳✳✳✳✳✳✳✳✳✳✳✳✳✳

Good Morning!! How Are My College Buddies?

"Maximizing the Trivial."

It's easy to fall into this trap, but the results are expensive! Here's what I mean, sometimes we look at a MINOR problem, inflate it's importance, then complain loudly! The problem is minor in the big picture, but because we have made it important, we then 'maximize the trivial!' This can happen in college, it can happen in a job, it can happen in a relationship. The end result is that we may be living in an ocean of blessings but we're upset over a teacup of problems.

College Buddies, it takes God's wisdom to realize that not all issues are equally important. Some issues are VERY important - some aren't worth a hill of beans, God can help us respond accordingly. Ask God to help you save your energy and concentration for the important stuff and to let go of the trivial stuff:

> "But the wisdom that is from above is first pure, then reasonable, gentle, open to reason, full of compassion and good deeds." James 3:17

Love You!!   Praying for You!!   Proud of You!!   Bro. Post

✱✱✱✱✱✱✱✱✱✱✱✱✱✱✱✱✱✱✱✱✱✱

Good Morning!! How Are My College Buddies?

"You don't have to say EXACTLY what is on your mind!"

If you had guests for dinner, you would never allow them to use your silverware that was tarnished and stained, you would first polish them and make them presentable.

Ok, College Buddies, remember this: When irritated, the first words that pop into our minds are always tarnished and unpresentable!! I am sure that you know what I am talking about. :-) The amazing thing to me is how God helps us in the PRACTICAL stuff, the day in, the day out struggles that we ALL face. God will help us here, He will give us the restraint to hold our words, to consider them, to rephrase them, to 'polish' them before we present them! This work of God, where He changes our words, may only take a few seconds, but it pays huge dividends. You will benefit vocationally, socially and greatly with your future spouse if you learn now to allow God to veto, substitute and 'polish' your words:

> "The righteous man can suit his words to the occasion; but the mouth of the wicked speaks perverse things." Proverbs 10:32

Love You!!   Praying for You!!   Proud of You!!   Bro. Post
✳✳✳✳✳✳✳✳✳✳✳✳✳✳✳✳✳✳✳✳✳

"If you live your life without compassion, your life will become a dry, barren desert."

You'll find yourself lonely in this desert, the only people you will tolerate are people who are 'together' - who are free from vocational, emotional or physical shortcomings. What about the people who are struggling? A person without compassion usually finds a standard reason for their 'failure' - often it heaps blame on the very person who is struggling. College Buddies, I believe with all of my heart that compassion is an absolute necessity for us to share God's love. Have you ever seen someone with problems and thought how easily you could have been in the same position? I sincerely hope that you have. Having compassion doesn't mean you can solve the problem…it does mean that you allow the person to lean on you until God solves the problem.

Instead of wondering how God can use you, why not ask God to fill your heart with compassion? You'll find an unbelievable joy and you will be walking in the very footsteps of Jesus:

> "When Jesus saw the crowds, he was moved with compassion for them, because they were harassed and helpless, like sheep without a shepherd." Matthew 9:36

Love You!!   Praying for You!!   Proud of You!!   Bro. Post

✶✶✶✶✶✶✶✶✶✶✶✶✶✶✶✶✶✶✶✶✶

"The Agony of Waiting."

God rarely answers our prayer immediately. There is almost always an interval, a time of waiting between the time that we begin praying and the time that He answers.

There are reasons why the Lord makes us wait but one reason is obvious in the Bible. Sometimes when I pray, I am trusting in God PLUS all of the other ways that I can think to solve the problem. I may even go as far as to latch on to MY solution and then pray and suggest to God that this is the best way to fix the problem!

The Lord rarely solves a problem with my solution, almost never. He has a much more awesome solution, and He wants us to recognize that HE did it, not ourselves.

So we wait. Our imagined solutions are like crutches that we lean on, something that we can try if all else fails. Our Father gently removes these crutches, and the spotlight shifts to Him, what HE will do in answer to our prayers.

Sometimes He waits until the very last hour! When the Children of Israel had to cross the Jordan River, our Father didn't first open a path and then invite them to walk through it. He waited and waited, until the last second, when their feet touched the water! Then He answered.

Our Father will not fail us, He will answer. However, He is removing the 'crutches,' so that we can be awed by His answer, not our feeble solutions:

"You have heard of Job's perseverance and have seen what the Lord finally brought about. The Lord is full of compassion and mercy." James 5:11

Love You!! Praying for You!! Proud of You!! Bro. Post
****

"Abandoning the Ship"

"There is nothing wrong or unnatural with feeling weary, but there is everything wrong with abandoning ship in the midst of a fight."
–Chuck Swindoll

That's the big issue, isn't it? Not whether we will become weary...we will. Not whether we will stumble...that will happen. Not whether we grow discouraged...there will be times when we will be. The BIG issue is whether we will quit - whether we will walk away from God, away from His people, away from His work. It's a sneaky ploy from the enemy - he is constantly urging and whispering, "Why don't you just quit?" If we throw in the towel, then the work that God intended for us to do is passed on to other Christians, making their load heavier. If we give up, then the whole church is weaker and Christ's witness is lessened. College Buddies, I hope you believe this, God wants to use YOU in His work. He can forgive us when we fail, encourage us when we're down, strengthen us when we're weary... HOWEVER, often it takes years for our Father to restore us when we simply quit and wander away. Many people today are no longer following the Lord - not because of a spectacular failure, they just became weary and quit. God's will for us is to be actively involved with His people in His work...let's not abandon the ship:

Good Morning!! How Are My College Buddies?

"Demas has deserted me, because he loved this present world..." II Timothy 4:10

"Be strong in the grace that is in Christ Jesus......Endure hardship like a good soldier of Christ Jesus." II Timothy 2:1, 3

Love You!!   Praying for You!!   Proud of You!!   Bro. Post
✶✶✶✶✶✶✶✶✶✶✶✶✶✶✶✶✶✶✶✶

Good Morning!! How Are My College Buddies?

"God nudges more than He pushes."

You may be considering expanding and growing in your life, yet your dream has been choked by the day-in, day-out stresses of life. You may have wonderful plans to fulfill in personal growth, yet the timetable always ends with 'someday'. I believe that God is the person who places these plans and dreams in our hearts, and He is constantly nudging us to get started! You may want to start a new hobby, want to exercise regularly, want to read and study the Bible, want to learn a musical instrument, want to ......the list is endless.

Guess where these dreams come from?!

God wants us to grow and flourish, not to be settled and stagnant. So He keeps bringing up these opportunities and gives us a desire to accomplish them - that's His way of nudging us. Maybe today's the day for you to start - life is fun when you're striving to achieve something. So if God is 'nudging' you, go ahead and start, He'll be there to help you finish.

"For it is God who is at work in you, enabling you both to choose and to work for His good pleasure." Philippians 2:13

Love You!!   Praying for You!!   Proud of You!!   Bro. Post
✳✳✳✳✳✳✳✳✳✳✳✳✳✳✳✳✳✳✳✳✳

Good Morning!! How Are My College Buddies?

"Caught Between Two Ticked Off People"

When two people are ticked off at each other, things can get rather ugly. It's not much fun to be around a friend or a family member who is nursing a grudge against someone else. You will be subjected to 'eruptions of anger,' usually verbal darts thrown at the person.

So how are we supposed to act around these people?! The least God expects us to do is to simply stay out of it. Just like you would avoid contact with a person with a bad cold, do NOT be infected by another person's bitterness. Another way we can help is to be a spiritual 'fire hose' - to use soft words, gentle reason, all in the hopes of reducing the fire of anger. This is not always possible, sometimes people are set on fanning the angry flames. Pray for a person caught in anger, God can deliver them when they repent. Ask God to use you, if possible, to slowly bring two people back together. When you do this, you will be doing the very work of Jesus:

"Blessed are the peacemakers, for they will be called children of God." Matthew 5:9

Love You!!   Praying for You!!   Proud of You!!   Bro. Post
✸✸✸✸✸✸✸✸✸✸✸✸✸✸✸✸✸✸✸✸

"A Travel Agent for Guilt Trips."

Job was experiencing a brutal and horrible time. He had lost his health to a miserable disease. Once wealthy, he now was bankrupt. By far the worse, ALL of his sons and daughters were killed at the same time. Job slumped alone in his grief, scraping the skin sores from the disease.

Job needed a friend, someone to comfort and encourage him. He did have three friends and when they came and wept with him, surely Job had hope that his friends would help him carry his burdens.

His friends' advice was disastrous. Instead of giving a hand to help Job up, their advice became a hammer which beat him down even lower. These friends were "Travel Agents for Guilt Trips" and their reasoning was simple: "God punishes evil, you have problems, so surely you have done something wrong."

Their advice was vicious, it was devastating, it was arrogant and self righteous.

Sadly, many Christians in America are "Travel Agents for Guilt Trips." They are disciples of Job's friends and their words are devastating to suffering Christians. Do you know the minister who has preached to more people in the last 50 years than any other minister? Did you know that for decades he has had serious health problems, carried incredible burdens and faced severe trials? And even now, he and his wife endure terrible health. Was it because of some sin or failure that Dr. Billy Graham has endured severe trials for decades? Hmm.

Good Morning!! How Are My College Buddies?

God wants us to love and encourage Christians who are suffering. Have you ever thought that we should respect them even more, since they still trust God in the middle of fiery trials? Surely we should consider them spiritual heroes, not inferior Christians.

Let's ask God to use us to refresh other Christians. Let's help carry their load and show them the gentle compassion of Jesus. Here's a wonderful promise to claim for them, it's a promise of hope, not a guilt trip:

"For I know the plans I have for you," declares the Lord, "plans to prosper you and not to harm you, plans to give you hope and a future." Jeremiah 29:11

Love You!!   Praying for You!!   Proud of You!!   Bro. Post

✳✳✳✳✳✳✳✳✳✳✳✳✳✳✳✳✳✳✳✳✳✳

"FORGIVEN...REMOVED...... FORGOTTEN"

College Buddies, the Lord wants us to remember these three verbs. These are the three things that God does with our sins when we ask for His forgiveness. If we are to succeed in our Christian lives, it is CRUCIAL that we remember this!

Our Enemy is an guilt expert and he loves it when he can pile a huge load of guilt on you...he whispers to you that you are a spiritual nobody, that you are unworthy of God's love and forgiveness.

Our Father knows how we struggle in this area, so He makes it very clear in the Bible how He deals with our sins. First, He forgives us...He truly forgives. Secondly, He removes the sins from us...we don't have to dredge them up and wallow in guilt. Lastly, since He is God, He has the power to actually FORGET them...the next time we pray, we don't have to worry if He is going to berate us with shame. If you have failed God and you are drowning in guilt, and you feel spiritually worthless and useless, please read carefully the following verses:

> "The Lord does not deal with us according to what our sins deserve, nor does he repay us for what our iniquities deserve. For as high as the heavens are above the earth, so great is his steadfast love to them who fear him; as far as the east is from the west, so far he removes our transgressions from us." Psalm 103:10-12

Good Morning!! How Are My College Buddies?

Love You!!   Praying for You!!   Proud of You!!   Bro. Post
✹✹✹✹✹✹✹✹✹✹✹✹✹✹✹✹✹✹✹✹

"Reshape, Not Ruin"

"Your Savior knows your breaking point. The bruising and crushing and melting process is designed to reshape you, not ruin you. Your value is increasing the longer He lingers over you." -Chuck Swindoll

It would be so nice if we didn't need the dark times, but we do. If our lives were free from worries and stress, we would slowly drift away from our Father. When these tough times do come, God is working on the circumstances that cause us the pain - He will solve the problem in His perfect time, in His perfect way. But He is doing something far more important on the inside of us! He is strengthening our faith by 'stretching' it, by allowing the tough times in which we must trust Him. He also is tenderizing our hearts, He is making us more like Jesus. We are now more likely to act like the Good Samaritan, to deeply care for others who are hurting. We are now less likely to walk on the other side of the road and ignore them.

Be aware of two lies that the enemy will whisper to you when you are struggling: "God is punishing you." and "This will break you." Ask God to help you resist these untruths and accept this truth from the Bible: Your Father is reshaping you, He is working to make you a very valuable person in His family, someone who can actually show others what Jesus is like:

"For He (the Lord) wounds, but He binds up; He injures, but His hands also heal." Job 5:18

Love You!! Praying for You!! Proud of You!! Bro. Post
✳✳✳✳✳✳✳✳✳✳✳✳✳✳✳✳✳✳✳✳

"She was an 'Expert at Rejoicing.'"

Two years ago, I was sitting with a family in the surgery waiting room at Arkansas Children's Hospital. I noticed a young family near us. You could tell it was a brutal time, the mom was emotional, the dad had tension etched all over his face. I found out later that their young child was undergoing a risky, intensive surgery. I glanced at them occasionally, feeling their tension, waiting for their surgeon to come out and report.

"YEAH!!!!!!!!!!!! THE SURGERY WENT VERY WELL!!!!!!!!! YEAH!!!!!!!!!!!!!!!!"

Startled, we looked at the surgery entrance door and there was a highly skilled surgeon, hands in the air, beaming as she yelled across the waiting room to this family. The response of the family was immediate and beautiful to watch - the mom streaming tears of gratitude, the dad slumping his shoulders in relief. Later, the surgeon would explain the intricate details of the surgery, but not now, it was a time of rejoicing.

What an incredible wise woman, as well as a gifted surgeon. An 'Expert at Rejoicing.'

College Buddies, our Father in Heaven crafts some incredible blessings for us each day. These blessings may be what He has done for us or what He has prevented from happening to us. Let's become experts at rejoicing, ok? Get alone, when you have been blessed, remember this surgeon, let your face light up with a grin, look up to your Father: "YEAH!!! YOU ARE AWESOME!! YEAH!!! "

"Praise the Lord. Praise the Lord, O my soul. I will sing praises to my God as long as I live." Psalm 146:1-2

Love You!!   Praying for You!!   Proud of You!!   Bro. Post
✷✷✷✷✷✷✷✷✷✷✷✷✷✷✷✷✷✷✷✷

"Rushing Away From an Opportunity."

Sometimes, when we are really pushed and in a hurry, we may rush right past an opportunity to serve God. It would be nice if these opportunities came at convenient times, but they rarely do. Often, right in the middle of our frantic pace comes the opportunity to show God's love to someone.

Then comes the Big Issue : Which is more important, my demanding schedule, or a needy person?

Jesus had the perfect pace to His life - there were times when He was extremely busy, daylight to dark. Other times, He deliberately withdrew from the hectic pace, for His spiritual renewal. It's fascinating to read about Him on a day when He was going at a frantic pace - a long day, a big crowd thronging around Him, he was summoned to hurry and go to a man's home. As He walked through the crowd, a sick woman, too weak to stand, just touches His garment. Amazingly, He instantly rearranges His schedule...the expectations of others can wait...He gives His full attention to the needy woman!

College Buddies, you may be 'running and gunning' today - plans to start early and go late, just to keep your schedule. Be aware, some person may likely reach out to you, be assured that it will probably be at the worst time, schedule wise. This is when Jesus can help us act like He did...the needy person first, the demanding schedule second:

"This is how we know what love is: Jesus laid down his life for us. And we ought to lay down our lives for our brothers." I John 3:16

Love You!!   Praying for You!!   Proud of You!!   Bro. Post
✴✴✴✴✴✴✴✴✴✴✴✴✴✴✴✴✴✴✴✴✴

"Spiritual Crosswinds"

Before the auto-pilot was invented the pilot was very busy! If he took off from Atlanta and wanted to fly to Philadelphia, he would know the exact direction to fly, 4 degrees north. However, if he flew that direction the whole flight, he would never find Philadelphia, he would probably end up in Baltimore.

The problem is crosswinds, a constant pressure pushing the plane off course, away from the pilot's destination. Therefore the pilot was frequently correcting, adjusting the plane's direction and keeping on course to Philadelphia.

College Buddies, until we get to heaven, we will constantly have to deal with 'spiritual crosswinds.' These are attitudes and temptations that will push us far off the course of living for the Lord. All of us want to live for God, but how well do we recognize the times when we are way off course? A person can be disappointed with a circumstance in life. But if we stay there, the crosswind of discontentment pushes us far away from God. A person may want to be generous in giving, but eventually the crosswind of American covetousness has pushed us way off course. A person may become upset and angry, and as the weeks go by, the crosswind of bitterness has caused them to drift far way from God.

The issue is not whether we are ever pushed off course by a 'spiritual crosswind', we all are. The issue is whether we recognize when we are off course and return to God.

Good Morning!! How Are My College Buddies?

Our Father is always ready to correct our direction in life, to help us redirect our course. Life is too short and your life is too precious to stay off course! King David once recognized that he was far off course and he prayed a simple prayer, a prayer that all of us can pray when we are struggling with 'spiritual crosswinds.'

"Create in me a pure heart, O God, and renew a steadfast spirit within me." Psalm 51:10

Love You!!   Praying for You!!   Proud of You!!   Bro. Post
✼✼✼✼✼✼✼✼✼✼✼✼✼✼✼✼✼✼✼✼✼

"Thinking vs. Doing"

"If I think about something that it is wrong, that is just as bad as if I had committed the wrong."

What a ridiculous statement.

Our true spiritual battles are fought in our thought life, in the way that we think. Fear, anger, jealousy, lust, envy, pride...these are a few of the battles that we fight in this realm. HOWEVER, just because we temporarily stumble in our thoughts does not mean that we have to sin in our actions - God can help us here. The Lord helps us when we wander off in Fantasy Land - He finds us, forgives us and restores us to walking with Him. He knows that if I am angry in my thoughts, eventually I will speak angry words... so He helps me BEFORE the wrong thoughts lead to wrong actions. I think this is so wonderful - our Father protects us by rescuing us before we make a grievous mistake!

College Buddies, it would be so wonderful if we never stumbled in our thought life...but the truth is, we all stumble, daily. However, it is a great comfort to know that our Father doesn't leave us there in Fantasy Land...He rescues and restores us so that we can live for Him. Notice how the Lord rescued David, when he struggled with fearful thoughts:

> "I said in my haste, I am cut off from before thine eyes; nevertheless, thou heard the voice of my supplications when I cried to thee. O love the Lord, all of his saints: for the Lord preserves the faithful..." Psalm 31:22-23

Good Morning!! How Are My College Buddies?

Love You!!   Praying for You!!   Proud of You!!   Bro. Post

✶✶✶✶✶✶✶✶✶✶✶✶✶✶✶✶✶✶✶✶

"Leo, Could You Hurry Up?"

The Mona Lisa didn't happen instantaneously. If we would have been watching da Vinci at the beginning, this painting would have been unimpressive, even ugly. This master painter knew that he had to paint the background, make the woman's outline, prepare patiently in order to produce the eventual masterpiece!

College Buddies, our Father is working patiently and preparing the foundation to send us His incredible blessings. But, you know, I just don't like waiting, I want the masterpiece now! Da Vinci spent many patient hours working at the beginning, but he was motivated by knowing the beautiful end result. Our Father refuses to send you a blessing until He has perfected it...until we will be awed by His incredible work. So He takes His time, patiently personalizing the blessing for you, His child whom He adores. Are you waiting for a 'Mona Lisa' blessing? A little down because it hasn't come yet? Keep trusting, your Father may well be finishing the last artistic strokes before He sends it. Tuck this verse in your heart and claim it, it was written for you.

"No good thing will he withhold from them who walk uprightly." Psalm 84:11

Love You!! Praying for You!! Proud of You!! Bro. Post

****

"Lord Jesus, you can have my sack lunch."

It's not much, it certainly can't meet the need of thousands, but Jesus, you can have it.

This little boy offered what he could, little did he know that Jesus had the ability to EXPAND the blessing, far beyond anyone's imagination.

Sometimes we feel like the need is so overwhelming, and the talents, gifts, and abilities that we have would make little difference, so why bother? Sometimes we hear others voicing their doubts, like the disciples did to this little boy's gift: "Here's a boy's sack lunch, but it won't make much difference."

College Buddies, God wants to use your 'sack lunch' every day of your life. There are two key words to remember when God leads you to serve Him: AVAILABILITY and EXPANSION.

God wants us to be available - to be ready to offer Him, no matter how small, our time, talents, abilities and service. DO NOT THINK THAT YOUR 'SACK LUNCH' IS UNIMPORTANT!! If this little boy had thought like that, the thousands would have gone home hungry. Is your 'sack lunch' available to God today?

Secondly, and this is so exciting: God will take your small 'sack lunch' and He will EXPAND IT! You will be amazed at the tremendous good that comes from our tiny, insignificant talents and abilities.

This miracle came, not because Jesus had a lot of assets - He only had a small lunch. This miracle came because Jesus had the ability to EXPAND the assets……and He will definitely do the same for your 'sack lunch' today.

"Jesus, it's not much, but you can have my sack lunch today."

> "So, my dear brothers and sisters, be strong and immovable. Always work enthusiastically for the Lord, for you know that nothing that you do for the Lord is ever useless." I Corinthians 15:58

Love You!!   Praying for You!!   Proud of You!!   Bro. Post
✶✶✶✶✶✶✶✶✶✶✶✶✶✶✶✶✶✶✶✶

"The Swirling Vat of Discontentment"

Sometimes a lot of our unhappiness comes from a 'swirling vat of discontentment.' No matter how well things are going, we can always imagine things that would, in our opinion, make things perfect. As we imagine, the unhappiness level rises and soon, we conclude that our life is miserable!!

College Buddies, there is no such thing as a Utopia until we get to heaven, there will always be stuff that we will endure in this life. The danger comes when we become snared by discontentment, it can cause us to do some weird things. Relationships are severed, careers are jeopardized, reputations soiled…all because we were motivated by the 'swirling vat of discontentment.' God can help us here, He knows our nature and He knows the solution. The solution is that He REFOCUSES our attention, away from the things we don't have and onto the things that we do have. He also REMINDS us - that He is control and that He will give us His best. He then RELEASES us from discontentment and helps us to enjoy the good life that He has given us:

> "Keep your life free from the love of money, and be content with what you have; for he has said, 'I will never fail you nor forsake you.'"
> Hebrews 13:5

Love You!!   Praying for You!!   Proud of You!!   Bro. Post

✶✶✶✶✶✶✶✶✶✶✶✶✶✶✶✶✶✶✶✶✶✶

"You're not important so it doesn't matter how I speak to you or treat you."

Hey, we wouldn't be caught dead saying that, would we?!

But think about it...often the basis for rudeness is an inside superior attitude. When a person has this attitude, they are very courteous to 'peers' - the ones they think are as 'important' as they are.

But watch how they treat people whom they feel are less important - they run over them verbally, treat them callously or with outright hostility. It doesn't matter whether it's on the phone, in a store, to a stranger on the street......arrogant Christians always offer consistent rudeness.

Many a Christian supervisor has ruined their testimony for Christ by internal pride and external rudeness.

Jesus was the perfect model of courtesy. He didn't differentiate – He treated the high ranking officials and the 'everyday folks' with equal courtesy. He didn't humiliate a woman who was caught in a public sin, He gently led her to salvation. At one point, He asked everyone to leave the room of a sick child whom He was about to heal - He knew the child would be terrified waking up to a room full of gawking adults, so He asked them to leave.

Jesus exercised perfect courtesy to everyone. Here is a incredible opportunity to live a sermon without saying a word! Let's ask God to make us as courteous and as thoughtful as Jesus. You'll be giving a powerful testimony in our acidic, abrasive culture.

"Love is not rude, it is not self-seeking." I Corinthians 13:5

Love You!! Praying for You!! Proud of You!! Bro. Post
✶✶✶✶✶✶✶✶✶✶✶✶✶✶✶✶✶✶✶✶

"How Well Do You Smell?" :-)

A delicate perfume has the ability to actually enhance a person's beauty - it causes the person to be more attractive. Interesting......but a beautiful fragrance has the quality of ATTRACTION.

On the other hand, a few years ago I boarded a plane for a long flight and was seated beside a young man who......well...he had incredible body odor. I looked around frantically, but the plane was full. I caught myself leaning away because the odor was repelling.

Look carefully at the verse below. The exciting truth is that others can be attracted to Christ through us!! When we speak with gentle words, act with Jesus' kindness and show Jesus' deep love to others, people without Christ can actually sense the presence of Jesus and be attracted to Him! Wow, what an opportunity for today.

Sadly, the opposite is true. If we live selfishly, slash people verbally, cut corners in our finances, burn with envy and jealousy......people can actually be repulsed and write off Jesus...because of us.

Today is an opportunity to let others enjoy the gentle fragrance of Jesus. You will probably never know anything about it, but God can use you to make Jesus more attractive to an unbeliever today.

"But thanks be to God, who always leads us in triumph, and THROUGH US SPREADS IN EVERY PLACE THE FRAGRANCE

THAT COMES FROM KNOWING HIM."
II Corinthians 2:14 (emphases mine)

Love You!! Praying for You!! Proud of You!! Bro. Post

✻✻✻✻✻✻✻✻✻✻✻✻✻✻✻✻✻✻✻✻✻

"You'll be fine; God will take care of you."

Wow, if anyone needed to hear these words at this particular time, it was the Apostle Paul. He had been through a horrible two weeks - a prisoner on a ship sailing to Rome. AND, that ship had been in a storm for those two weeks and now it was breaking up, about to sink. AND, the guards wanted to kill all of the prisoners, Paul included. AND, to top things off, after the ship had sunk and everyone was safe on an island, Paul reached for some firewood and he was bitten by a deadly snake!! (Acts 27)

The Lord is so compassionate to His kids; He knows how easily tough times can dispirit us and leave us floundering. So He will send a message of protection to you, a little reminder that He is still guarding you and protecting you. In Paul's case, an angel came and delivered this message of protection: "You will be fine, God will take care of you." However, the Lord may use a Bible verse, a devotional book, a word from another Christian...... there are many ways that He may choose to send it. But the reason is very clear - your Father wants to lift your fears and calm your panicky thoughts, so He sends a message of protection. If today the circumstances of your life make you feel like you're in a fierce storm, hanging on for dear life - just watch, your Father will deliver a message to you. After all, you are just as precious to Him as the Apostle Paul.

Good Morning!! How Are My College Buddies?

"For he will give his angels charge of you, to guard you in all your ways.......When he calls to me, I will answer him; I will be with him in trouble, I will rescue him and honor him." Psalm 91:11-15 (emphasis mine)

Love You!!   Praying for You!!   Proud of You!!   Bro. Post
✳✳✳✳✳✳✳✳✳✳✳✳✳✳✳✳✳✳✳✳✳

Good Morning!! How Are My College Buddies?

"Just because we don't know what He is doing does not mean that HE does not know what He is doing!"

If you look at a beautiful needlepoint, you can see the artist's skill and meticulous work. However, if you look at the backside, it is unattractive, disjointed, even rather ugly. The problem is that we can only see the backside, we do not share the artist's vision of producing something beautiful. God's work in our lives is identical to this - He does not share the specifics of what He is doing in our lives. However, He does promise us that His will for us is perfect and beautiful. He loves us so much that He will not give you second best, He plans the perfect for you. College Buddies, some things will happen in your life that you will not understand at all. We may understand it later in life, we may have to wait until we get to heaven. But be assured, your Father is working in the background, planning and implementing events that will make your life everything He wants it to be:

"For now we see in a mirror, and are baffled; but someday we are going to see Him in His completeness, face to face. As yet my knowledge is incomplete, but then I shall know in full, as I have been fully known." I Corinthians 13:12

Love You!!   Praying for You!!   Proud of You!!   Bro. Post
✵✵✵✵✵✵✵✵✵✵✵✵✵✵✵✵✵✵✵✵✵✵

"'Nagging' 'Stewing' 'Terror'"

These words describe the three stages of fear, and the Lord will help us as we have to face these during our lives. 'Nagging' fear is when we are having a good day, but a troubling thought keeps popping up in our mind. 'Stewing' is a more frightening concern, and we catch ourselves thinking and worrying about the problem almost all of the day. 'Terror' is when we or a loved one is in imminent danger and we are terrified and shaken.

I am amazed at how we think our Father is disappointed in us when we struggle here - don't you think He knows that this is a BIG issue in our lives? Of course He does, He rarely scolds His kids, He always helps His kids. God can help us first turn the spotlight on our fears, to identify them and pray about them. "Father, this is what is scaring me…" The Holy Spirit can then remind us of our Father's promises of protection in the Bible. Then our Father gently encourages us to give this fear to Him - again and again, all through the day…then His peace comes. Instead of our Father being disappointed in us, today He is longing to help us; He hurts when His kids hurt. He will help us today. We will find God's promises to be a soft pillow for a weary worrier. Here's one of our Father's wonderful promises, enjoy it.

> "In all their affliction he was afflicted, and the angel of his presence saved them; in his love and in his pity he redeemed them; he lifted them up and carried them." Isaiah 63:9

Good Morning!! How Are My College Buddies?

Love You!!   Praying for You!!   Proud of You!!   Bro. Post
✳✳✳✳✳✳✳✳✳✳✳✳✳✳✳✳✳✳✳✳

Good Morning!! How Are My College Buddies?

"Maybe you're wearing the wrong yoke."

A yoke is a leather collar placed upon a mule or a horse. If the collar fits well, the animal can function very well, accomplishing the purpose of it's master. However, if the animal is wearing the wrong yoke, it chaffs its neck. The animal becomes agitated and weary.

Today, a lot of people miss out on God's purpose in life because they insist on wearing a yoke from a different master. Our culture wants us to wear the yoke of accumulated wealth, or the yoke of instant pleasure, or the yoke of acting superior to others.

The world has hundreds of different yokes that you may choose to wear, but be informed... these yokes do not fit, these yokes will leave you agitated, weary, and unhappy. Jesus offers us the perfect yoke, walking in His will, loving and serving Him. The amazing thing is that when we do this, we have a sense of joy and purpose in life. So if the Enemy has coaxed you into wearing the wrong yoke, take it off and claim this promise from Jesus:

> "Come to me, all who are exhausted and heavy burdened, and I will give you rest. Take my yoke upon you, and learn from me, for I am gentle and lowly in heart, and you will find rest for you souls. For my yoke is easy and my burden is light." Matthew 11:28-30

Love You!!   Praying for You!!   Proud of You!!   Bro. Post

✳✳✳✳✳✳✳✳✳✳✳✳✳✳✳✳✳✳✳✳✳✳✳

Good Morning!! How Are My College Buddies?

"Know where you're weak, know who can help."

College Buddies, I believe you will excel in whatever vocation the Lord leads you. However, please remember that in your vocational responsibilities, there will always be one or two areas where you are weak. Now you can deny this fact, rationalize this fact...OR you can enjoy God's solution to this fact!

Please remember this: There will always be someone near you who can help you, God has planned it that way! I love what I do, but I am painfully aware of two areas where I am weak. I struggle in these areas, I have a tough time. However, God has brought some wonderful Christians in my life who are excellent in the very areas where I struggle. I value their advice, I listen to them carefully. And this is precisely God's solution, one of the ways that God makes us the best that we can be. College Buddies, please read carefully the following verse and enjoy this huge blessing in your life:

"Without counsel plans are disappointed; but in the multitude of counselors they are successful." Proverbs 15:22

Love You!!   Praying for You!!   Proud of You!!   Bro. Post
✸✸✸✸✸✸✸✸✸✸✸✸✸✸✸✸✸✸✸✸✸

"Levels of Thanksgiving"

There are different types of thanksgiving in the Bible, and God wants us to use all of them! The first is the simplest, it is giving thanks for the way God provides for us.... food, clothing, all of our needs. We should do this, especially in the light of the many who are desperately needy. The second type of thanksgiving is what I call the 'whew!' thanksgiving, like: "Whew! Thank you God for straightening out that mess!" We should do this after God delivers us from a problem. The next two take more faith. Next is the "Things are a real mess God, but I thank you NOW that you will solve my problems." I think this prayer is very pleasing to God, and often He waits until this prayer until He answers.

The last one is the best. It's when we simply are overwhelmed how much God loves us and we thank Christ for dying a brutal death so we could be forgiven. We go to bed and before we go to sleep, we pray, "Father, I don't understand why, but I am amazed at how much you love me. I cannot repay you, but I want to say 'Thank you.'" Now you are really thrilling your Heavenly Father's heart.

"I will bless the Lord at all times, His praise shall continually be in my mouth." Psalm 34:1

Love You!!   Praying for You!!   Proud of You!!   Bro. Post

✽✽✽✽✽✽✽✽✽✽✽✽✽✽✽✽✽✽✽✽

Good Morning!! How Are My College Buddies?

"Like a mother humming a lullaby, God whispers gently to His children. Listen for the whispers of God - let them give you rest and peace." Chuck Swindoll

Our Father always knows exactly what He needs to whisper to us; He knows us totally and completely. He knows when we are discouraged, so He gently reminds us of His power and His plans for our future. He knows when we have failed Him, so He gently reminds us that He has cleansed us and removed our sins. He knows when we are frightened, so He gently whispers His protection and care. As a perfect Father, He knows how to soothe and calm His troubled child...He does this for all of His kids. College Buddies, if you're struggling today, your Father knows all about it. Get alone, pray and ask your Father to help you...listen as He whispers in your soul. He will help you and reassure you of His love and care. Read and enjoy this beautiful promise.

"My sheep hear My voice, and I know them, and they follow Me. And I give them eternal life, and they shall never perish; neither shall anyone snatch them out of My hand." John 10:27-28

Love You!!   Praying for You!!   Proud of You!!   Bro. Post
✶✶✶✶✶✶✶✶✶✶✶✶✶✶✶✶✶✶✶✶✶

Good Morning!! How Are My College Buddies?

"Praying doesn't help much, praying mixed with believing does wonders."

College Buddies, how much believing do you add to your praying? Just praying a lot doesn't do anything, it's not like God has a calculator, adding up how many times you ask Him! As you pray, do you REALLY believe God has the power to answer your prayer? Do you really think that He will? Can you 'see' the answered prayer in your heart, even before it comes? Can you thank Him, in advance, for the way He will surely answer? Often we try to 'hedge' our prayers...after we ask, we make disclaimers: "It must not be God's will"..."I guess it's not the right time."

College Buddies, God never told us to try and decide what is His will - God DID tell us to pray with faith, expectantly, enthusiastically eager for our Father's answer. Starting today, ask God to make you a man/woman of faith and mix your faithful praying with anticipating faith...you'll be delighted with this potent combination:

> "Truly I tell you, if you have faith the size of a mustard seed, you shall say to this mountain, 'Move from here to there,' and it will move; and nothing will be impossible for you." Matthew 17:20

Love You!!   Praying for You!!   Proud of You!!   Bro. Post
✸✸✸✸✸✸✸✸✸✸✸✸✸✸✸✸✸✸✸✸✸✸

"Lose the word 'lucky.'"

It insults your Father.

Okay, think with me. When I went to college, my dad and mom both worked hard to pay for it. They even borrowed money to see that I could earn a degree. I remember their coming to my graduation; they seemed happier than I did! Now imagine, at that graduation, if a friend came up and congratulated me. Now imagine if I were to say, in the presence of my parents, "Thank you. I was really lucky to have enough money to get my degree." Hmm......I can't imagine how my parents would have felt.

The Bible says that ALL good blessings and gifts come from our Father in heaven. To ascribe a blessing to an esoteric idea of 'luck' is to simply place the credit in the wrong place.

Ask God to give you a 'Blessing Antenna' - that spiritual ability to recognize a blessing from your Father throughout the day. They don't have to be dramatic blessings; just develop the ability to spot them and identify them. When we practice this, our whining decreases and our gratitude increases.

Lucky? Come on...don't go there. You are BLESSED!!!

Good Morning!! How Are My College Buddies?

"EVERY good and PERFECT gift is from ABOVE, coming down from the FATHER of lights, who does not change like a shifting shadow." James 1:17 (emphases mine)

Love You!!   Praying for You!!   Proud of You!!   Bro. Post
✶✶✶✶✶✶✶✶✶✶✶✶✶✶✶✶✶✶✶✶✶

"Ruining a Good Funeral"

Jesus knew how to ruin a good funeral. He came upon a funeral procession, with the family grieving, and chose to bring the person back to life! The family was transformed from grief to joy, from despair to hope, the funeral service was the only thing that suffered. (Wonder what the preacher said after THAT happened! :-)

College Buddies, you may have spent a long time praying for a blessing, and it has not come. You may have given up hope, disappointed that you will never see that blessing. In effect, you have taken you dream and performed a funeral in your soul, burying it, thinking God will never send it. These 'soul funerals' can come in thousands of ways, from job hunt discouragement to giving up on someone's salvation. Always remember: The blessing that God sends you is PERFECT and the timing of the blessing is always PERFECT. If God sees the perfect time is down the road, then we should wait and still pray, still trust. Don't bury your dream just because God waits in answering.

Are there any funerals in your heart that Jesus is planning to ruin? Yeah, I know, we all have them. Memorize this verse, tuck it in your heart.

> "NO GOOD THING will he withhold from them who walk uprightly." Psalm 84:11 (emphasis mine)

Love You!! Praying for You!! Proud of You!! Bro. Post

✶✶✶✶✶✶✶✶✶✶✶✶✶✶✶✶✶✶✶✶✶✶

"Trust In His Heart"

"When you don't understand
When you don't see His plan
And when you can't trace His hand
Trust in His heart."

College Buddies, your Father's heart is filled with an incredible amount of deep love for you! His heart overflows with affection as He thinks of you and that's why, as a doting Father, He constantly is blessing you......He just can't help himself. However, as much as He loves you, He does not always explain His plans, and sometimes we are totally confused! It's in these times of confusion that we must "trust in His heart."

Are you bewildered by life? Trust in His tender heart. Are you hurt and disappointed in a dream that you had, and now that dream is dashed? Trust in His heart...as hard as it seems, He does have something better. Are you weary from carrying painful burdens? Trust in His protective heart that would never allow you to be broken in despair. Are you hurting for another person's heartache? Trust in your Father's heart who loves that person as much as anyone.

It's easy, in tough circumstances, to look only at the tough circumstances. But now's the time to force ourselves to think about our Father's heart toward us - filled with gentleness, deep affection and tender compassion:

Good Morning!! How Are My College Buddies?

"For I know the plans I have for you, declares the Lord, plans to prosper you and not to harm you, plans to give you hope and a future." Jeremiah 29:11

Love You!!   Praying for You!!   Proud of You!!   Bro. Post
✷✷✷✷✷✷✷✷✷✷✷✷✷✷✷✷✷✷✷✷✷✷

Good Morning!! How Are My College Buddies?

"You're trying to serve the Lord, but look at your problems! It seems like God promised you blessings, but He has only given you burdens. Is it really worth it?"

Ok, College Buddies, let me warn you. You will hear this whisper from our enemy thousands of times in your lifetime. You won't hear it when you are doing fine - you will hear it when the burdens are heavy, the temptation battles are intense and your fears about the future are raging.

It really depends where we shine the spotlight. At times, I shine the spotlight on present burdens - I elevate them, study them, magnify them and then resent them. Other times, we shine the spotlight on our Father's promises - we look beyond our present misery to His future solution and blessing.

It would be nice if we only placed the spotlight on God's promises, but truthfully, we go back and forth between the two.

Our Father deeply wants us to trust Him, to believe that He is in control of the present and that He has wonderful plans for the future. He often sends 'reminder blessings' to us when we struggle - He is trying to bring us back to believing Him.

Where is your 'spotlight' as you read this devotional? Ask God to help you focus it on His promise. Here is a beautiful one to claim for yourself and others:

> "For I know the plans I have for you, declares the Lord, plans to prosper you and not to harm

you, plans to give you hope and a future." Jeremiah 29:11

Love You!!   Praying for You!!   Proud of You!!   Bro. Post
✳✳✳✳✳✳✳✳✳✳✳✳✳✳✳✳✳✳✳✳✳

Good Morning!! How Are My College Buddies?

"Come back to Me...Come as you are."

It's interesting, when we stumble and fail, how we feel a pressure to punish ourselves, mentally reviewing our sin and giving ourselves the appropriate amount of shame and guilt. It's almost like we feel that God will be more inclined to forgive us if we pummel ourselves with shame and remorse. Imbedded in this process is a spiritual time bomb - if we continue doing this, often we are more obsessed with our own failures than we are with God's gentle, forgiving grace. When we continue like this, our Enemy will encourage us to quit, he will assure us that we are lousy Christians and he will explain any future hardship as a punishment from God!! Many Christians have fallen for this lie.

College Buddies, the reason our Father forgives us is because of Jesus' death on the cross - our Savior's death is the reason that our Father so graciously and lovingly forgives us daily. When our Father looks at you, He has the same intense and perfect love that He has for His Son. (This truth just floors me.)

Have you failed your Father? Wondering if He will forgive you? Just return to Him and ask for forgiveness, you will amazed at happily and joyfully He will cleanse you:

> "I, I am He who blots out your transgressions for my own sake, and I will not remember your sins." Isaiah 43:25

Love You!!   Praying for You!!   Proud of You!!   Bro. Post

✳✳✳✳✳✳✳✳✳✳✳✳✳✳✳✳✳✳✳✳✳✳

"The Boring Habit of Praying Safely."

It's easy to do, isn't it? Occasionally our prayer lives become monotonous, tedious and uninspired. The problem is not that we don't have faith, the problem may be that we pray 'safely' - generic, general prayers. There's nothing wrong with praying "Lord bless _____" or "Be near them" or "Lord, help _____." But do we really want to be that vague when we pray?!

Focus your prayers, make them very specific, ask your Father to work in a particular way when you pray. Let's pray like we REALLY believe that God is God. Don't be afraid to 'go out on a limb' when you pray - if our Father doesn't answer exactly as we ask, He will answer in a even better way! Today, let's all thank God that He is God, that He has the power to do anything. Then let's pray specifically for the need of someone and ask our Father to intervene and help in a specific way. Then let's start watching and expecting......our Father will answer perfectly, He always does. Let's not bore ourselves spiritually by 'praying safely':

> "Elijah was a man of like nature with us. He prayed earnestly that it would not rain and it did not rain on the land for three and a half years. Again he prayed, and the heavens gave rain, and the earth produced its crops." James 5:17-18 (He prayed specifically. God answered specifically)

Good Morning!! How Are My College Buddies?

Love You!!   Praying for You!!   Proud of You!!   Bro. Post

✶✶✶✶✶✶✶✶✶✶✶✶✶✶✶✶✶✶✶✶

"Brutally Honest."

College Buddies, one way to enrich your prayer life is to practice brutal honesty...telling your Father exactly what you are feeling. Often we couch our hurt, pain, anger and fears in 'religious' phrases - we never open up and unload, maybe because we think our Father will be disappointed? Have you ever unloaded your anger on your Father? What about your pain? What about your fears? Have you ever told your Father how unfair this is...and asked why He allowed it? Have you ever unloaded your pain upon your Father? Maybe you think that is unspiritual. Hmm, I don't think so.

The day before Jesus died is called Maundy Thursday. On this Thursday, in Jesus' life, He unloaded to His Father. He was brutally honest. He begged and pleaded in prayer until He was drenched in sweat. He was overwhelmed in sorrow...so He unloaded and released it to His Father...and THEN, our Father helped him!

College Buddies, have you had about as much as you take? Are you even a little angry at your Father? Disappointed in Him? Tell Him about it...get on your knees and 'let it fly'. He won't disown you, I promise you that this type of praying is what He loves to hear from His child. Tell Him about it...be 'brutally honest'...then He will amaze you how gentle He is. God helped Jeremiah in a tough time AFTER Jeremiah had prayed and 'unloaded.' Here is Jeremiah's brutally honest prayer...the one His Father quickly answered:

Good Morning!! How Are My College Buddies?

"I sat alone, because your hand upon me, and you have filled me with indignation. Why is my pain unending and my wound without hope of being well? Will you really disappoint me, like a stream that runs dry?" Jeremiah 15:17-18 Wow, 'brutal honesty!' (Yes, God helped him.)

Love You!!   Praying for You!!   Proud of You!!   Bro. Post
✳✳✳✳✳✳✳✳✳✳✳✳✳✳✳✳✳✳✳✳✳✳

"Let Your Nets Down...Today"

The disciples were bone tired, hungry and sleepy. They had worked all night, dropping and retrieving fishing nets. Hard work! Problem is, they had not caught a fish...they had had enough! Then Jesus appeared to them and told them to do something that they didn't understand. "Lower your nets again, on the other side of the boat." I love this story! There are times when you and I have struggled and worked ourselves into exhaustion, trying to create a blessing or solve a problem. We get discouraged, just like the disciples! Even though it didn't make sense, the disciples obeyed, they lowered their nets and the miracle was wonderful! A record catch.

College Buddies, when you pray today, 'let your nets down'...pray in a way that shows that you really believe God will bless you. Anticipate God's answer, look forward to it coming. Jesus knows the perfect time to perfectly answer your prayer of faith:

"Now faith is being sure of what we hope for and certain of what we do not see." Hebrews 11:1

Love You!! Praying for You!! Proud of You!! Bro. Post

✶✶✶✶✶✶✶✶✶✶✶✶✶✶✶✶✶✶✶✶

Good Morning!! How Are My College Buddies?

"A Spiritual Tug of War."

It's easy for us to place a problem into the Lord's hands...as long as we can still cling to it, hang on to it. We have a frustrating tendency to tug the problem out of God's hands - we try to resolve it, rethink it, rework it, analyze it to death - only to place it back in His hands when we are exhausted. A 'Spiritual Tug of War'......we have all been there, done that.

College Buddies, the Lord does allow some problems to come our way that we just can't solve, we don't have the ability. He invites us to give it to Him - He wants to show us a clear picture of HIS power. He doesn't get angry when we tug it out of His hands...He gently waits until we are ready to give it back to Him. I wonder, in my lifetime, how many hours of sleep I have forfeited. I can't sleep and worry at the same time. Take a piece of paper, date it, write out the problem, give it to the Lord. When you realize that you have pulled it out of God's hand, stop yourself, go back and give it back to Him. Don't get down on yourself...ALL Christians do this at times! One more thing, here's a delightful promise to write on that piece of paper:

> "Cast your burden on the Lord, and he will sustain you; he will never permit the righteous to be moved." Psalm 55:32

Love You!!   Praying for You!!   Proud of You!!   Bro. Post

✳✳✳✳✳✳✳✳✳✳✳✳✳✳✳✳✳✳✳✳✳✳

"Father, I ask you this for your Name's sake."

Our Father does indeed love us dearly and He does indeed still answer our prayers in wonderful, miraculous ways. However, He does not appreciate it when we neglect to give Him all of the credit. He is offended when we attribute something that He has done to other reasons.

College Buddies, even when God answers our prayers, it is ultimately not about us - it's about Him, showing His power and His grace to others. Now when God answers our prayers, how do we tell others about it? Do we couch our testimony in a way that implies that the answer came because of our great faith, our persistence in prayer? PLEEZE!! DON'T GO THERE!! IT IS ABOUT HIM, NOT US!!!

Be like a little wide-eyed child, brag about your Father, be thrilled as you tell how wonderful He is. "Father, I ask you to answer this prayer for your Name's sake. I can't wait to see your wonderful answer to this prayer. I promise to tell others how wonderful you are and to give you ALL of the credit."

> "Yet He saved them for His name's sake, that He might make known His mighty power. So He saved them from the hand of the foe, and delivered them from the power of the enemy... Then they believed His words; they sang His praise." Psalm 106:8, 10, 12

Good Morning!! How Are My College Buddies?

Love You!!   Praying for You!!   Proud of You!!   Bro. Post

✶✶✶✶✶✶✶✶✶✶✶✶✶✶✶✶✶✶✶✶

"God does not scare His kids."

He would never fill our hearts with terrifying thoughts, dread over future scenarios. What kind of Father would He be if He tormented His own children? However, there is another person who is a master at frightening us, Satan. He not only slyly suggests future troubles, he sometimes tricks us into believing that these thoughts come from God!

College Buddies, this is very common to all Christians, it is a universal struggle of all who want to serve the Lord. Recently I was flying home and throughout the flight, I was troubled, edgy and miserable. The reason was because the enemy was suggesting a lot of frightening troubles and I was... well, I was listening. Now today, none of the things that I was troubled about have happened - but that's not the point. The point is that I was miserable, troubled and worried about things that were all untrue. Does any of this sound familiar? :-)

College Buddies, the next time you go to bed and your heart is troubled and frightened, that is NOT your Father. Remember who is trying to trouble you, ask your Father to help you ignore the enemy's 'whispers' that frighten you:

> "May the God of hope fill you with great joy and peace as you trust in him, so that you may overflow with hope by the power of the Holy Spirit." Romans 15:13 (Think about this verse...God wants to give us 3 things)

Good Morning!! How Are My College Buddies?

Love You!!   Praying for You!!   Proud of You!!   Bro. Post
✳✳✳✳✳✳✳✳✳✳✳✳✳✳✳✳✳✳✳✳✳

Good Morning!! How Are My College Buddies?

"Highlight The Strength!"

Suppose your child, a straight A student, brought home a C. Would you put the child's report card on the fridge, circle the C, then call all your relatives to inform them? Of course not. Yet some people always maximize the mistakes of others. Regardless of how the person has previously excelled, let them slip up once and some people will be there to shine a verbal spotlight on the misstep.

Why not ask God to make you the opposite? Be quick to speak well of someone. Highlight a strength. Compliment an achievement. Praise a godly character. In this society of toxic words and acidic criticism, be the first to encourage someone with a sincere compliment of appreciation:

> "We give thanks to God for you, because your faith is growing abundantly, and the love of every one of you for one another is increasing. THEREFORE WE OURSELVES BOAST OF YOU in the churches of God for your faithfulness and faith..." II Thessalonians 1:3-4 (emphasis mine)

Love You!!   Praying for You!!   Proud of You!!   Bro. Post
✶✶✶✶✶✶✶✶✶✶✶✶✶✶✶✶✶✶✶✶

"Pain and a Pearl"

The origin of the pearl is steeped in pain. A piece of sand is caught inside the oyster, causing irritation and pain. Slowly and methodically the oyster coats the sand, layer after layer, producing the beautiful pearl. The final beauty would never be seen without the beginning – the experience of pain.

College Buddies, we all have points of pain in our lives, things we wish were completely different. Our first inclination is to resent the intrusion and pray that God would remove the problem...and sometimes He does, after a while. However, many times the present stress produces future blessings: gentleness, patience, compassion for others. God has the beautiful ability to transform the frightening circumstances of the present into the invaluable beauty of a godly character. There is a plaque that we have hung in our home for many years, please read carefully the words:

> "Sometimes God calms the raging storm in the life of His child. Sometimes He lets the storm rage and calms His child." (Author Unknown)

Love You!! Praying for You!! Proud of You!! Bro. Post
✶✶✶✶✶✶✶✶✶✶✶✶✶✶✶✶✶✶✶✶✶✶✶

"Borrowing Tomorrow's Trouble."

Imagine a caravan of camels, trekking across a desert. Each camel carries an identical load of cargo. It would be foolish to stop the caravan, unload 6 camels, then pile all of the six loads on the back of one camel. Yet that is exactly what we do when we borrow tomorrow's troubles. God says that each day does have responsibilities and concerns, and with His help, we can manage the troubles of each day. HOWEVER, if we look ahead, into the coming week, and worry about tomorrow's troubles, as well as facing today's troubles, then we become weary and discouraged. "Borrowing trouble" is common to all of us and our Father wants to remind us: "My child, we will worry about Friday when Friday comes. Let's face Thursday together."

"Therefore, be not anxious about tomorrow, for tomorrow will be anxious for itself. Let the day's own trouble be sufficient for the day." Matthew 6:34

Love You!!   Praying for You!!   Proud of You!!   Bro. Post
✳✳✳✳✳✳✳✳✳✳✳✳✳✳✳✳✳✳✳✳

Good Morning!! How Are My College Buddies?

"The First Step"

If you're facing a tall mountain, the Lord will help you scale it. There may be times when you have given up, times when you are exhausted, even times when He has to carry you...but He will get you over it. College Buddies, there will be mountains in your life...obstacles that you think are totally impossible. These mountains can appear in hundreds of different varieties. You may be facing one right now......things were going fine until this happened! It's wonderful how the Lord helps us to take one step, than another step. If we stumble, or even fall backwards, He helps us stand up again. After a while, you see a little progress and you feel encouraged. I'm not saying this is enjoyable, it's not. But there will come a time when the obstacle is gone, the path is straighter, the journey easier. So if you're struggling today, let God take your hand and help you - remember "a journey of a thousand miles begins with the first step."

> "We are afflicted in every way, but not crushed; perplexed, but not driven to despair; persecuted, but not forsaken, struck down but not destroyed." 2 Corinthians 4:8-9

Love You!!   Praying for You!!   Proud of You!!   Bro. Post
✳✳✳✳✳✳✳✳✳✳✳✳✳✳✳✳✳✳✳✳✳✳

"Open up the faucet."

The fact that you love someone doesn't help much. You may love a friend, a family member, another Christian…that nice, but not very beneficial. Imagine a large wheat field in July, shriveling up because it needs water. Now the farmer has irrigation pipes all through the field and the pipes are connected to a well. That's nice, but useless, right? It's only when the farmer opens the well's faucet that the water can then benefit the crops!

If you have God's love in your heart, then you need to ask God to help you EXPRESS it to others! Just having it your heart is pretty much irrelevant. You can 'turn on the faucet' in the way that you speak to others, how you treat them…you can show them on the outside how you feel about them on the inside. The great thing about God is that He not only loves us, He EXPRESSES that love to us daily! Ask God today to help you 'turn on the faucet'…to let His beautiful love flow through you to others:

> "How does God's love abide in anyone who has the world's goods and sees a brother or sister in need and yet refuses help? Little children, let us love, not in word or speech (only), but in truth and action." I John 3:17-18

Love You!!   Praying for You!!   Proud of You!!   Bro. Post

✶✶✶✶✶✶✶✶✶✶✶✶✶✶✶✶✶✶✶✶✶✶✶✶

Good Morning!! How Are My College Buddies?

"I don't want to, but I have to."

It would be nice if your chosen vocation was free of responsibilities that you really dislike, but that just doesn't happen. Whether you're in college or working full-time, there are always the parts that you really dread to do, but you have to do. It helps to remember that God has placed you in your present circumstances in life, He knows the parts you like and the parts that are a pain! As a Christian, God gives us the power to discipline ourselves to face the days when we're tired, mildly irritated, and we're looking at some things we really don't want to do. Interestingly, after we go ahead and finish these type of responsibilities, we often feel a deeper sense of satisfaction than when we accomplish the tasks we enjoy. The Christian faith is extremely practical, the Lord waits to help us with the jobs that "we don't want to, but we have to.":

> "the fruit of the Spirit is love, joy, peace, PATIENCE, kindness, goodness, FAITHFULNESS, gentleness, SELF-CONTROL; against such there is no law." Galatians 5:22-23 (emphases mine)

Love You!!　Praying for You!!　Proud of You!!　Bro. Post
✳✳✳✳✳✳✳✳✳✳✳✳✳✳✳✳✳✳✳✳✳✳

"Stop badmouthing yourself…you're talking about my child."

God can help some Christians stop the terrible sin of judging others – He can also help other Christians stop the terrible sin of harshly judging themselves. We sometimes think that humility means that we turn a spotlight on every flaw that we have…we wallow in guilt and pummel ourselves. This has nothing at all to do with humility - humility is an intense desire to see that our Father receives the credit and praise, not ourselves. The sad result of this practice is that a child of God, loved intensely and adored by the Father, washed totally clean by the blood of Christ, adopted into the most prestigious Family ever, an heir to unbelievable blessings now and later……this child of God is now regretting rather than relishing, rehashing rather than rejoicing.

When I need a reminder of God's love, I often think of my two daughters – I am absolutely crazy about them, I love them dearly. Then I remember that God loves you and me even greater than this…wow, that is amazing. College Buddies, I pray that you will learn the 3 R's of God's love. RELAX: Stop trying to earn God's love, He already adores you.

RELISH: Imagine your Father's arms around you, holding you tightly.

REJOICE: Let this awesome truth cause you to grin on the inside:

"How great is the love the Father has lavished on us, that we should be called children of God! And that is what we are!" I John 3:1

Love You!! Praying for You!! Proud of You!! Bro. Post
✶✶✶✶✶✶✶✶✶✶✶✶✶✶✶✶✶✶✶✶

'Tear down the Facade of Perfection.'

College Buddies, some days are just tough days, we struggle in our walk with God. However, it is interesting how we often feel a pressure NOT to let another Christian know this - so we fight the battles alone, wearily presenting the facade of having it all together. I can understand not letting a judgmental Christian know about your struggles...who wants to be hammered, judged, and sent on your way with a cliché? However, there are many Christians who will not judge you, they themselves experience rough days, so they will encourage you, pray for you and help carry part of the burden with you. This process of sharing your need and receiving encouragement from another Christian is God's plan and it can be a tremendous help and encouragement. But if you insist on 'going it alone,' wow, tough days can be REALLY tough!! God never intended for us to always present a picture of spiritual perfection - living this way is so tiring. Check out the verses below, open your heart and let God help you through the encouragement of another Christian:

> "Practice bearing one another's burdens, and in this way fulfill the law of Christ." Galatians 6:2

> "Confess your faults to each other and pray for each other so that you may be healed." James 5:16

Good Morning!! How Are My College Buddies?

Love You!!   Praying for You!!   Proud of You!!   Bro. Post

✶✶✶✶✶✶✶✶✶✶✶✶✶✶✶✶✶✶✶✶

Good Morning!! How Are My College Buddies?

"God doesn't miss the runway."

Years ago, a friend asked me to fly with him from Charlotte, N.C. to Spartanburg, S.C.. To him, it was just a 45 minute short hop. To me, it was 45 minutes of torture!! It was pouring rain, windy and dark. I kept looking out the window, praying for lights! He was very calm, looking at an instrument called a glide scope. The instruments were telling him that he was perfectly on course, the runway was straight ahead. The fact that he couldn't see anything didn't rattle him, he trusted his instruments. A few minutes later we broke through the clouds and the runway was right in front of us! (I felt like kissing the ground!:-)

College Buddies, God has a plan for your life that is perfect - He wants the very best for you. Sometimes His plans and destination for you is not clear at first...He wants you to trust Him. At the right time, you'll see that God's plans are better than yours, He was in control when you were panicking. So if you are a little confused and bewildered at circumstances, that's ok, just keep trusting. Our Father has been guiding His children for ages...and He never misses a runway.

> "For I know the plans that I have for you, says the Lord, plans for good and not for evil, to give you a future and a hope." Jeremiah 29:11

Love You!!   Praying for You!!   Proud of You!!   Bro. Post

✶✶✶✶✶✶✶✶✶✶✶✶✶✶✶✶✶✶✶✶✶✶

"Having trouble forgiving someone?"

In the mid-90's, a Baptist church in rural North Carolina was set on fire. It was that horrible time when many black churches were destroyed by arson. This church was not completely burned down, but totally ruined. The pastor called for his congregation to meet the following Sunday in the burned out sanctuary, to sit in the charred pews. The man who had torched the church had already been arrested, and the pastor had arranged for the sheriff to bring him to the Sunday service, where he sat on the first row. The pastor preached and said that yes, the man had sinned against the God and His people. However, the pastor then told the congregation that this man was still a creation of God. The pastor then told the church that forgiveness was the business of God's people. He then turned to the man and assured him that this church had forgiven him. Then the pastor told the congregation that the man didn't have a lot of money and that his family would be needy as he awaited trial. The pastor then called forward the ushers and they took an offering and gave it to the man's family.

College Buddies, are you still having trouble forgiving someone? God can help us do this.

Forgiveness is the business of God's people:

> "And when you stand praying, forgive, if you have anything against any one; so that your Father also who is heaven may forgive you your trespasses." Mark 11:25

Good Morning!! How Are My College Buddies?

Love You!!   Praying for You!!   Proud of You!!   Bro. Post
✷✷✷✷✷✷✷✷✷✷✷✷✷✷✷✷✷✷✷✷✷

Good Morning!! How Are My College Buddies?

"Join the Club!"

College Buddies, if you have done some things and you're ashamed...if you have fallen flat on your face in your walk with God...if the Enemy is whispering that you are a lousy Christian...all I can say is: Join the Club!! Welcome to God's Family!! God's Family is composed of imperfect sinners and we all stumble, we all occasionally fail. Ok, think of the great Christian, the Apostle Paul. Remember what he did before he became a Christian? He imprisoned Christians and actually caused some of them to be put to death. Then he became a Christian. Then he preached in the churches of that day and almost certainly, he met some of the friends and family members of Christians whom he had previously helped put to death!! How could he do that? I would have been paralyzed with shame.

There's only one answer, he accepted God's forgiveness, he allowed God to cleanse him, he put the past failures behind him. I have been a Christian for 40 years, and I have never met ONE Christian who didn't deeply regret some past sins, myself certainly included. That's why we need God to forgive us. So here is the verse for today, read it, relish it, claim it and rejoice:

> "Their sins and their iniquities I will REMEMBER NO MORE." Hebrews 10:17

Love You!!   Praying for You!!   Proud of You!!   Bro. Post

✱✱✱✱✱✱✱✱✱✱✱✱✱✱✱✱✱✱✱✱✱✱✱

"As Pure as Jesus."

Often we struggle because we do not clearly understand the word 'forgiveness.' We mistake 'forgiveness' with 'probation.' All of us daily need God's forgiveness because we daily stumble in our walk with God. The Bible teaches us that our Father cleanses away the spiritual stain of our sins - He removes them and actually forgets them. Awesome, right? It gets even better. When our Father looks at us, He does not even see our failures and sins. He actually sees the purity of His Son Jesus, He sees Him when He looks at us. This beautiful truth in theology is called IMPUTATION......in our Father's eyes, we are as righteous and holy as Jesus. Absolutely amazing.

The number one problem with Christians is not how bad we are, the number one problem is that we don't realize how intensely loved we are. Languishing in our failures shackles us - living in God's love releases us, to accept His forgiveness and to love Him in return. Have you sinned and stumbled? Ashamed, hard to pray, thinking that God will not listen to you again? God the Father longs to cleanse you, remove your failures and restore you. He will welcome you back to Himself, He will love you and assure you that, in His eyes, you are as pure as His Son Jesus:

"He (Jesus) who knew no sin became sin for us, that we might be made the righteousness of God in him." II Corinthians 5:21

Good Morning!! How Are My College Buddies?

Love You!!   Praying for You!!   Proud of You!!   Bro. Post

✶✶✶✶✶✶✶✶✶✶✶✶✶✶✶✶✶✶✶✶✶

Good Morning!! How Are My College Buddies?

"Could have happened...Should have happened...Didn't happen."

College Buddies, our Father sends many blessings to His children, He is a doting Father who loves to see His children smile. It's pretty easy to praise Him for these type of blessings that He sends to you, straight from His heart. However, there is another very important blessing that God sends to you...the things that He prevents from happening. This does not mean that Christians never face trials - some Christians face brutal, intense trials. It does mean that our Father knows our breaking point, and He will never allow the 'straw that broke the camel's back.' He steps in, and because of His love, He prevents things, He stops them.

Ok, think back to some of the frightening or difficult circumstances that you have faced. I bet you can think of a hundred bad things that could have happened......but because of God's goodness, it didn't happen. When we thank God today, let's certainly praise Him for the things that He has done for us. But also, like the Apostle Paul in the verse below, let's thank Him for things that He prevented - for things that could have happened, but didn't happen:

> "We are pressed on every side, yet not crushed; we are perplexed, but not in despair; persecuted, but not forsaken, cast down, but not destroyed......" II Corinthians 4:8-9

Love You!!   Praying for You!!   Proud of You!!   Bro. Post

✶✶✶✶✶✶✶✶✶✶✶✶✶✶✶✶✶✶✶✶✶✶

"The Sour Suspicion of a Cynical Person."

College Buddies, let's be careful here, ok? One of the more dangerous attitudes that can infect our souls is cynicism - that inward suspicion of someone's good motives and the constant poison of harsh criticism. A person caught in cynicism is often a verbal fountain of poison - the toxic words can harm families, ruin friendships and alienate coworkers. Compliment someone in front of a cynic and the cynic will remind you of that person's past failure. Share your dreams for the future and the cynic will give you reasons why your dream won't happen. If all of this is not enough, cynicism can weaken our faith in God - if we always doubt others, we will certainly doubt Him.

None of us are immune to cynicism, but God can deliver us. It always starts when we ask for forgiveness, then our Father starts to remove the poison and replace it with faith. Notice below the conversation between the Lord and Jeremiah, a great prophet who at one point was poisoned by cynicism:

> "Why is my pain unending and my wound grievous and incurable? Will you be to me like a deceitful brook, and like a spring that fails?" This is what the Lord says, "If you repent, I will restore you that you may serve me...for I am with you, to rescue and save you," declares the Lord." Jeremiah 15:18

Good Morning!! How Are My College Buddies?

Love You!!   Praying for You!!   Proud of You!!   Bro. Post

✷✷✷✷✷✷✷✷✷✷✷✷✷✷✷✷✷✷✷✷

"Dear Lord, please help me to be more stubborn."

Sounds weird, right? Actually there are three areas in the Bible where God can give us a 'godly stubbornness.' Stubborn in our PRAYING...Stubborn in our TRUSTING.......Stubborn in Showing GOD'S love to others.

Be stubborn in your praying. It's sometimes easy to pray for a day or even a week, to ask God to work in His special way. But after a while, when the answer hasn't come quickly, it becomes easy to spiritually 'throw in the towel' - to just assume that what we had asked was not God's will. Then we just stop praying. Hmm.......let's think about that.

Have you ever thought that God already knows the solution to the problem, but He wants to help US grow? To help us learn to pray better, to pray stubbornly?

Here's an example of stubborn praying. "Ask, and it will be given unto you; seek and you will find; knock and the door will be opened to you." Luke 11:9

Please remember two things about this beautiful verse. First, this verse is a COMMAND from God, just as much as the Ten Commandments. Interesting.

Secondly, this verse is in the PRESENT tense. Ok, you can read it this way: "I am commanding you to keep on asking, to keep on seeking and to keep on knocking."

Then come the beautiful promises...'it will be given unto you...you will find...the door will be opened unto you.'

Stubborn praying.

It's up to us —we can ask once or twice, tap lightly on the door a few times and then give up. OR, we can keep on asking and keep on seeking and keep on knocking until our knuckles are sore.

Let's ask God to make us stubborn in our praying.

Love You!!   Praying for You!!   Proud of You!!   Bro. Post
✶✶✶✶✶✶✶✶✶✶✶✶✶✶✶✶✶✶✶✶

"A Foul Weather Faith."

Some days it seems like the Lord is right beside us - we pray and He answers quickly, we read the Bible and it comes alive to us. Other days, it seems like the Lord is a million miles away - reading the Bible does not help us, our circumstances are tough, we cry out to God and we receive......silence. It's like He doesn't hear and He doesn't care anymore.

College Buddies, ALL Christians have times like this, there's nothing wrong with your faith. Our Father is actually doing something very special in these occasional times when He seems a million miles away. He is gently moving us away from the trap of a 'Fair Weather Faith.' You know, "Things are going great today, I know God loves me!" (Does He love you less when things are going terrible?) Or, "I know my Father loves me, I feel it in my heart!" (What about the days when you feel nothing?) The trap of a fair weather faith is that we think God loves us on the good days - but on the bad days, we become discouraged and suspicious, wondering if He truly cares for us. God wants us to trust Him regardless of the circumstances, so He allows us to have days in which He seems a million miles away.

Tough day today? Think your Father has forgotten about you? Look closely at the following verse, this is where your Father is taking you:

"We walk by faith, not by sight. (circumstances)." II Corinthians 5:7

Good Morning!! How Are My College Buddies?

Love You!!   Praying for You!!   Proud of You!!   Bro. Post
✶✶✶✶✶✶✶✶✶✶✶✶✶✶✶✶✶✶✶✶✶

"Falls are not Fatal...Failures are not Permanent"

College Buddies, our Father loves us even after we have failed - He seeks us, He gently leads us back to Him. Once we ask for forgiveness, He cleanses us completely and gives us a renewed walk with Him. However, after we have received this forgiveness, we often face a VERY dangerous temptation from our enemy. Ok, let me explain this way. Our Father forgives our sin...Satan reminds us of our sin. Our Father welcomes us back as His son or daughter... Satan whispers that you are now a 'second-class Christian.' Our enemy will suggest that your prayers will no longer be answered...He will convince you that tough times are God's way of punishing you... He will whisper that you are not loved as much now as you were before you failed...He will have you cringe at the future, expecting a retaliation from your Heavenly Father!!

It is crucial that we DO NOT listen to these lies - if we do, we will wander away from our Father. If you have stumbled, as we all have done, go back to your Father. He will forgive you, He will cleanse you...He will wrap His arms around you. He will welcome you back...and one more thing, He will throw a party in heaven...just for you:

> "But while he was a long way off, his father saw him and was filled with compassion. He ran to his son, threw his arms around him and kissed him......the father said to his servants,

Good Morning!! How Are My College Buddies?

'Quick! Bring the best robe and put it on him. Put a ring on his finger and sandals on his feet. Let's have a feast and celebrate.. for this son of mine was lost, and is found." Luke 15:20-24

Love You!!   Praying for You!!   Proud of You!!   Bro. Post
✷✷✷✷✷✷✷✷✷✷✷✷✷✷✷✷✷✷✷✷

"Walk Toward the Blessing"

They could see the blessing, God had promised the blessing, but they didn't have a clue how to claim the blessing! God had brought the Children of Israel right up to the beautiful Promised Land. The problem was that it was on the other side of the Jordan River. They had no idea how to get 2 million people across the river. The Lord spoke to them and told them to start walking toward the edge of the river. They started and as soon as the soles of the feet of the priests touched the water, the river parted and they enjoyed the blessing.

College Buddies, this is my favorite story in the Old Testament. You have hopes and dreams of special blessings from God; a college degree, a good job, a Christian home...the list goes on. God is telling you the same today: "Start walking toward the blessing!" Don't wait until the river is parted, until all the obstacles are gone; start walking now. The Lord will send the blessing, but first He wants you to believe it, claim it, get off your rear and walk toward it:

> "Now faith is a confident assurance of that for which we hope, and makes us certain of realities we do not see." Hebrews 11:1

Love You!!   Praying for You!!   Proud of You!!   Bro. Post

✻✻✻✻✻✻✻✻✻✻✻✻✻✻✻✻✻✻✻✻✻✻✻

Fulfillment: "I can do this. I enjoy doing this. This is what I'm supposed to do, what God wants me to do."

College Buddies, did you feel that way about anything that you did today? God leads us to serve Him every day, and when we do serve Him, we feel His inner sense of FULFILLMENT.

Some Christians serve the Lord when all of the circumstances are favorable. They have to see a 'green light' from heaven, then they serve. God wants us to rise to another level of service - cultivating a 24/7 servant attitude.

When you think about it, why in the world would God leave us here after we have become a Christian? He could just beam us to heaven, out of the trials and temptations of this world. But He leaves us here so that all of His children each day can serve Him by showing others an example of His love.

The closest that you will ever feel to God is when you allow Him to share, through you, a small portion of His love with others. If you keep this love tightly tucked in your soul, that soul will shrivel in fear, dryness and negative thoughts.

Don't hope that God uses you today......ask and expect Him to use you today!

'One Day...One Person... One Love Act'...... You'll go to sleep tonight with a godly sense of fulfillment:

> "...always abounding in the work of the Lord." I Corinthians 15:58

Good Morning!! How Are My College Buddies?

Love You!!   Praying for You!!   Proud of You!!   Bro. Post

✶✶✶✶✶✶✶✶✶✶✶✶✶✶✶✶✶✶✶✶✶

"Function in the Fire."

You remember the story of the fiery furnace, and Shadrach, Meshach and Abednego. What a great miracle for God to deliver them! However, I am fascinated with what happened before they were delivered, while they were still IN the furnace. The Bible simply says that they were "walking in the middle of the fire, unhurt…" Wow.

You see, College Buddies, there was now another person in the furnace with them, and I believe it was Jesus. They entered the furnace bound with ropes, now they are walking around IN the fire, talking with Jesus. Two things fascinate me:Jesus didn't stay in heaven and help them from there…He actually came down, entered the furnace with them and encouraged them! The second thing is that His presence allowed the three men to 'function in the fire'; instead of cowering in fear, they walked in the middle of it, waiting until they were delivered. College Buddies, you may be in a fiery furnace of tough circumstances today and you just want to quit. But wait a minute, Jesus is in there with you and He will help you today, to get dressed, go to work/school, do your work - He will help you 'function in the fire.'

> "In all their distress He too was distressed, and the angel of His presence saved them. In His love and mercy He redeemed them, He lifted then up and carried them all the days of old." Isaiah 63:9

Good Morning!! How Are My College Buddies?

Love You!!   Praying for You!!   Proud of You!!   Bro. Post

✶✶✶✶✶✶✶✶✶✶✶✶✶✶✶✶✶✶✶✶

"Flying Without Fear"

It was the best flight of my life. I really don't care too much for flying and I hate the last 5 minutes of a flight! Before we took off in Chicago, a United pilot sat beside me. He had flown a plane from San Francisco and was 'dead-heading' back to Memphis. We talked, I asked him a hundred questions about flying, he patiently answered them. :-) Before long we were in Memphis, I had thoroughly enjoyed the flight, no jumpiness toward the end of the flight. The reason is simple: If he was not nervous, I was not nervous. This pilot had 'seen it all', he was not alarmed or rattled, even when we flew by a line of thunderstorms.

College Buddies, the secret in situations that make you jumpy is to remember that your Savior is right beside you. NOTHING rattles Him, He is in absolute control of your circumstances. If He is not nervous, He can certainly help us not to be nervous:

> "Fear thou not, for I am with you, be not dismayed, for I am your God; I will strengthen you, I will help you, I will uphold you with my victorious right hand." Isaiah 41:10

Love You!!   Praying for You!!   Proud of You!!   Bro. Post

✶✶✶✶✶✶✶✶✶✶✶✶✶✶✶✶✶✶✶✶

"Dream Monsters"

"Come out from under the covers. God has chased away the dream monsters from the closets of your life." Chuck Swindoll

Wow, some of these 'dream monsters' can terrify us, can't they?! I guess our enemy knows how vulnerable we are between the time that we go to bed and arise, and that's when he tries to torment and discourage us with imagined future disasters. These 'dream monsters' usually take two forms: First, what we fear will happen, (bad stuff to us or family, or friends), and secondly, what we fear won't happen, (dreams dashed, unanswered prayers, no joy in the future.)

College Buddies, do not let this discourage you... I assure you that almost all Christians fight this battle. I stumble here as often as I overcome, but there is one verse that I quote when sleep won't come and my imagination is in overdrive and the 'dream monsters' have scared me to death. It is a simple verse from the Psalms, and I think David wrote it for all of us. The next time you get a visit from the 'dream monster', claim this verse:

"I will both lie down and sleep in peace; for thou alone, O Lord, makes me to dwell in safety." Psalm 4:8

Love You!!   Praying for You!!   Proud of You!!   Bro. Post

✶✶✶✶✶✶✶✶✶✶✶✶✶✶✶✶✶✶✶✶✶✶✶

Good Morning!! How Are My College Buddies?

"Misreading the Mirror."

College Buddies, our Father wants us to think of ourselves as HE thinks of us - He wants us to have a godly self-image. Sadly, there are two extremes of self image that our enemy would love for us to have: "I am awesome!" and "I am worthless." We tend to drift toward one of these extremes, based on our life experiences.

Ok, let's talk about the last one. It's true, before we come to Christ, that we are unworthy of His love. UNWORTHY does not mean WORTHLESS! How can that be? The story of salvation is that of God always taking the first step - creating us, seeking us, dying for us, forgiving us, adopting us, blessing us. God is the stubborn lover, the one who loves us intensely and constantly lavishes His love on us. There will be an eternal marriage between Jesus and the church, and YOU are part of that church! How could you possibly be worthless?

Your true worth is linked to the person you are - a son/daughter of the greatest King. Unworthy we are, but worthless we are not.

Our enemy loves to remind us of past sins and mistakes, then he whispers that God couldn't possibly love you! He then tries to convince you that bad stuff is coming, a 'divine payback' for your mistakes.

Ok, here's what the Bible teaches about God forgiveness: He forgives us, He cleanses us, He removes the sin from us, He takes away the guilt AND He forgets our sins...He can't even remember the past sins that wrack us with guilt. Wow, think about that.

You are incredibly valuable in God's family...... after all, a King died for you. Ask God to flood your heart and remind you how much He loves and adores you...here is a great verse to get you started:

> "How great is the love the Father has lavished on us, that we should be called the children of God! And that is what we are!" I John 3:1

Love You!!   Praying for You!!   Proud of You!!   Bro. Post

✷✷✷✷✷✷✷✷✷✷✷✷✷✷✷✷✷✷✷✷✷

"The School of Lingering Burdens"

When we come to Christ, the Lord does allow us to experience temporary burdens - those short lived times when the burdens are heavy or the fears are intense. Then He relieves the burden by answering our prayers, our life seems to settle back down, it returns to normal.

However, all of us will be enrolled at some point in the 'School of Lingering Burdens.' That's when we have unresolved problems, frightening circumstances or heavy loads to daily bear. We pray...we ask others to pray...and guess what? Our Father leaves us in that school and the burdens continue.

Will we always be in these tough times? No, but the Lord is teaching us some valuable lessons in that school. Here's a few:

1. It stretches us - our faith grows out of necessity, we have to grow in faith or we give up.
2. It tenderizes our heart - this school makes us more sensitive and caring to the hurts of others.
3. It isolates our faith - we stop trusting in our ability to fix things, our confidence shifts to God only.
4. It displays our faith - the best sermons are preached by the Christian with heavy burdens, who continues to trust and serve the Lord.

It would be nice if we could learn these lessons without time in this school, but we can't. The Apostle

Good Morning!! How Are My College Buddies?

Paul spent time in the 'School of Lingering Burdens' and he definitely did not like it. But God helped him, just like He helps us. If your burdens linger, they do not go away and you're wondering what's going on, claim this wonderful promise:

> "But the God of all grace, who called us by Christ Jesus to share in his eternal glory, will himself, after your brief suffering, restore, establish, and strengthen you on a firm foundation." Peter 5:10

Love You!!   Praying for You!!   Proud of You!!   Bro. Post
✶✶✶✶✶✶✶✶✶✶✶✶✶✶✶✶✶✶✶✶✶

"Walk this way, I know it's scary, but it's perfectly safe. God will soon bless you."

The priests in Joshua chapter 3 could have easily made that statement. God had promised His people a huge blessing, a new land to live in. The problem was, the new land was on the other side of the swollen and deep Jordan River. But you know the story, when the feet of the priests touched the water, God rolled back the water and gave the people a dry path to walk across. What's so scary about that? Think about it, the dry path was beside the huge wall of water. If they started to cross, would the water come crashing down on them?!! Scary stuff…have we ever wondered that our lives would crash, that a flood of tough times would destroy us? Hmm………

The way God encouraged His people was wonderful. After the water rolled back, those same priests walked down the path and stood by the wall of water as the people passed by. They stood there, they stayed there…the people saw them and were encouraged, they then walked across to the blessing. Now these priests didn't yell from the safety of the bank…'Keep walking!" No, they stood right beside the people, in the middle of the danger, encouraging them, giving them hope in God.

College Buddies, you know someone who is facing some scary stuff in their life. Now you can try to encourage them from a distance, but it won't work. Go to them, stand with them in their scary times, pray with them, encourage them that God will work. Here's a good promise to claim for them as you pray for them:

> "The salvation of the righteous comes from the Lord; He is their stronghold in time of trouble. The Lord helps them and delivers them;......because they take refuge in Him." Psalm 37:39-40

Love You!!   Praying for You!!   Proud of You!!   Bro. Post
✻✻✻✻✻✻✻✻✻✻✻✻✻✻✻✻✻✻✻✻✻

"God's power is not limited by the lack of fair play." Chuck Swindoll

But it really stings, doesn't it? One of the reasons that it hurts so much for Christians is that we are committed to fairness, it comes from the perfectly fair nature of our Father.

A man in the Book of Genesis knew all about the lack of fair play. His mother had deceived his father - he had watched that happen as a young child. Later, he fell madly in love and agreed to work 7 years for the woman's father as a dowry - the father deceived him, he gave him his other daughter to marry. This man toiled for his father-in-law for 20 years, he watched as his father-in-law lied, tricked and deceived him. Even though his hard work had enriched his father-in-law, he received no appreciation or reward.

Ok, no advice here, I'll just tell you what happened. This man, stung by unfairness, was helped by God. He wrestled with God all night, he came from that experience a changed man. Then he was spiritually able to be forgiving and even act unselfish to a man who had treated him horribly.

That's the only way, with God, there is no way we can fight and win this battle! Maybe you live in a personal world of unfairness - the bitterness is engulfing you. Take it to God...ask Him to deliver and change you, just like He did for Jacob:

"I can do all things through Christ who strengthens me." Philippians 4:13

Good Morning!! How Are My College Buddies?

Love You!!   Praying for You!!   Proud of You!!   Bro. Post
✷✷✷✷✷✷✷✷✷✷✷✷✷✷✷✷✷✷✷✷

"Intensely Loved."

College Buddies, do you have any idea how much your Father loves you?

He absolutely adores you. He really does.

Some Christians teach that we can live the Christian life better if we love God more. So we try to conjure up love for God.......and guess what, it just won't work.

The secret to the Christian life is to understand more and more how much He loves US. When we grow in this love, understanding it more and more, then and only then will we love Him.

Think about a mom or a dad - God is compared to both in the Bible. Now the love of a parent is incredibly intense, beginning at the first sight of the child. The parent becomes a constant nurturer, tending to the needs of the child. (Sound familiar? :-) The parent lavishes affection upon the child, just the sight of the child thrills the parent. (God feels the same way.) The Parent is always intensely protective - the parent will gladly forfeit their life to protect the child. (Didn't God do this very thing for you?!) The parent is emotionally linked to the child - the parent assumes the child's happiness, hurt, fear or joy! (Check out Isaiah 63:9, awesome verse!)

Hey the list of love promises is long in the Bible, and there is a very good reason: It is so hard for this truth to sink in! But our Father, deeply and intensely in love with you, will not give up. Through His actions and His words, He is the Perfect Parent and

He has a message for you today: "I absolutely love and adore you. Please believe me."

> "The Lord your God is with you,....... He will take great delight in you, he will quiet you with his love, he will rejoice over you with singing." Zephaniah 3:17

Love You!!   Praying for You!!   Proud of You!!   Bro. Post
✳✳✳✳✳✳✳✳✳✳✳✳✳✳✳✳✳✳✳✳✳

"Job's Comforters."

They teach us a very important lesson:

"Beware of giving unsolicited advice......to a struggling Christian...when we don't know anything about what we're talking about."

The hurt can be deep and lasting. Imagine a struggling Christian, with a battered faith, hoping for God to give them guidance. Now imagine another Christian, with little knowledge and no experience with the problem. But this Christian goes ahead anyway and gives clichés, simplistic solutions or just shallow 'encouragement.' It's happened before, in the Book of Job, and it still happens today. It leaves the struggling Christian either deeply hurt, or disappointed and or further in despair.

Ok, think with me here. I have a very good friend who is an gifted surgeon. He and I can encourage and help each other in a lot of ways. But suppose he was facing an intense and difficult surgery. Suppose I walked in the operating room in the middle of this surgery, stood by him and said, "Doc, I'm right here beside you, let me advise you on the right way to do this." (I can't imagine. :-) Now he may benefit from another surgeon, with more experience in these surgeries...but he definitely will not benefit from me! I lack the medical knowledge and I lack the experience.

College Buddies, there are areas in your life where you can be a great blessing to others! If the

Lord opens the door, share your encouragement with them. However, if you share with someone and you have little knowledge and no experience...that's ok......hold the advice, because there are other Christians who are experts in this area. Don't feel like you've let God down if you fail to give advice! Love them, tell them you're praying, refer them to another person - but by all means, don't give shallow advice to a person needing deep spiritual help. Look closely at these verses, notice the damage done by Job's 'comforters.' They had many words, little compassion:

> "Miserable comforters you are! Will your longwinded speeches never end? What ails you that you keep on arguing?......But my mouth would encourage you, (if you had my troubles), comfort from my lips would bring you relief." Job 16:2,3 & 5

Love You!!   Praying for You!!   Proud of You!!   Bro. Post

✸✸✸✸✸✸✸✸✸✸✸✸✸✸✸✸✸✸✸✸

"Love just won't let go."

God would never let go of us, He is faithful during our rough times, our disobedient times, our times of failure. He gives that very same quality to us when He fills us with His love. While others may give up on a person, we won't. We love them when they are at their spiritual worst, we look forward to them returning to God. Often, during this time of a person's disobedience, we have to put up with a lot of junk - they unfairly criticize, they are sometimes angry at us, they often blame us for the misery of their life. Hey, that's ok, we'll endure that stuff, after all, we are EXPECTING God to work in their life. When it comes to a Prodigal person, sometimes we naively think that we can pray for them and they will immediately return to God. That may happen, but often there is an interval before it happens. During this time of their sin, love them, don't let them go, endure their verbal darts. God willing, you will rejoice in the future when they return to the Lord:

"There is nothing love cannot face, there is no limit to its faith, it hopes under all circumstances. Love gives us power to endure everything." I Corinthians 13:7

Love You!!   Praying for You!!   Proud of You!!   Bro. Post
✶✶✶✶✶✶✶✶✶✶✶✶✶✶✶✶✶✶✶✶✶✶

"The Miserable Interval."

College Buddies, sometimes when we pray, our Father quickly answers our prayer - almost immediately! But these times are rare, the majority of the time there is a waiting period, an interval between when we begin to pray and when He answers.

It's no fun in that waiting period!! It's easy to get discouraged when the Lord waits and waits, when the circumstances are not any better and may even be getting worse.

It's easy to stop praying and think that it is not God's will. It's easy to think that God will not answer because we have failed Him in the past. It's easy for our faith to weaken : "If God doesn't answer that prayer, why should I expect Him to answer any of my prayers."

God is still God, even in the 'miserable interval.' He definitely has heard your prayer and He is fashioning His answer, in His own time. Will He answer exactly as I have asked? Probably not, He always answers in a better way.

Is it miserable to wait? Of course it is, but our Father is actually busy, working in the background. He's carefully crafting His answer, and it will be perfect. Notice these two verses about trusting God in the 'miserable interval.'

"My expectation is from him." Psalm 62:5

"Delight yourself in the Lord and he will give you the desires of your heart." Psalm 37:4

Good Morning!! How Are My College Buddies?

Love You!!   Praying for You!!   Proud of You!!   Bro. Post
✷✷✷✷✷✷✷✷✷✷✷✷✷✷✷✷✷✷✷✷✷

Good Morning!! How Are My College Buddies?

"On a Need to Know Basis"

We make a mistake when we want all the details about the future! God has not opened that window, He never promised to tell us all of the particular events that await us. If He told us the future, the dark times would scare us, the good times would make us apathetic. College Buddies, God gives PROMISES for the future, He doesn't reveal the particulars all at once. He reveals the particulars on a 'need to know' basis, when the timing is perfect.

King David was obviously thinking about the future, he wrote a beautiful psalm about it. Notice that he included three promises from God in the verse below. College Buddies, these three promises assure us that God will make sure that everything in the future turns out fine:

"Surely goodness and unfailing love shall follow me all the days of my life: and I will dwell in the house of the Lord forever." Psalm 23:6

Love You!!　Praying for You!!　Proud of You!!　Bro. Post
✶✶✶✶✶✶✶✶✶✶✶✶✶✶✶✶✶✶✶✶✶

Good Morning!! How Are My College Buddies?

"Their life plans were ruined, their hopes were dashed, and their future was scary!"

I wonder if at times they were bewildered. These three young men, in the Book of Daniel, had their life turned upside down. Enslaved away from home, they were told what to do, when to do it. They had no hopes of a career, they would die as slaves. To marry and love a wife? To father a child? It was physically impossible for them. And when they tried to live for the Lord? The king tried to kill them.

It's easy to say this, but the Lord's hand was behind their suffering. The Lord does sometimes scatter our plans and disrupt our future. Like Shadrach, Meschach and Abednego, we are left bewildered and have to fight a fierce battle in our soul: Will we still be faithful to God when NOTHING MAKES SENSE?

Good question! And College Buddies, there will be times in your life when little or nothing makes sense. God is still totally in control, but it surely doesn't look like it and it doesn't feel like it! God is pleased by His child who trust in the sunshine - however, He is THRILLED by His child who trusts in the pitch darkness of confusion.

Confused today? Not much makes sense? Choose to trust…even when you don't feel like trusting… decide to trust:

> "Because the Lord helps me, I will not be disgraced. Therefore I have set my face like flint, and I know I will not be put to shame."
> Isaiah 50:7

Good Morning!! How Are My College Buddies?

Love You!!   Praying for You!!   Proud of You!!   Bro. Post

✶✶✶✶✶✶✶✶✶✶✶✶✶✶✶✶✶✶✶✶

"To be a burden bearer, you have to have a burden of your own."

This is the REAL reason that God allows us to have tough times. (Satan will try to tell you that God is punishing you!) What our Father is really doing is enrolling us into a spiritual academy where He can gently prepare us and mold us into effective ministers of His love to others.

This process involves stress. It seems that the heat of tough times is the process that God uses to 'tenderize' our heart. The nights of anxiety cause us to cry out to God and then He helps us. We live through these times with a faith that is being strengthened - but the tough times ARE real, the heartaches truly hurt.

After this process, we are changed people. We now have a spiritual antenna, an ability to sense in our hearts when another person is hurting. We feel a degree of their hurt, we consider what it would be like if we were in their condition. We then start praying and considering any practical ways that we can encourage that person. When we pray and care and encourage and help another person weighed down.......wow, it's beautiful ministry to be involved in.

Here's a couple of things to remember. Embrace this ministry, don't shun it. If the Lord has brought you through tough times, then you are now uniquely qualified to encourage others! To encourage others, don't worry if you have not experienced their exact problem. Remember this: hurting people long for your compassion, to know that you care! Finally, just like angels encouraged Jesus at His lowest hour, God will use you to be an 'angel of hope' to others in their lowest hour.

This is why our Father occasionally allows us to have tough times. Do not think your Father is punishing you, believe that He is preparing you for a higher form of service in His kingdom. Ask God to use you in the following 'comfort cycle':

> "Blessed be the God of all comfort, who comforts us in all our troubles so that we can comfort those in trouble with the comfort that we ourselves have received from God."
> II Corinthians 1:4

Love You!!   Praying for You!!   Proud of You!!   Bro. Post

✶✶✶✶✶✶✶✶✶✶✶✶✶✶✶✶✶✶✶✶

"It's better to light your candle than to curse the darkness."

Sometimes we feel our candle is pretty small, don't we? "What good would it do? This person won't change......those bad circumstances are permanent......if God wants to do something, He will, but I won't get my hopes up."

'Cursing the darkness.' I don't mean profanity, I mean a RESIGNATION to the status quo...a life looking around and never looking up.

Have you ever been in darkness so deep that you can't see your hand in front of your face? A very small light, in the middle of this kind of darkness, projects a very piercing beam!! God wants us to use our small faith, to be a tiny light of hope in a dark abyss of impossible circumstances.

God specializes in circumstances of deep darkness. He loves to wait until things are so dire that we cannot see anyway that the person or circumstances will be saved. Then He works...always in a way that glorifies HIM.

Just like God is not afraid of the darkness, so there are some Christians who are not intimidated. God bless them, they refuse to despair and they shine their tiny light of faith in the middle of hopeless circumstances. They just KNOW God will act - they refuse to 'throw in the towel.'

College Buddies, take your tiny pen light of faith and turn it on! You may the only light some people will ever see. Shine it around the scary circumstance and believe that God WILL act. God doesn't listen only to people with strong faith, He also listens to people with 'pen light faith.'

> "Help me, O Lord my God; save me in accordance with your love. Let them know THAT IT IS YOUR HAND, THAT YOU, O LORD, HAVE DONE IT." Psalm 109:26-27 (emphases mine)

Love You!!   Praying for You!!   Proud of You!!   Bro. Post
✶✶✶✶✶✶✶✶✶✶✶✶✶✶✶✶✶✶✶✶

"Looking into the eyes of someone you have helped."

College Buddies, when it comes to experiencing joy as a Christian, it doesn't get any better than this. To go to bed at night and know that another person has been helped, another person encouraged, another person has experienced our Father's agape love...and you were the one whom God used to do this.

You see, it's easy for us to magnify everything we do, to emphasize it's importance. But that's just not true, it is the times when we directly show agape love to others, when we can look into their eyes, that is the most important thing that we do in this life.

Today, at Arkansas Children's Hospital, I was rushing to visit 3 people who are fighting tough battles. Walking through the lobby, I noticed a wheelchair with an eight year old boy. His hair was gone, he was very pale, he had IVs in his arm and a feeding tube in his nose. Unless the Lord does a miracle, this child will not live much longer.

We would do anything if this child could be healthy, but we don't have that power. However, God may be calling us to encourage others, to show them that gentle agape love of our Father. That child in a wheel chair was taken back to his room, and there in the bed beside him was a stuffed animal. Someone looked into this child's eyes as they delivered that stuffed animal. That child had nice cards taped on his wall. Someone delivered those cards and gave it to him, and looked into the child's eyes. Those parents, like most parents at this hospital are financially strained. Someone got some money together and delivered that money to the parents, and looked into the parents' eyes. There are Christmas decorations in that child's room. Someone took the time to decorate his room. And yes, they were able to 'look into the eyes' of this child whom they had helped.

College Buddies, always remember that God's love is PRACTICAL - not a beautiful theory in the clouds. Whether you help build a home for Habitat, whether you work in a food pantry, visit a Children's Hospital, visit a rehab center, baby sit free for an exhausted single mom, collect toys to brighten a needy child's Christmas, gather coats for children who can't buy them.......you are doing Jesus' work. Let's ask God to give us these opportunities, to look into the eyes of someone whom we have helped, for Jesus' sake:

"Whoever shall give to drink to one of these
little ones a cup of cold water, truly I tell you,
he shall not lose his reward." Matthew 10:42

Love You!!   Praying for You!!   Proud of You!!   Bro. Post
✳✳✳✳✳✳✳✳✳✳✳✳✳✳✳✳✳✳✳✳✳✳

"If you try to do God's work on the outside without having God's love on the inside, you do a lot more damage than good!"

Have you ever heard someone screech their fingernails down a chalkboard? The sound is annoying, grating and irritating. Amazingly, even if we do the greatest works for God, give all of our earthly goods to the needy, even suffer martyrdom for Jesus, it is all for nothing UNLESS we love the very people whom we serve. Without God's love, we come across to people in an annoying, grating manner! God can fill us so much with His love that we can actually love someone in a beautiful manner.

How do I know if I have God's love? It is mainly a deep sense of care and affection and also, a strong desire for the person to experience the very best in life! A 'Love Person' is thrilled when others do well and grieves when others experience hurt. A 'Love Person' is quick to offer you their time, their possessions and their help, simply because you need it. Let's ask God to fill us abundantly with His love so that it will easily flow out to others:

> "If I speak in the tongues of men and of angels...
> If I have prophetic powers, and understand all mysteries..
> If I have all faith so to remove mountains...
> If I give away all I have, and deliver my body to be burned...

Good Morning!! How Are My College Buddies?

IF I DO NOT HAVE love
I am a noisy gong or clanging cymbal…
I am nothing…
I gain nothing.
I Corinthians 13:1-3

Love You!!   Praying for You!!   Proud of You!!   Bro. Post
✶✶✶✶✶✶✶✶✶✶✶✶✶✶✶✶✶✶✶✶✶✶

"'From' and 'Out Of.'"

Life is full of snares, or traps. It seems that things can be going ok and life seems to be fine. We cannot see them, but in our day-in and day-out activities are hidden traps, circumstances that would harm us spiritually, physically, or both.

Your Father can see these traps! When we walk with Him, He has a way of guiding us away from things that can harm us. The problem here can be stubbornness - not heeding His warning signs. (In dating relationships, stubbornly resisting God can lead to years of heartache.) Notice the verse below, David had confidence that God would protect him from walking into a snare. In addition, David believed that God could rescue him when he DID get caught in a snare.

College Buddies, if you tend to walk through life getting caught in one snare after another, ask your Father to guide you. He can gently lead down a path of safety, He dearly wants the best for you in your life:

"Surely he will save you from the snare of the fowler." Psalm 91:3

Love You!!   Praying for You!!   Proud of You!!   Bro. Post
✴✴✴✴✴✴✴✴✴✴✴✴✴✴✴✴✴✴✴✴✴✴

"I'll keep reminding you…and I won't stop."

The most difficult task that God does for us, after we become Christians, is to help us understand how much He loves us. We seem to get it, then we lose it - that inner 'settledness' that comes when we experience our Father's lavish love. There are two reasons why we struggle here: 'circumstance oriented' and 'feeling oriented.' We subconsciously tend to link how much our Father loves us to our circumstances, we think He loves us more when things are going well, we wonder why He doesn't love us when things are rough. Now we know this isn't true in our minds, but in our hearts we stumble here, we start doubting. In addition, we also link our Father's love to how we feel that day…we know better, but we tend to do this.

So what does our Father do to help us? One of the things that He does is to send us 'Love Reminders', little events or circumstances that He uses to remind us how much He cherishes you. These 'Love Reminders' can come in thousands of different ways, but the spiritual results are the same - we feel encouraged, uplifted, our confidence is renewed. All of us need these every day, you may especially need one this day. Ask your Father to send one to you, ask Him to remind you how much He loves you. Then watch for His 'Love Reminder', it will come soon, your Father is eternally in love with you:

"And I pray that you may have power to understand how WIDE and LONG and HIGH and DEEP is the love of Christ,...and to KNOW this love that surpasses knowledge." Ephesians 3:17-19 (emphases mine)

Love You!! Praying for You!! Proud of You!! Bro. Post
✶✶✶✶✶✶✶✶✶✶✶✶✶✶✶✶✶✶✶✶

"A Blessing in Installments."

Suppose someone gave me a cashier check for a million dollars. Wow, I would be really grateful! However, suppose the same person offered to give me fifty thousand dollars once each month, for 20 months. The blessings would be the same, it's just that the latter one would come in installments.

It's true that God often sends us blessings 'instantaneously' when we pray, and it is wonderful to receive them. However, much more often, God sends a blessing in steps, or installments. This is even more wonderful to receive. (And fun to watch!!) Sometimes we pray for someone or for some thing and we become frustrated because the prayer is not answered quickly. However, have you ever thought that the prayer is indeed being answered, just not all at once! Don't become impatient with the Lord's timing. Instead of looking for the big check, thank Him for each installment. The full blessing is coming, don't worry about it:

> "Every good and PERFECT gift comes from above, from the Father of lights, with whom there is no variation nor shadow turning."
> James 1:17

Love You!!   Praying for You!!   Proud of You!!   Bro. Post
✳✳✳✳✳✳✳✳✳✳✳✳✳✳✳✳✳✳✳✳✳

"Hope and Compassion."

These two words enter my mind every time I walk through the halls of the Arkansas Children's Hospital. The children here are facing intense, fierce battles - the parents try to present an encouraging picture to their kids, but inside, they fight an tremendous battle with fear and terror. The staff has a wonderful way of offering hope to these children - they will be treated with the latest procedures to restore the child's health. If the parents cannot pay, that doesn't matter. The staff also offers gentle compassion to the child and the parents when the child will not recover - this compassion comes from their hearts, it's real, it's spiritual and it's God sent. I always sense God's presence when I walk through the halls.

It seems to me that all of us should offer these godly attitudes to everyone: hope and compassion. Some Christians are beaten down by their burdens, they wonder if God has forgotten them - we can gently restore their faith. Others have deep heart wounds, they are hurting from a wound we cannot imagine...but still, their burdens are lighter when we stand beside them and love them. We rub elbows with people needing these two blessings every day. Want to serve God today? Ask God to intersect your path with someone who needs hope and compassion - straight from His heart, dispensed by you.

> "Praise be to God...the Father of compassion, who comforts us in all troubles, so that we can comfort those in any trouble with the

comfort we ourselves have received from God." II Corinthians 1:3-4

Love You!!   Praying for You!!   Proud of You!!   Bro. Post
✶✶✶✶✶✶✶✶✶✶✶✶✶✶✶✶✶✶✶✶✶

"Walk, Not Drown"

Sometimes, when God leads us to walk down a certain path, all of the circumstances are encouraging. When the Hebrews left Egypt, God led them to cross the Red Sea. God made all of the circumstances at this time encouraging - the waters parted, there was a dry path through the center! However, sometimes God will lead us down a path where NONE of the circumstances are encouraging.

Years later, Joshua would lead the Hebrews through the Jordan River. Now it was really frightening! The Jordan River was flooded and deep and most discouraging, God had not yet parted the waters! Actually God would wait until the last second, when the feet of the priests actually touched the water, then He would make the pathway through. My point? Sometimes, as you follow God, you look around and the circumstances say: "Yes! This will work! Keep Walking!" Other times, the circumstances say: "If you take another step, you will drown!"

College Buddies, God will lead you safely through out your life, but be prepared, sometimes, it won't look too safe! When His path seems to make no sense, or even looks disastrous, He can roll back the dangers, He can protect you when you follow His path. Follow Him - He alone has the power to make your life safe, productive and meaningful for all eternity:

> "When you pass through the waters, I will be with you; and when you pass through the

rivers, they will not sweep over you......For I am the Lord, your God, the Holy One of Israel, your Savior." Isaiah 43:2-3

Love You!!   Praying for You!!   Proud of You!!   Bro. Post
✷✷✷✷✷✷✷✷✷✷✷✷✷✷✷✷✷✷✷✷

"What goes around, comes around. I can't wait to see them get it!"

While Joseph was in that dungeon, he most certainly faced a fierce battle with unforgiveness. I'm sure he mused about his brothers' cruel treatment and I'm sure that there were times when his anger flared. FLASH.......TEMPORARY....... PERMANENT - these are the three types of resentment. When we are wronged, we all experience 'flash' resentment – the type that lingers for a few minutes. Sometimes it lingers for a few days, it becomes a temporary resident in our heart. If not dealt with, it can become permanent - scarring and poisoning our life and attitude. It's always best to be totally honest with our Father, don't hold back, tell Him all about it. I would love to hear some of Joseph's prayers to God...surely he asked for help when the bitterness was overwhelming. And that is the only way, we humans are too flawed to invent true forgiveness.

Maybe you want to take a piece of paper and write your hurt - then be honest, ok? Tell God how ticked off, bitter and hurt you are, He knows perfectly. Take the paper and grip it tightly in your fist...pray...and slowly release the paper on the table as you release it to your Father. He will help us, He will deliver us:

"I can do all things through Christ who strengthens me." Philippians 4:13

Love You!!   Praying for You!!   Proud of You!!   Bro. Post

✷✷✷✷✷✷✷✷✷✷✷✷✷✷✷✷✷✷✷✷✷✷

Good Morning!! How Are My College Buddies?

"Be gentle...Be gentle...Be gentle."

It's fascinating to watch a young mom interact with her child. The mom is a picture of gentleness. When she speaks or holds the child, the child experiences tender words and a gentle touch. Even if the child is overtired, the mom expresses patience, knowing the source of the child's irritability. When the child is sick, the child receives the best nursing attention possible......24/7...from mom. College Buddies, when you deal with others, your family, friends or coworkers, the purest witness that you can be for Christ is to show them gentleness. Offer gentleness when others are doing fine, offer it to them when they are struggling. When their soul is tired, be gentle...remember the times when you were not spiritually at your best.

Think of some of the Christians who were the greatest help to you - I bet they were gentle to you. Think about the Apostle Paul – a powerful preacher, fearless evangelist and an excellent Christian. Now notice carefully how he treated other Christians:

> "As apostles of Christ, we could have been a burden to you, but we were gentle among you, like a mother caring for her little children." I Thessalonians 2:7

Love You!!   Praying for You!!   Proud of You!!   Bro. Post

✹✹✹✹✹✹✹✹✹✹✹✹✹✹✹✹✹✹✹✹✹

"FEAR. DREAD. PRESSURE..."

'The Big Three'. Few things can help us more in our Christian lives than these three uncomfortable emotions. Do not always consider them an enemy.

These 'Big Three' act like a magnet, drawing us to God, and helping us learn to trust HIM. We experience these attacks from the 'Big Three' hundreds of times, in hundreds of differing circumstances. College Buddies, let's be honest, even though we may have wondered at the time, GOD HAS NEVER LET US DOWN.

If we never had an attack from the 'Big Three', we simply would have a weak, anemic faith. It's in the throes of the struggle that we see God's Fatherly care, His love and His compassion.

Some Christians teach that a victorious Christian Life means that we are immune to fear, or that we never struggle with dread or with pressure. I don't think so. It's like when we see a storm coming and we automatically assume that our Father will steer us around it. Sometimes He says, "Not around it, my child, here's my hand, we will walk though it."

College Buddies, if today you are experiencing a huge storm from the 'Big Three', maybe you're a little jumpy, and that's ok. However, if you still are trusting your Father, and deep down in your soul, you still believe that He will protect you...to protect others dear to you...Has it ever dawned on you that you are indeed experiencing God's victory right now?!

"I sought the Lord, and he answered me, and delivered me from all my fears." Psalm 34:4

(Notice that David had to experience fear in order to experience God's deliverance from fear.)

Love You!!   Praying for You!!   Proud of You!!   Bro. Post
✸✸✸✸✸✸✸✸✸✸✸✸✸✸✸✸✸✸✸✸

"A Simmering Burn."

It's fascinating how the Bible addresses so many of human weaknesses. Have you ever thought about something in your life, or someone else's life, that you really do NOT like? Then, have you ever mulled this unfairness over and over in your mind, making you even more ticked off?! Have you caught yourself irritable with others, projecting your inner anger upon them? Hey, all of us have been there, done that.

The Bible describes this condition exactly - it uses the word 'fret'. The Hebrew word for 'fret' means a 'simmering burn.' Ok, I'll talk about myself here. When I get this way, I am blinded to God's goodness, I pray less, read my Bible less and want to stop everyone and tell them, "Unfair!" God can help us here, He knows how vulnerable we are to inner discontent and anger. He first forgives us when we ask. Then He restores our perspective - He gently reminds us of His goodness and kindness to us. One of the easier ways for our spiritual enemy to sidetrack us is to frequently remind us of things that we wish were different...over and over again. But our Father helps us, He restores us and helps us. He has the ability to quench the 'simmering burn' of the anger of discontentment:

> "Refrain from anger and turn from wrath; do not fret - it leads only to evil." Psalm 37:8

Love You!!   Praying for You!!   Proud of You!!   Bro. Post

✶✶✶✶✶✶✶✶✶✶✶✶✶✶✶✶✶✶✶✶✶✶

"Behind every Former Failure is a God-sent Barnabus."

I bet John Mark was wracked with guilt. If he looked in a mirror, he would see the words 'failure' and 'quitter' on his face. He was convinced God would have nothing more to do with him. His church has given him money, prayed over him and sent him to the mission field, with the Apostle Paul! He excitedly left, but soon he faced tough times and overwhelming discouragement. So......he failed...he left the Apostle Paul in a bind and returned home. He left for the mission field encouraged and excited - he returned dispirited and filled with guilt. Even Paul had placed the 'Failure' sign on him - Paul would never take him back.

Now God could have left John Mark to spend the rest of his life in guilt, but God had other plans. He sent Barnabus, a gentle apostle who quietly encouraged John Mark. While Paul wrote him off as a failure, Barnabus could see God forgiving, restoring and blessing John Mark again. Barnabus, by his actions and gentle words, brought God's message to John Mark: "I forgive you, let's start all over again."

College Buddies, all of us have worn the sign 'Failure' - all of us have stumbled in our walk with God. Think back to the 'Barnabus' that God placed in your path, who encouraged you and gently persuaded you to return to the Lord. Now, ask God to make you a Barnabus this coming year - to be the source of spiritual encouragement to people who think that God has written them off. I wish that I could have

Good Morning!! How Are My College Buddies?

seen it - a restored John Mark, a FORMER failure, going BACK to the mission field, now successful, now doing work for the Lord. God did this - he restored John Mark - but never forget, God did it by using a Barnabus. God bless you as you become a 'Barnabus' to someone today:

> "Now instead, you ought to forgive and comfort him, so that he will not be overwhelmed by excessive sorrows. I urge you, therefore, to reaffirm your love for him." II Corinthians 2:7-8

Love You!!   Praying for You!!   Proud of You!!   Bro. Post
✶✶✶✶✶✶✶✶✶✶✶✶✶✶✶✶✶✶✶✶

Good Morning!! How Are My College Buddies?

"Look for a Love Token"

When we are struggling with a problem, very often the Lord waits a while before He solves it. He does this for a number of reasons, one being that waiting often stretches our faith and helps it grow. However, sometimes in the middle of a problem, it's easy for our faith to get shaken, for us to wonder if God is still in control and if He is still looking out for us.

In days like these, be looking for a 'love token,' a small sign from God that shows you that He still loves you and that He is still taking care of you. A 'token' does not solve the problem, but it does renew our wavering faith. A 'token' is an unexpected blessing, a load lightener. These love tokens can come in thousands of different ways, but out Father has one goal in mind when He sends them. It's a gentle reminder that He is still God, that He adores you and that He wants to remind you: "I know your problem, I WILL solve it in the future, here's a sign to show you I am working on it."

Be on the lookout for a 'love token' today:

"Show me a token of your favor, …….. because you, Lord, have helped me and comforted me." Psalm 86:17

Love You!!   Praying for You!!   Proud of You!!   Bro. Post

✸✸✸✸✸✸✸✸✸✸✸✸✸✸✸✸✸✸✸✸✸✸✸

"The Take It Back Test."

College Buddies, God will bless you throughout your life, He has promised to do this. Occasionally, He sends a blessing to you that is so awesome that it leaves you breathless, you are overwhelmed at His goodness and kindness. When this type of blessing comes, we are always fully happy and fully thankful and rejoicing, right? Well, not always.

Actually, sometimes we face a very severe test right after a wonderful blessing - the 'Take It Back Test.' This is when we fight inner suspicions, we actually wonder if the blessing is temporary, like our Father would thrill us with a blessing and then remove it. Or, we may think that God has blessed us in one area, so things will get really bad in another area!! 'The Take It Back Test'.......this is common to all Christians.

God is a perfect Father, He does not torment us by sharing a blessing for a while, then removing it. His favor is not based upon our worthiness – He loves us with the EXACT degree of love that He loves His Son, Jesus. Our enemy does not want us to revel and rejoice in a blessing - he would rather divert our attention away from God by making us wonder if we will continue to enjoy the blessing...so he whispers: "It's only temporary, it won't last." By faith, accept happily and joyfully God's blessings to you, it came from His heart, a visual aid to show you how much He adores you:

"Gladness and joy will OVERTAKE them, and sorrow and sighing will flee away. I, even I, am He who comforts you." Isaiah 51:11, 12

Love You!! Praying for You!! Proud of You!! Bro. Post
✶✶✶✶✶✶✶✶✶✶✶✶✶✶✶✶✶✶✶✶

"Sometimes we can't see the forest for the trees."

Here's what I mean, sometimes we nitpick and cannot see the whole picture. Especially when it comes to ourselves! The Bible tells us that God is involved in our life for a lifetime - He's not going to leave us or cast us away. He is involved in the process of changing us, making us more like Jesus Christ. This lifetime work is the 'forest', the big picture of what God is doing in us. But sometimes we focus in on an individual 'tree' - we isolate one of our faults, beat ourselves up, get discouraged. Ask God to help you stop doing this!

Try this. Look back at where you were when you first became a Christian - you were happy to be a Christian, but you certainly weren't a mature Christian. Now take a minute and look back at how you have grown since then. There you go…see what I mean? Give God time to mature you. If God wants to grow a weed, He takes a few months. If God wants to grow a massive oak tree, He takes a lifetime.

Take your eyes off of your faults, back up and look at the big picture:

> "I am confident of this, that the One who began a good work in you will bring it to completion by the day of Jesus Christ."
> Philippians 1:6

Love You!!   Praying for You!!   Proud of You!!   Bro. Post
✼✼✼✼✼✼✼✼✼✼✼✼✼✼✼✼✼✼✼✼

"He was standing to show His concern, His compassion and His power."

After Jesus died and returned to heaven, He sat down at the right hand of God the Father. Everywhere in the Bible, it refers to Him sitting at this highest place of honor. Except for one place - in Acts 8.

One of His servants, Stephen, was enduring a horrible time of trouble and trial. When Stephen looked up into heaven, he saw Jesus standing. Seeing this, Stephen was given the encouragement and confidence to endure. Try to imagine how much love and concern Jesus had for Stephen - a man suffering because of his faith in Christ. Imagine Jesus actually standing up and closely watching Stephen. Jesus was showing Stephen that He was in total control, that Stephen's misery had His total attention, He would help Stephen and welcome him to heaven.

College Buddies, Jesus is watching you at all times, 24/7. He's in total control and He is listening for you to call out to Him. On the tough days when life has beaten you down, Jesus is standing to give you His perfect help. Look at this beautiful verse from the Bible - it applies to each of us:

"The eyes of the Lord are on the righteous and his ears are listening for their cry." Psalm 34:15

Love You!!   Praying for You!!   Proud of You!!   Bro. Post

✽✽✽✽✽✽✽✽✽✽✽✽✽✽✽✽✽✽✽✽✽✽✽

Good Morning!! How Are My College Buddies?

"The mountain is not as high as you thought, once you start climbing it."

The problem is that we make the task of climbing much worse by dreading it!! We worry, we fret and we doubt that the Lord will help us. College Buddies, ALL of us occasionally face mountains of hardships or obstacles in life. The first step is to remember past 'mountains' that you have scaled...the Lord didn't let you down, did He? The second step is to remember that God knows all about this mountain...He knew about it before you were born. You may be panicky, but your Father isn't. Lastly, now is the time to get up, stop dreading the future and start climbing. When you do, the Lord starts walking right beside you, steadying you, guarding you, showing you the best route. When the hardship is over, you'll be amazed at your Father's help and care along the trek:

> "Do not fear, for I have redeemed you... When you pass through the waters, I will be with you; and through the rivers, they shall not overwhelm you; when you walk through fire you shall not be burned, and the flame shall not consume you." Isaiah 43:1-2

Love You!!   Praying for You!!   Proud of You!!   Bro. Post

✽✽✽✽✽✽✽✽✽✽✽✽✽✽✽✽✽✽✽✽

Good Morning!! How Are My College Buddies?

"God rarely fixes things in fifteen minutes."

If He did, why would we need faith? Think of a massive ocean liner, the captain doesn't turn it around immediately - often it takes up to 15 miles!! College Buddies, these areas of your life that need repair, God often waits before He fixes them. He's waiting while our spiritual muscles are toned and strengthened. None of us enjoy this process, quite frankly these needy areas cause us real pain!!

The good news is that our Father does plan to end the dark night of tough circumstances - at the right time, He allows the dawn of better days. However, this work of His, easing our pain, will not happen in 15 minutes! The wait makes our faith stronger, the blessing sweeter and His plan more beautiful. Have you been praying for relief and nothing has happened? Your Father is working on it, He has started turning the ship of your life. His name is linked to your welfare - what kind of master neglects his servants? He will rescue you, He will help you, He will relieve the pressure…but likely it won't happen in the next fifteen minutes:

> "And God, the giver of every spiritual blessing, who has called us by Christ Jesus to share in his eternal glory, will himself, after your brief suffering, restore, establish and strengthen you on a firm foundation." I Peter 5:10 NEB

Good Morning!! How Are My College Buddies?

Love You!!   Praying for You!!   Proud of You!!   Bro. Post
✶✶✶✶✶✶✶✶✶✶✶✶✶✶✶✶✶✶✶✶

Good Morning!! How Are My College Buddies?

"God, save me from myself...especially on a day like today!"

Very honest praying, right? College Buddies, our faith in Christ works wonderfully on the sunny days, the days when everything is going well. However, our faith in Christ works even better on the rotten days, those days when circumstances are lousy!! God will help us, He knows that on days like these, we desperately need His help.

It may take a while but God helps us in our PERSPECTIVE - He helps us to see that our present misery is temporary and less than many others. He then acts as our PROTECTOR - He can protect us from our self, the wrong things we want to do, the wrong words we want to unload...we may WANT to, He helps us NOT to. Lastly, He acts as our SHEPHERD - He comes and finds us when we have wandered away in self pity, frustration, anger or discontentment. Think your faith is just for the sunny days? Watch how your faith works on the lousy days...notice how your Father will help you. Tough day today? "Father, save me from myself..."

> "But you, O Sovereign Lord, deal well with me for your name's sake; out of the goodness of your love, deliver me. For I am poor and needy, and my heart is wounded within me."
> Psalm 109:21-22

Love You!!   Praying for You!!   Proud of You!!   Bro. Post

✶✶✶✶✶✶✶✶✶✶✶✶✶✶✶✶✶✶✶✶✶✶

"Crossroads of Faith."

Mary and Joseph certainly saw God work in a miraculous way! To be visited by angels, to conceive a baby miraculously, to see God Himself born... wow, they were certainly blessed! However, in the middle of these blessings were some frightening, scary times! It was like God was bringing them to a crossroad - choose to believe me and walk the road of faith, or choose not to believe me and walk the road of doubt.

One crossroad Mary faced was the crossroad of public perception - would she trust God when no one else believed how she was expecting a child? Another crossroad was the crossroad of provision - would Joseph trust God to provide for his family when he was moving them at night to a foreign land! Maybe the biggest crossroad was the crossroad of protection - would Mary trust God to protect her baby when the most powerful man in the country wanted to slaughter Jesus. God sends His greatest blessings, not on the sunny days but on the stormy days. His light shines the brightest when it pierces the darkness of tough times, scary events, and pressure cooker circumstances. God didn't fail Mary, He didn't fail Joseph and He certainly won't fail you:

> "All who rage against you will be surely be ashamed and disgraced; those who oppose you will be as nothing and perish......For I am the Lord, your God, who takes your right

Good Morning!! How Are My College Buddies?

hand and says to you, Do not fear; I will help you." Isaiah 41:11, 13

Love You!!   Praying for You!!   Proud of You!!   Bro. Post
✸✸✸✸✸✸✸✸✸✸✸✸✸✸✸✸✸✸✸

Good Morning!! How Are My College Buddies?

"Praise the Master, not the brushes."

Ok, think about this. You can enter one of two rooms. In the first room are the very brushes that da Vinci used to paint the Mona Lisa. That would be great, but in the second room, you could meet the master himself, Leonardo da Vinci. Not a hard choice is it? It's ok to appreciate the brushes but you want to compliment the master!!

Sometimes Christians get confused here - they compliment the method that God blesses you, but forget the PERSON who blesses you. Behind each blessing that you have ever received, your Father is the Master who created the blessing, waited for the perfect time and then delivered the blessing to you. He deserves, at the least, our sincere thanksgiving. Let's do that this week, let's not get confused, let's appreciate His methods but let's thank and praise the Master:

> "Praise our God, O peoples, let the sound of his praise be heard; he has preserved our lives and kept our feet from slipping." Psalm 66:8-9

Love You!!   Praying for You!!   Proud of You!!   Bro. Post

✶✶✶✶✶✶✶✶✶✶✶✶✶✶✶✶✶✶✶✶✶✶

"Scaring the Heck Out of Ourselves'"

Have you ever met a Christian who DOESN'T do this occasionally? It's like sometimes our imagination runs wild and it becomes a factory which churns out terrifying scenarios. We then mull over the terrifying scenarios and embrace them, and then we cringe at the coming disaster......which we have created solely in our own minds.

It's both comforting and fascinating to read in the Bible of some very wonderful Christians who, at times, 'scared the heck out of themselves.' These panic times were brief but very intense. Interestingly, these panic times often came after a period of deep exhaustion and intense stress. From Jeremiah questioning whether God was lying, Elijah hoping to die, Abraham lying about his wife, David feigning a mental illness.......it's not a pretty picture when we scare the heck out of ourselves.

Our Father understands these panic times and He doesn't throw us away or even scold us harshly. Our Father has the gentle maternal quality of calmly His frightened kids and He does this perfectly. He does this by different ways but the most important one is that He gives you His PRESENCE. He is right beside you at 1 AM, when you are mentally scaring yourself to death. He is there when you start a busy day carrying an extra load of worry. He is there when you see a terrifying mountain in the future that you must climb and you see no way to do it.

My oldest daughter used to be terrified of thunderstorms when she was a little girl. She couldn't sleep so I would take a chair and sit by her bed. Now I could have lectured her that the storm wouldn't hurt her, or I could have told her to try hard and just stop being afraid.......but that would have been a waste of breath. But when I sat beside her for ten minutes so she could touch my arm several times, even though the storm was still raging outside, she quickly went to sleep......because she knew that her father was right beside her.

Our Father wants to calm your mind by reminding you that HE is right beside you. The next time you terrify yourself, imagine yourself touching Him by reciting this verse:

"So do not fear, for I am with you; do not be dismayed, for I am your God. I will strengthen you and help you; I will uphold you with my righteous right hand." Isaiah 41:10

Love You!!   Praying for You!!   Proud of You!!   Bro. Post
✴✴✴✴✴✴✴✴✴✴✴✴✴✴✴✴✴✴✴✴

Good Morning!! How Are My College Buddies?

"Lord, help me to back off."

When it comes to the Serenity Prayer, it's a lot easier for us to change the things that we can change than it is for us to accept the things that we cannot change! Sometimes God is working in ways that we cannot see and at this stage God doesn't need our help, therefore it's time for us to back off.

The Prodigal Son's father is the best example I know for this truth. When his son left, he could have begged and pleaded for him to stay, but he let him go. This father knew that God had to work in his son's life, so even though it was very hard, he backed off. When we back off, it doesn't mean that we have no faith, actually it means that we are focusing our faith: "Lord, I'm helpless here, I can do nothing. Father, I'm trusting you to work in this situation."

College Buddies, you may have been praying for a problem and you may have tried everything you can think of to solve the problem. Maybe it's time for you to be like the Prodigal's Son's father, maybe God is speaking to you. "I know what's going on, my child, and I am working on the problem. Why don't you back off and trust me?"

"I waited patiently for the Lord; he inclined to me and heard my cry." Psalm 40:1

Love You!!   Praying for You!!   Proud of You!!   Bro. Post
✳✳✳✳✳✳✳✳✳✳✳✳✳✳✳✳✳✳✳✳✳✳

"Who Do You Think You Are?!"

Sometimes we are tentative and reluctant to serve the Lord. It's like Satan is whispering: "Who do you think you are?! Don't you remember when you did......" We listen to the replay of past faults and invent an excuse to avoid a present opportunity.

Think with me on this. If God needs perfect Christians to do His work, then nothing would ever get done! He uses people who are painfully aware of their shortcomings, people who know that they need God's forgiveness. HOWEVER, when we imperfect people go ahead and serve the Lord, the Lord blesses our feeble efforts and we then KNOW that He did it, not us. And that is what humility is all about. When God gives you an opportunity to serve Him, be aware of two lies that Satan will whisper: "You're not good enough" or "You can't do that well enough". College Buddies, go ahead, serve the Lord, God's forgiveness cleanses you completely:

"Serve the Lord with gladness,......Know that it is the Lord, no other, who is God, we are His..." Psalm 100:2,3

Love You!!   Praying for You!!   Proud of You!!   Bro. Post

✳✳✳✳✳✳✳✳✳✳✳✳✳✳✳✳✳✳✳✳✳

Good Morning!! How Are My College Buddies?

"Faith, not Feelings."

College Buddies, it's great to serve the Lord when we are spiritually pumped up, excited and motivated. It's easy to read our Bibles and pray when we wake up feeling God's presence.

But this is the easy stuff, isn't it? God wants to move us to another level of maturity in our lives - trusting, obeying and serving Him when we definitely don't feel like it. When we wake up tired and pushed, and we DECIDE to read our Bibles and pray anyway...... now we're really growing! When we believe that God is right beside us when it feels like He is a million miles away......congrats, we are really making spiritual strides. When we trust that God will solve our problem even when everything around us is getting worse... now our faith is maturing.

Living the Christian life when we 'feel' that God is close? That's ok, but it is really spiritual kindergarten stuff. But being faithful when the feelings aren't there, when the circumstances are tough, when we feel like we're in a 'spiritual desert'......that's where God is leading us. Look carefully at the verse below:

"I solemnly urge you: proclaim the message, be faithful whether the time is favorable or unfavorable........." II Timothy 4:2

Love You!!   Praying for You!!   Proud of You!!   Bro. Post
✶✶✶✶✶✶✶✶✶✶✶✶✶✶✶✶✶✶✶✶✶

Good Morning!! How Are My College Buddies?

"You lean on me and I'll lean on you and we will be ok."

It may take a while, but eventually this truth will sink in: you just can't go it alone as a Christian. If we try, the concerns are more terrifying, the burdens far heavier, the fatigue is deeper, and our faith becomes much weaker. God intended for us to lean on each other - to show genuine concern, to pray for mutual needs and to love each other deeply, with God's love.

Think about Moses in the Bible - a great man of God, fearless and bold. Yet, at several times, he needed someone to help him. At one point, God gave him 100 wise men to ease the pressure of his job. Another time, God gave him Aaron and Hur, to hold his arms up when he was too exhausted to continue. Hmmm, if Moses needed God's people......you get my point.

Today our American culture values 'rugged individualism' - go it alone, tough it out. This philosophy will lead you to spiritual disaster because NONE OF US ARE STRONG ENOUGH TO GO IT ALONE!! If your path is weary and your burdens are very heavy, you are very blessed if you have another Christian to help carry the load. If you're stumbling in exhaustion and you can't take another step, look around - God has placed someone there to help you, to encourage you and to pray for you.......lean on them:

> "Two are better than one...If one falls down, his friend can help him up. But pity the man

Good Morning!! How Are My College Buddies?

who falls and has no one to help him up...... though one may be overpowered, two can defend themselves." Ecclesiastes 4:10, 12

Love You!!   Praying for You!!   Proud of You!!   Bro. Post

✻✻✻✻✻✻✻✻✻✻✻✻✻✻✻✻✻✻✻✻✻

Good Morning!! How Are My College Buddies?

"Pre-Blessing, Imagined Disasters."

When it comes to God sending a blessing to His child, I have noticed an interesting trend. Sometimes, right before the blessing comes, the circumstances start to fall apart. It's almost as if we get our hopes up, then circumstances dash those hopes. And no, I don't believe that these discouraging circumstances are always from Satan. I believe our Father is sometimes responsible, He allows the circumstances to look more and more impossible, just before He works the miracle.

Why would He do this? If we prayed and everything went smoothly right up to our Father's answer, guess who we would be tempted to credit? Either ourselves or others. But our Father waits until there is NO DOUBT who sent the blessing, then He acts. So if things have gone to you know where in a handbasket lately,.. God is still in control. Very likely, He is getting ready to send you a blessing so wonderful that you will be overwhelmed:

> "Blessed be the Lord, for he has wondrously shown his steadfast love to me. I had said in my alarm, 'I am cut off from God's sight.' But God heard my prayers, when I cried to him for help." Psalm 31:21-22 (Wonderful verses!!)

Love You!!   Praying for You!!   Proud of You!!   Bro. Post
✶✶✶✶✶✶✶✶✶✶✶✶✶✶✶✶✶✶✶✶✶

"911 Christians"

God's people just didn't get it - they only walked with God in the bad times, the times in which they were frightened, troubled and afraid. Then God would deliver them and guess what? They started 'drifting' again: they ignored God, they forgot about His goodness, they went back to their previous way of life. So they would drift along until more trouble would come - then they would pray and plead with God again until the new emergency passed. '911 Christians'.......faithful only when they were in trouble. (The Book of Judges)

College Buddies, the easiest time to live for the Lord is in the tough times...but it is VERY difficult to live for the Lord when the sky is blue, the problems are small, the future is bright. 'Spiritual Drifting' is a common temptation that we face, but God is willing to help us. Even in the best of days, the Lord still has a claim to our lives: our time, our talents and our possessions. The best of days should be filled with frequent thanksgiving to our Father – not wasted days in which we offer Him benign neglect.

If you're struggling today, I know you feel God especially near you, He is there to reassure you. However, He is just as near to you if you are having a wonderful day! He still wants to walk with you, bless you and fellowship with you. Be careful that you refuse the temptation of drifting, don't be a '911 Christian' :

Good Morning!! How Are My College Buddies?

"Bless the Lord, O my soul, and FORGET NOT all his benefits." Psalm 103:2

Love You!!   Praying for You!!   Proud of You!!   Bro. Post
✶✶✶✶✶✶✶✶✶✶✶✶✶✶✶✶✶✶✶✶✶

Good Morning!! How Are My College Buddies?

"Please try again."

One of the harder things to do as a Christian is to accept God's forgiving grace. It's a free gift, but we keep trying to feel like we deserve it - we often try to 'earn' it. God's forgiving grace cleanses us when we have failed miserably, when we think God doesn't care for us anymore. Very often, in times of embarrassment or shame, God meets us in a special way, He forgives us and lifts us up.

I heard a wonderful testimony a year ago about a Christian woman who had failed God in her life. She struggled with guilt and wondered if God would give her another chance. As she was driving to work, the Enemy was making her miserable, assuring her that she was at best a lousy person, at worst, she wasn't even a Christian. God broke through this person's guilt and encouraged her and restored her. As she opened a diet 16 oz. Dr. Pepper bottle, she glanced inside the lid. God spoke to her as she read the words "Please Try Again." And that is exactly what God may be saying to you: "I forgive you, my child, I cleanse you...now let's try again."

> "If we confess our sins, he is faithful and just to forgive us our sins, and cleanse us from all unrighteousness." I John 1:9

Love You!!   Praying for You!!   Proud of You!!   Bro. Post
✶✶✶✶✶✶✶✶✶✶✶✶✶✶✶✶✶✶✶✶✶✶

"Pray yourself to sleep."

One of our most vulnerable times is when we go to bed. Especially if we have had a grinding, rough day. It is uncanny how the enemy can whisper into our ears, causing us to imagine frightening scenarios, imagined disasters. The result? Our body needs sleep, but it is held hostage by our overactive imagination.

In the Book of Acts, the Apostle Peter was in prison facing a likely execution the next day. When God sent an angel to rescue him, the angel found Peter in his prison cell, asleep!

Why not pray yourself to sleep? Start by thanking God for His protection and care throughout your life - remember and thank Him for specific examples. Then thank Him that He loves you so much...spend a lot of time doing this. Then start praying for others who have needs, thank Him that He is working in their lives. Then pray for yourself, for the needs you have, thank Him that He will work in His perfect time. As you are doing this, you will sense God's fatherly 'soothing' of your soul - your body relaxes, your fears decrease, your confidence returns. Then you will experience what King David meant when he said these words:

"In peace I will both lie down and sleep;
for thou alone, O Lord, makes me dwell in safety." Psalm 4:8

Love You!!   Praying for You!!   Proud of You!!   Bro. Post

✷✷✷✷✷✷✷✷✷✷✷✷✷✷✷✷✷✷✷✷✷✷

Good Morning!! How Are My College Buddies?

Always remember this: "Sometimes, it's not what you're saying, it's how you're saying it."

All of us need to constantly add two ingredients to our speech: gentleness and tact. These two qualities allow your message to get through. Soften your tone, lower your voice, take away any accusation in your voice, speak gently. Think about HOW to say something, the best way to phrase it - speak tactfully. If you practice this manner of speech, you will benefit at home, at work and at school. Many a time a person's true message has been rejected because it was packaged in immature, incendiary words. Deliver your message in a way that gives it the best chance for it to be received properly.

"The mind of the wise makes his speech judicious, and adds persuasiveness to his lips." Proverbs 16:23

Love You!!　　Praying for You!!　　Proud of You!!　　Bro. Post
✳✳✳✳✳✳✳✳✳✳✳✳✳✳✳✳✳✳✳✳✳

Good Morning!! How Are My College Buddies?

"Lord, help me stop this RIGHT NOW."

When it comes to wrong attitudes, it is always best to be very aggressive! If we nurture the attitude, and allow it to stay inside of us, it always grows. After a few days, our whole outlook on life has been poisoned. God can help us deal aggressively with a wrong attitude, it doesn't matter whether it's bitterness, worry, discontentment, self pity, jealousy...... the list is quite long.

There is a large oak tree near my home. This large tree was once a small sapling. Now the only time I could have uprooted this tree was at the beginning of it's life, many years ago. Today, it is impossible to uproot, for many years now it has grown and has been nurtured by the soil.

College Buddies, be VERY careful what attitudes you allow to grow in your heart. All of us have wrong attitudes that come into our hearts, but we don't have to allow them to live and grow there! God can uproot the wrong and replace it with a Christian attitude:

"Let the words of my mouth and the meditation of my heart be acceptable to you, O Lord, my rock and my redeemer." Psalm 19:14

Love You!!   Praying for You!!   Proud of You!!   Bro. Post
✳✳✳✳✳✳✳✳✳✳✳✳✳✳✳✳✳✳✳✳

Good Morning!! How Are My College Buddies?

"I have a right to this!!"

Ok, that may be true, but aren't you glad Jesus didn't insist on His rights? If He had, we would be in deep trouble! Can you imagine what would have happened when they slapped Him, spit in His face, publicly humiliated Him...what if He said, "Hey! I built this world, I don't have to take this!"

College Buddies, there will be times when we will need to set aside our 'rights' and serve others. If you go through life howling when others slight you, your life will become a vast, egocentric wasteland. Jesus gladly set aside what He deserved: honor, worship and respect. He also endured what He didn't deserve: ridicule, rejection and a brutal death. Let's follow His example the next time others slight our rights.

> "Have the same attitude that Christ Jesus had. He did not cling to his prerogatives as God's equal, but He impoverished himself and took upon the nature of a servant...he humbled himself and became obedient unto death, even the death of the cross." Philippians 2:5-8

Love You!!   Praying for You!!   Proud of You!!   Bro. Post
✶✶✶✶✶✶✶✶✶✶✶✶✶✶✶✶✶✶✶✶✶✶

Good Morning!! How Are My College Buddies?

"Naive to believe it, foolish to pass it on."

These are the twin dangers when we hear gossip. Gossip is so dangerous because it has an element of truth, just enough to give some legitimacy to the falsehood. The problem is, the truth gets twisted, altered and embellished as it passes from one person to another. To accept a rumor as the absolute truth, free from distortion, this is so naive! And yet, I have done this many times. To pass it on is simply foolish; that rumor that you spread is like a verbal bullet, once you fire it, you cannot retrieve it. Sadly, I have foolishly done this at times.

College Buddies, the most valuable possession a person owns is their reputation; many a person has suffered professionally, personally and socially because of gossip. Avoiding this sin is easy. When you hear gossip, pray one of the best prayers you can ever pray: "Father, help me keep my mouth shut."

"Whoever belittles another lacks sense, but an intelligent person remains silent. A gossip goes about revealing secrets, but one who is trustworthy in spirit keeps a confidence."
Proverbs 11:12-13

Love You!!   Praying for You!!   Proud of You!!   Bro. Post
✶✶✶✶✶✶✶✶✶✶✶✶✶✶✶✶✶✶✶✶✶✶

Good Morning!! How Are My College Buddies?

"Unseen Protectors"

Elisha could see them, his servant could not. The city where Elisha lived was surrounded by an army who wanted to capture and kill him. The servant was freaking out! Finally, Elisha prayed for his servant, that he could see. The servant's eyes were opened and all around them were thousands of angels in fiery chariots, sent by God to protect them.

College Buddies, you are just as important to God as the prophet Elijah. When it comes to your safety, God is watching you very carefully; He knows the dangers, the traps, the snares of life. God would never let Jesus die for you and then abandon you to the dangers and temptations of life. I guess you could say that God has way too much invested in you, He gave His only Son for you. If you are troubled or frightened, ask God to help you relax. Once you see God's wonderful love and care, the threats in life aren't nearly as frightening:

> "The angel of the Lord keeps guard around those that fear him, and delivers them." Psalm 34:7

Love You!!   Praying for You!!   Proud of You!!   Bro. Post

✷✷✷✷✷✷✷✷✷✷✷✷✷✷✷✷✷✷✷✷✷

Good Morning!! How Are My College Buddies?

"The Room of Unanswered Questions."

College Buddies, I strongly recommend that you open such a room in your heart. You'll need it in your lifetime, there will be a few times when something will happen and you will be totally baffled and confused. You will think it through a hundred times: "Why?", "I don't understand!" "Where is God?" You will even pray, but God will not explain. THEN it's time to place this issue in the "Room of Unanswered Questions." When you place it there, pray: "God, I just don't understand, but I do believe that you are still in control of this. I'll trust you."

College Buddies, it is true that our Father, for our own good, does not always show us the 'why'. He does know, He does care, and He is working on the problem, solving it in His perfect way. The fact that He chooses not to tell us the details means that we MUST trust Him. Think of all of the ways He has taken care of you…I assure you that He will work out the problems in that room in the same way. Today, as you place some issues in that room, imagine the following words written over the door:

My Father is too kind to be cruel,
My Father is too wise to make a mistake,
My Father is too profound to be understood.

Love You!!   Praying for You!!   Proud of You!!   Bro. Post
✶✶✶✶✶✶✶✶✶✶✶✶✶✶✶✶✶✶✶✶✶✶✶

"Repair Specialist"

"God is a Specialist at making something useful and beautiful out of something broken and confused." - Chuck Swindoll

Actually He does this for all of us - our Father comes to us in our times of hurt, disappointment and failures. Now when He comes, He DOESN'T come to scold us, to rebuke us, to shame us. He comes as a gentle Father, filled with concern for His son/daughter who is struggling.

College Buddies, to think that we will live a life without heartaches, fears and bitter disappointments is spiritual naive - the points of pain will come. Broken and confused - our Father actually allows this to happen to us at times. Then He starts His wonderful process of rebuilding our hope, picking up the pieces of our heart and reshaping our lives for the future. You are far too precious to your Father for Him to allow your life to be destroyed...He future plans for you may be different, but far better. At the end of our lives, even though it may be tough to believe it now, we will be amazed at the beautiful life He reshaped, using the broken pieces of our heartaches that we are enduring today. Take the broken pieces and place them in your Father's hands, trust Him, the Master Repairman is already working in the background for you:

"Before they call I will answer; while they are still speaking, I will hear." Isaiah 63:24

Good Morning!! How Are My College Buddies?

Love You!!   Praying for You!!   Proud of You!!   Bro. Post
✻✻✻✻✻✻✻✻✻✻✻✻✻✻✻✻✻✻✻✻

Good Morning!! How Are My College Buddies?

"A Transfusion of Hope"

"Every time we encourage someone, we give them a transfusion of hope." (Chuck Swindoll)

College Buddies, always remember that every Christian is carrying at least one private burden - an unresolved issue that either frightens them, frustrates them or discourages them. These burdens can range from trivial to life-threatening, but ALL Christians have them. The longer the person carries the burden, the more weary they become. God is nudging all of us to be a spiritual lifeline to them - to use our gentle words, our caring actions and our consistent prayers to infuse a new confidence in them.

You may think that your encouraging actions are insignificant, but to a Christian who is fighting a fierce battle, your acts of kindness are extremely helpful! Don't hide behind clichés or trite words... go to them, open your heart to them, love them, encourage them, pray for them. If you're longing to serve the Lord in a special way today, ask God to make your path cross with a person fighting a fierce battle...our Father will use you and your gentle actions to infuse a renewed sense of faith and hope in Him:

"An anxious heart weighs a man down, but a kind word cheers him up." Proverbs 12:25

Love You!!   Praying for You!!   Proud of You!!   Bro. Post
✻✻✻✻✻✻✻✻✻✻✻✻✻✻✻✻✻✻✻✻✻✻

Good Morning!! How Are My College Buddies?

"All of us occasionally get a case of the 'Frenzies'."

A day with the frenzies is tough because you seem extra jumpy, edgy and irritable. You look at all you have to do and panic, dreading and resenting your normal responsibilities. People easily get on our nerves when we have the frenzies - we catch ourselves either sullen or with a verbal hair-trigger. Hey, we all get that way!!

You can see some people in the Bible who had the frenzies, God didn't give up on them, He helped them. The Lord will help us settle down, He has the amazing ability to replace the inner whirlwind with a peaceful calm. He also helps us to be very careful how we act and speak until we are back to normal. Don't beat yourself up when you get a case of the frenzies, but don't go it alone either!! Ask your Father to help you, you'll be amazed how much better these tough days can be:

"He (the Lord) said to me, "My grace is sufficient for you, for my power is made perfect in weakness." II Corinthians 12:9

Love You!!   Praying for You!!   Proud of You!!   Bro. Post
✳✳✳✳✳✳✳✳✳✳✳✳✳✳✳✳✳✳✳✳✳✳✳✳

"Think About It Carefully...You're Making a Huge Mistake"

College Buddies, the Lord has been so good to us, and He has blessed us so much, we'd would never leave Him, right? Hmm, let's think about that. Throughout our lives, there will be times when our enemy presents a temptation...a wrong road that he wants us to take. The problem is that this wrong path often looks exciting and wonderful at the beginning... "Hey it won't hurt anyone, no one will know."

You see, when we turn down the wrong road, we make two huge mistakes. The first is the wrong attitude or action that we commit. But the greater mistake is that we turn our backs on God and His plan for our lives. The wrong road looks VERY appealing and our old nature in us very much WANTS to go down it. Being tempted like this means that you are a normal Christian, all Christians occasionally fight these tough battles. God spoke through Jeremiah and gave us very excellent advice -think about it first, before you make a HUGE mistake. Today, if you're fighting a tough battle of temptation, and you really want to take a wrong road away from your Father, read carefully Jeremiah's words. Our Father gave us this warning because He loves us dearly and doesn't want to see us get hurt:

> "Consider then and realize how evil and bitter it is for you when you forsake the Lord your God and have no awe of me", declares the Lord, the Lord Almighty." Jeremiah 2:19

Good Morning!! How Are My College Buddies?

Love You!!   Praying for You!!   Proud of You!!   Bro. Post
✶✶✶✶✶✶✶✶✶✶✶✶✶✶✶✶✶✶✶✶

"As Low As It Gets."

If I were Jeremiah, I would be ready to quit! He had served the Lord faithfully, he had done nothing wrong. However, some people, upset with him, took him, tied his hands and feet, and dumped him into a huge water cistern. No way to get free, he settled in the mud, waiting to starve to death. However, our Father does His best work in hopeless situations, it seems like our Father waits until He ONLY will get the credit and praise. So God sends Ebed-Melech, an officer in the King's Court, to rescue and save Jeremiah. (Jeremiah 38)

College Buddies, there will be times like this in your life, count on it. There will be times when you think you are sinking in the 'mud' of tough circumstances and even worse, you can't do a thing about it, your hands are tied. Hopeless...unless God works. God was watching Jeremiah closely in the cistern - when he went into the mud, God already knew when and how He would get him out. The same is true of all of us...He waits, we trust, He acts, at His perfect time. Here is a wonderful promise about that from the Bible. You may want to write it out and place it on your mirror:

> "And the God of all grace, who called you to his eternal glory in Christ, after you have suffered a while, will himself restore you and make you strong, firm and steadfast." I Peter 5:10

Good Morning!! How Are My College Buddies?

Love You!!   Praying for You!!   Proud of You!!   Bro. Post
✴✴✴✴✴✴✴✴✴✴✴✴✴✴✴✴✴✴✴✴

Good Morning!! How Are My College Buddies?

"Speak kind words and you will hear kind echoes."

Ok, not everyone feels like they can tell others about Christ, they feel nervous and intimidated. For some Christians, to speak publicly would cause them to faint! :-)

Here's an even better way to witness for Christ: Ask God to fill you with His gentleness and kindness. Gentleness is not a weakness, gentleness is a sign of spiritual strength! When we show kindness to others, we are living the very life of Jesus. Kind words, gentle actions, these are probably the best sermons ever preached. People will notice the difference - after all, we live in a highly abrasive society. People will open their hearts to you, they will feel safe because they sense the very gentleness of Christ in you. Jesus was gentle, and He can make us gentle. Jesus was kind, and He can make us kind. Let's ask God, even on a tough day, to display His gentle kindness today:

"Make sure that nobody pays back wrong for wrong, but always be kind to each other and to everyone else." I Thessalonians 5:15

Love You!!   Praying for You!!   Proud of You!!   Bro. Post
✵✵✵✵✵✵✵✵✵✵✵✵✵✵✵✵✵✵✵✵✵

Good Morning!! How Are My College Buddies?

"Hold their head up."

The Louisiana Deputy Sheriff was amazed at what he was seeing. He had just responded to an auto accident and a young mom, (my cousin,) was unconscious in a ditch, she and her son had been thrown from their vehicle. The mom was paralyzed and definitely would have drowned in the ditch. When the officer arrived, the 4 year old was standing in the ditch beside his mom, holding her head up out of the water. This little boy couldn't move his mom, somebody else would do that. This little boy couldn't give emergency care and rehab to his mom, that would come later. However, he could hold her head out of water until help came.

College Buddies, you will meet some Christians in your life who are drowning in tough circumstances, their faith has taken a battering, they find it hard to believe God still cares for them. Now you can't solve their problems, only God can do that, but you can spiritually 'hold their head up' until God eases their problems. You can encourage them, love them, give compassion to them - God can use you to give them a glimmer of hope that their Father will indeed rescue them:

> "And we exhort you.......comfort those who are frightened, give a helping hand to the weak, be patient with everyone." I Thessalonians 5:14

Love You!! Praying for You!! Proud of You!! Bro. Post

✶✶✶✶✶✶✶✶✶✶✶✶✶✶✶✶✶✶✶✶

"Through a Lover's Kind and Gentle Eyes."

The writer of Proverbs was intrigued and enthralled at the love process between a man and a woman. The man becomes the 'initiator', the one to first express, usually by his actions, his affection for the woman. Eventually the man becomes 'smitten', looking for opportunities to be with the woman he loves, as often as possible. He looks for ways to express that love to his beloved, being inwardly thrilled when she is happy. He verbally elevates her, highlighting her points of beauty and ignoring her weaknesses. He is quick to praise her, quick to please her, quick to forgive her...all because he is now crazy about this woman! Then eventually, this true love leads the man to commit himself to her for a lifetime and then, we have a wedding!!

Ok, here's where I'm going with this: the Bible says that when we get to heaven, the first thing we will do is have a wedding!! Jesus himself will marry His beloved, the Church...and that is you! Jesus loves you more than you can possibility imagine, so He will be your husband for all eternity. I am praying that each of us will receive a fresh insight into how deeply we are loved:

> "For this reason I bow my knees before the Father,...that you, being rooted and grounded in love, may have power to understand what is the width and length and height and depth, and to KNOW the love of Christ, which

surpasses understanding, that you may be filled with all the fullness of God." Ephesians 3:17-19

Love You!!   Praying for You!!   Proud of You!!   Bro. Post
✶✶✶✶✶✶✶✶✶✶✶✶✶✶✶✶✶✶✶✶✶✶

"A Dad Thing"

I couldn't understand why I couldn't go to sleep, something kept nagging in my mind. Then I remembered that I hadn't talked to one of my daughters in a few days. I felt she was okay, but I just wanted to hear her voice. Knowing she stayed up late, I called her. "Hi Daddy! Good to talk to you! I'm doing fine, love you too!" I hung up the phone, laid back down, and went to sleep. I guess checking up on your kids is a dad thing, we do it a lot.

College Buddies, did you know that your Heavenly Father is constantly 'checking up' on you? He's watching you closely, He knows your mood, your circumstances, your joys, your fears...He's constantly monitoring how you're doing. He does this so that He will know EXACTLY how to encourage you, bless you, help you. As He is watching you, He is also working in the background, His unseen hand crafting the solution to the very problem you're enduring...or, He's crafting a blessing to give you that will lighten your load and bring you joy! Wow. One more thing, in case you doubt it at times, He also does this because He absolutely adores you:

> "Do not fear, for I have redeemed you, I have called you by name, you are MINE. When you pass through the waters, I will be with you, and through the rivers, they shall not overwhelm you, when you walk through fire, you will not be burned." Isaiah 43:1-2 (emphasis mine)

Good Morning!! How Are My College Buddies?

Love You!!   Praying for You!!   Proud of You!!   Bro. Post

✸✸✸✸✸✸✸✸✸✸✸✸✸✸✸✸✸✸✸

Good Morning!! How Are My College Buddies?

"<u>Confused</u> is Good. <u>Bewildered</u> is very Good. <u>Helpless</u> is excellent."

College Buddies, often the Lord gets us to this place and then He answers. Jehoshaphat was an OT king who faced an incredible problem and even though he was a godly man, these three words described his condition: Confused…Bewildered…Helpless.

You see, I don't know about you, but I have this awful tendency to pray and think that God will help <u>me</u> solve the problem……so God waits and waits and waits. He is waiting until we trust HIM…only. This is why sometimes we feel so boxed in, we wrack our brains and frantically search for a solution!! When we turn to Him only, He may calm our outside storms, OR He may calm the storm inside of us - but He will always help us and we will know that He alone did it. And the way that He answers is ALWAYS far better than the best that we could imagine. I don't ask you to do this often, but would you memorize the verse below? It is one of my favorite verses in the Bible, it is part of Jehoshaphat's prayer. In our lifetimes, we will need to pray like this thousands of times:

> "We are powerless against this great multitude that is coming against us. We do not know what to do, but our eyes are on you." II Chronicles 20:12

Love You!!   Praying for You!!   Proud of You!!   Bro. Post
✷✷✷✷✷✷✷✷✷✷✷✷✷✷✷✷✷✷✷✷✷✷

"You can hide, but the Lord will find you."

Elijah had 'had it', so he found a nice cave to hide in. Now there is no way that God will leave a child of His in a cave, dispirited and struggling. So God finds him. It's interesting how gentle and kind God treated Elijah - He didn't scold him, He lovingly gave him the exact help that Elijah needed.

You know, all of us find a favorite cave to hide in on occasions, don't we? These caves can have a thousand different names, but the characteristics are often the same - frustration, (sometimes with God), discouragement, jumpiness and fear, despair, disappointment, sometimes bitterness. Our Father knows our 'cave' times and He quietly finds us, He gently encourages us, He promises to help us, He forgives us and gently takes our hand and leads us out of the cave...... just like with Elijah. There are thousands of different types of 'spiritual caves', and you may be hiding in one today. And that's ok, because Someone is coming to help you. Here's what He will do:

"He restores my soul." Psalm 23:3

Love You!!   Praying for You!!   Proud of You!!   Bro. Post

✶✶✶✶✶✶✶✶✶✶✶✶✶✶✶✶✶✶✶✶✶✶✶✶

"What's Behind the Door?!"

Opening a new door in life sometimes scares the heck out of us!! It's only normal to dread changes, we stress about what's behind that new door. Some changes are minor inconveniences, other changes jolt us to the core. Before I open a new door, I usually ask God to explain in detail what's behind that door! :-)

College Buddies, as Christians, it is your Father who brought you to this new door and He wants you to open it. He DOES know exactly what's ahead, He is not rattled. Let me tell you what's NOT waiting behind that door: failure, disaster, abandonment, embarrassment…you get the picture. The great thing is that Jesus is standing beside you when you open that new door, He is encouraging and assuring you. We may balk, but He is whispering: "Trust me, I will be with you. I have some blessings waiting behind that door, go ahead and open it."

> "For surely I know the plans I have for you, says the Lord, plans for your good and not for your harm, to give you a future with hope." Jeremiah 29:11 (emphasis mine)

Love You!!   Praying for You!!   Proud of You!!   Bro. Post

✽✽✽✽✽✽✽✽✽✽✽✽✽✽✽✽✽✽✽✽✽

"Look at the Big Picture."

Some Christians can easily forgive other people's sins, but they have a tough time forgiving themselves. These are usually very sensitive and compassionate Christians, they can easily forgive others but they are incredibly harsh upon themselves. Guilt is their constant struggle, beating up on themselves is a daily event.

College Buddies, if we are like this, then once again, we need to look at the Big Picture. Look back at your Christian life 2 years ago......I bet you have made good progress since then! Think of the ways that God has helped you grow and mature, think of the ways the Lord has used you in His work. In addition, force yourself to think about what grace is, a free gift to the <u>totally undeserving</u>. Do NOT listen to your Enemy, who is an expert with the 'Hammer of Guilt'. Believe what God says is true, that you are in Christ and God the Father loves you as much as He loves Jesus. Sit down, open your Bible and let Jesus speak to you about His love for you......He can dissolve your guilt and literally set you free to love Him in return:

"Yea, I have loved you with an everlasting love and therefore with loving kindness have I drawn thee." Jeremiah 31:3

Love You!!   Praying for You!!   Proud of You!!   Bro. Post
✶✶✶✶✶✶✶✶✶✶✶✶✶✶✶✶✶✶✶✶✶✶

"You can't live your life without getting hurt."

As much as we try not to, we run into circumstances that leave us heartbroken, discouraged, grieving. When you become a parent, you'll realize that this is when you feel the most helpless, when your kids are hurting and you can't make it go away.

The Bible tells us that our Heavenly Father performs a special miracle in these times of misery. He could build a protective umbrella around us, to shield us from any and all hurts. Instead, the tenderness and kindness of God is clearly seen when life has left us dazed and bewildered. College Buddies, your Father will, in time, heal your grief, your disappointment and your heartache. In the meantime, He doesn't send help, He comes to you. He is especially near His struggling child, supporting you, helping you. "I'll help you get through this, just trust me."

"The Lord is near to those whose heart is broken and He saves those who are crushed in spirit." Psalm 34:18

Love You!!   Praying for You!!   Proud of You!!   Bro. Post

✽✽✽✽✽✽✽✽✽✽✽✽✽✽✽✽✽✽✽✽✽✽

"The Ghost of Past Sins"

All of us have a room in our lives where lurk the ghosts of past sins. The problem is that we sometimes visit that room, we sit down and we relive, rehash and re-blame ourselves for past mistakes. Young people, all of us have done things that we are totally ashamed of doing. "Bro. Post, I have asked God to forgive me a hundred times!" I understand, but have you asked God to help you forgive yourself?

It's sad how we Christians, people of grace, can find God's grace so hard to accept for ourselves. The enemy of our faith is behind this, he loves to cripple us with guilt, he loves to ruin our hopes for the future because we are drowning in a sea of guilt and shame. The result? We really don't expect our Father's goodness in the future, we're too busy torturing ourselves over past failures! Tonight, write out that past sin you frequently revisit. Pray and give it to God one last time. Shred the paper and then say with faith: "I am forgiven and I am free."

> "The Lord does not deal with us according to our sins, nor repay us according to our iniquities. As far as the east is from the west, so far he removes our transgressions from us." Psalm 103:10,12

Love You!!   Praying for You!!   Proud of You!!   Bro. Post

✶✶✶✶✶✶✶✶✶✶✶✶✶✶✶✶✶✶✶✶✶✶✶

Good Morning!! How Are My College Buddies?

"'It Never Fluctuates"

We make a huge mistake when we think that God's love is like a thermometer, fluctuating, changing each day. When things are going great, we may subconsciously think that God really loves us! When things go downhill, we may subconsciously feel that our Father is angry, His love has diminished.

College Buddies, both of these subconscious feelings are <u>very</u> wrong! Here's what the Bible teaches us: It is impossible for God to love you more than He loves you at this very moment. He loves you intensely, constantly, forever. You can't earn His love, so why not enjoy it? You can't earn His forgiveness, so why not stop trying and just accept it? Today, let your heart feel the warmth of knowing your Father in heaven is crazy about you, He has you in His forever embrace:

"The Lord, your God, is in your midst,……
He will rejoice over you with gladness, He will renew you in His love; He will rejoice over you with singing..." Zephaniah 3:17

Love You!!   Praying for You!!   Proud of You!!   Bro. Post
✵✵✵✵✵✵✵✵✵✵✵✵✵✵✵✵✵✵✵✵✵✵

"A Grace Encounter"

Thomas had a "Grace Encounter." He is the one who said he would not believe Christ's resurrection unless he could touch the Savior's wounds. Jesus later appeared and invited him to do just that, to inspect His recent wounds. It was at that point that Thomas was overwhelmed by the love of Christ.

College Buddies, a lot of our struggles and problems are eased when we realize how much God loves us. Some Christians believe that a mature Christian is someone who strives to keep a list of do's and don'ts. The problem is, all of us occasionally break that list......then we wallow in guilt, grit our teeth, resolve to try harder! What a <u>tiring</u> way to live! Today, Jesus gives you the same invitation He gave to Thomas; "look closely at my wounds, I suffered them for you." Once this sinks in, I promise you that you will love the Lord and love others. You will gladly serve the Lord because you will be in awe that this Person would be so kind to you. This is a "Grace Encounter", the difference between enjoying your life or enduring your life:

> "For this reason I bow my knees before the Father,......that you, being ROOTED and GROUNDED in love, may be able to understand what is the breadth and length and height and depth, and to know the love of CHRIST...so that you may be filled with all the FULLNESS of GOD." Ephesians 3:14-19 (emphases mine)

Good Morning!! How Are My College Buddies?

Love You!!   Praying for You!!   Proud of You!!   Bro. Post

✱✱✱✱✱✱✱✱✱✱✱✱✱✱✱✱✱✱✱✱

"To the world you might be one person, but to one person you might be the world."

Young people, there are a lot of people whom you encounter who are wearing a facade of happiness hiding a heart of sadness. It is true that God will help them, but God wants to help them through you! Let God borrow your eyes so that you can see their unhappiness. Let God borrow your heart, so you can give them love and compassion. Let God borrow your hands, to reach out and meet their need. You will become a 'human lifeline", a person who gives them hope in the middle of despair. If you allow God to use you this way, the person will connect to God through you. In addition, they'll always love you and think the world of you:

"the fruit of the Spirit is love, ... KINDNESS, GOODNESS, GENTLENESS, ...against such things there is no law." Galatians 5:22-23 (emphases mine)

Love You!!   Praying for You!!   Proud of You!!   Bro. Post
✼✼✼✼✼✼✼✼✼✼✼✼✼✼✼✼✼✼✼✼✼

Good Morning!! How Are My College Buddies?

"Go ahead and peek, you'll be pleased."

Many young children cannot resist the temptation to take a sneak peek and unwrap a gift - it's hilarious how they try to wrap it back up and hide their tracks. In the Bible, our Father actually tells us to use our faith and 'peek' into the future - He has some special gifts in store for us. Remember two things about 'faith peeking', something that we should do often. First, our enemy tries to get us to look ahead, then he tells us a pack of lies. He wants to terrify us with future disasters, disgraces, failures and miseries that break us. <u>It will not happen</u>. Our Father wants us to 'peek' into the future and believe that it will hold His tender love, His protective care and His daily goodness. Our Father has the biggest heart of anyone and He is like any doting parent, He loves to give special 'love gifts' to His kids. College Buddies, why not take a peek into the future, use your faith and actually BELIEVE what God is promising you! Memorize the verse below, it is what David wrote after he used his faith and peeked in the future:

"Surely goodness and loving kindness shall follow me <u>all</u> the days of my life and I shall dwell in the house of the Lord forever." Psalm 23:6

Love You!!   Praying for You!!   Proud of You!!   Bro. Post

✷✷✷✷✷✷✷✷✷✷✷✷✷✷✷✷✷✷✷✷✷✷

"You First."

College Buddies, these two words contain the key to incredible joy as a Christian! I know it sounds weird, but the greatest joys in life come when you give yourself to other people, in the name of Christ. Some Christians never discover this; they lose themselves in a lifelong pursuit of their own interests. Two problems here: First, when we get one thing for ourselves, another interest pops up - it's a constant pursuit. Secondly, getting something else for ourselves never really satisfies very long, it's like a eating cotton candy.

However, when we follow Jesus' example, and practice daily giving ourselves to others, it's like an incredible fountain of great joy. Sure, it takes time and effort and energy to serve others, but the internal joy and satisfaction is incredible. It's like we feel that we are doing what God placed us on this earth to do. Tired of the relentless pursuit of stuff to please yourself? If you really want to get a kick out of life, take a towel, wrap it around your waist, pray and ask God to bring you in contact with someone whom you can serve today. You'll go to bed grinning tonight:

> "Stop looking after your own interests only, but practice also looking out for the interests of others." Philippians 2:4

> "...we must help the weak, remembering the words of Lord Jesus: 'It is more blessed to give than to receive.'" Acts 20:35

Good Morning!! How Are My College Buddies?

Love You!!   Praying for You!!   Proud of You!!   Bro. Post

✱✱✱✱✱✱✱✱✱✱✱✱✱✱✱✱✱✱✱✱✱

"The clinging hand of His child makes a desperate situation a delight to Him."

It's only natural for a frightened child to cling to the hand of a parent, to 'transfer' the threat from the child to the mom/dad. Almost always there is a calming of the fears, the child will settle down and remain calm - as long as the child knows the parent is near.

College Buddies, all of us occasionally find ourselves in frightening situations in life - we long to feel safe, we long to cling to our Father's hand and to know that He is protecting us. It is situations like these that are an absolute joy to our Father, He loves to show how deeply He loves us and how fiercely He protects us. Sadly, sometimes we think that He is disappointed in us when we are frightened, so we add guilt to our fears. (Our enemy loves it when we do this!) Actually, just the opposite is true...He looks forward to when we cling to His hand, He has such a tender heart toward you that He loves to protect you. I bet He was thrilled to protect Daniel from the lions! Frightened today? Go ahead, pray and cling to His hand, experience His deep love and fierce protection:

"Because he cleaves to me in love, I will deliver him; I will protect him, because he knows my name. When he calls to me, I will answer him; I will be with him in trouble, I will rescue him and honor him." Psalm 91:14-

15 (Notice the underlined words - that's what your Father will do for you. :-)

Love You!!   Praying for You!!   Proud of You!!   Bro. Post
****

"Human sweat never made a rainbow. When you think about it, it makes little sense to try to impress God."

Wow, we really try though, don't we? We seem to make a terrible mixture of God's grace, (His undeserved kindness), and our spiritual efforts. (Our prayers, Bible reading, good works, etc.) This is a terrible mixture because it pollutes the pure water of God's love - we mix God's beautiful gift with stuff we do, and often, we divide the credit. Really sad.

Ok, College Buddies, please remember this: we have <u>never</u> deserved one blessing from God, from the time we became a Christian until today. These blessings come our way because our Father has a huge heart of love - it's almost like He can't help Himself, He has to bestow wonderful gifts and blessings upon His kids! He's even a little stubborn about this - He adores you so much that He will bless you even if you really don't believe He will bless you. You see, it's about Him, and His huge heart of love - it's not about us. Once this sinks in, this truth sets us free. We're now free to love Him dearly because He loves us. We're free to pray and believe because we know how much He loves to bless others! If we mix in our efforts, and think He answers because we pray so well, or know so much about the Bible, we are simply missing out. He blesses us, not because we deserve it, but because He adores us. This is what GRACE is all about. Get it?

Good Morning!! How Are My College Buddies?

"The Lord is <u>merciful</u> and <u>gracious</u>, slow to anger and <u>abounding</u> in steadfast love. He does deal with us according to our sins, nor requite us according to our iniquities. For as a father has tender compassion upon his children, so the Lord has tender compassion upon those who fear him." Psalm 103:8,10,13 (emphases mine)

Love You!!　　Praying for You!!　　Proud of You!!　　Bro. Post
✶✶✶✶✶✶✶✶✶✶✶✶✶✶✶✶✶✶✶✶

"Don't give up on your day, the Lord can salvage it."

Everybody knows what it's like to have a day going nowhere fast, and by 10 AM, it is spiraling downward. My tendency sometimes is to write off a day like this, to assume that the total day will be lousy!! So I spiritually hunker down and go into the survival mode, praying that <u>tomorrow</u> will be better.

I am learning that our Father has a beautiful tendency to salvage <u>today</u> - that He can bless us in a way that restores our confidence, evaporates our doubts and deepens our thanksgiving to Him. Now these blessings, right after our struggles, can come in thousands of different forms, but the results are the same - we feel encouraged, refreshed...like a cool drink of water on a blistering hot day. When you think about it, it makes perfect sense for Him to do this, His heart is unbelievably tender toward all of His kids, He loves to encourage us and lighten our loads. So, if by 10 AM today, your day is really lousy and rotten, it's very likely that by 10 PM tonight, your Father will have sent you a special blessing, just for you. You'll go to sleep smiling, not grimacing:

> "Incline thy ear, O Lord, and answer me, for I am poor and needy. Thou art my God, be gracious to me, O Lord, for to thee do I cry all the day. Gladden the soul of thy servant, for to thee, O Lord, do I lift up my soul." Psalm 86:1,3

Good Morning!! How Are My College Buddies?

Love You!! Praying for You!! Proud of You!! Bro. Post

✵✵✵✵✵✵✵✵✵✵✵✵✵✵✵✵✵✵✵✵✵

Good Morning!! How Are My College Buddies?

"You can't love someone on an empty tank."

College Buddies, if you want to truly show God's love to others, you first need to bask in God's love, allow Him to fill your heart. You need to take time to personalize God's love, to remind yourself how much He loves YOU. Then you will be amazed and full of your Father's love and it will <u>easily</u> flow out to others! I promise you that this works. If you are needing a fresh awareness of your Father's love, it is impossible to 'grit your teeth' and love others.

Let's start at the beginning: take your Bible, get alone, pray and ask your Father to remind you and to refill you with His incredible love. He may gently take you on a journey to the cross of Calvary where He will show you Jesus' death for you……or He may lovingly remind you of what could have happened to you, but didn't -because He has preserved and protected you. Whatever it takes to refresh you with His love, He will do it. He waits as your lover who adores you, He really does. Once God fills your heart, you will be amazed at the way your heart goes out to others:

> "There is no fear in love, for perfect love casts out fear…….and whoever fears has not reached perfection in love. WE LOVE BECAUSE HE FIRST LOVED US." I John 4:18-19 (emphasis mine)

Love You!!   Praying for You!!   Proud of You!!   Bro. Post

✶✶✶✶✶✶✶✶✶✶✶✶✶✶✶✶✶✶✶✶✶✶

"DECISIONS! WHAT TO DO AT THE CROSSROADS OF LIFE"

"I have to make up my mind." "I've got to choose." "I have to say yes or no."

Decisions. You'll have to make thousands of them in your adult life. And always remember, a decision always carries a consequence, good or bad. But the neat thing is that God doesn't leave us alone when we face decisions; He's waiting there at every crossroad to guide you to the right choice! Notice this verse from the Bible: "Trust in the Lord with all of your heart, and do not depend upon your own understanding. Commit all of your ways to Him, and HE WILL DIRECT YOUR PATHS." Proverbs 3:5-6 (Emphasis mine)

Young people think of every decision as a crossroad. You have to choose which road you'll walk on. Now imagine at that crossroad you see some flashing signs that read: "PRAY!" "THINK!" "THINK AHEAD" "NOW DECIDE!"

And that is exactly what this article is about. I ask you to try this process the next decision you face; I am confident that the Lord will clearly guide you.

Before we consider these steps, let me share with you some WRONG ways to make a decision:

1. "I LIKE THIS CHOICE!" That's nice, but the real issue is: "Is it the right choice?" "Is this God's choice?" Making a decision based solely on the fact that you want to do something, or because you like that option, is VERY

risky. I remember a few years back walking through DFW airport. Braniff had just unveiled their newly painted jets. Suppose I boarded a Braniff jet, didn't check the flight number, just boarded because I liked the color of their jets? Suppose it didn't take me where I wanted to go? You see, I needed FACTS about the flight, not just the feeling of PREFERENCE! Yet some people, when they face a decision in life, will immediately do what they want, what they like! Then ten years later, they don't like where that decision carried them! Happens all the time.

2. "I JUST FEEL THIS IS THE RIGHT DECISION!" Again, you need to be very careful here. Our feelings are very fickle, they can change rapidly. I may wake up one morning and love being a pastor. I have awoke a few mornings and wished I had never heard of this profession! :-) Beware of making decisions based solely on your feelings!

3. "THE LORD TOLD ME TO DO THIS!" Well yes, He does do that, sometimes. He certainly can, and sometimes He does give 'instant direction.' But young people, He doesn't always guide us this way. Sometimes, our faith grows more as we pray and wait and go through a process of finding the right choice. We'll talk about that more in a minute. Also, as a Christian, you don't need pagan devices. Tarot cards, astrology, Ouija boards, PLEEZE! Come on, you know better than this! I won't

insult your intelligence by telling you why a Christian should have nothing to do with this.

Instead, use these steps for God's guidance:

PRAY THINK THINK AHEAD CHOOSE

Let's think about these steps.

PRAY FIRST!!

Do you really believe that God wants the very best for you in life? I really do. Do you believe He wants you to make foolish mistakes when you face a decision? Of course not. Are you willing to obey and follow Him when He shows you the right choice? Then pray about a decision, put it in is hands. When you come to a crossroad and you have to decide, let prayer be your first step. Ask Him to show you His choice for you. You'll never regret it! Beware of asking God for a "sneak preview". What I mean is, "God, please show what you want me to do so I can decide whether I like it or not!" As a father, I can't imagine wanting anything but the very best for my two daughters. However, no one loves you as much as your Heavenly Father! Not even close! If you follow Him in all of your decisions, He will see to it that you experience the best life possible! After you have prayed about a decision, now go to the next step.

Good Morning!! How Are My College Buddies?

THINK!!

If you have prayed and committed your decision to the Lord, and you still are not sure which decision is correct, go to the next step. THINK!! Make a concentrated effort to find out everything you can about the options you face. Which college to go to? Write down what you find out about the colleges. You really like someone you're dating? Thinking this relationship might lead to marriage? Learn about the other person as you're dating! Think it through. A choice of job offers? Carefully study and write down the facts.

Don't be jumpy in a decision. Take time to think it through! Yesterday I was sitting on the bank of a huge, beautiful rice reservoir, writing notes about this article. Right behind me, about 50 ducks came flying over the treetops, wanting to land near me. But they didn't rush to a decision! They circled three times first. Why? They were gathering facts! Is there food there? Are there any natural predators? Are there any risks? Is this a good place? On the third circle, they spotted me and instantly flew to the other end of the reservoir. There they circled and eventually landed. Here's the point: they made their decision based upon the facts! If God gave ducks the intelligence to live by facts, then surely He wants the same for us! Facts can be like the runway lights at an airport, guiding the pilot accurately to a safe landing. One more thought: there is rarely an option that is 100% perfect. There are pro's and con's to any choice. Take a piece of paper and make two lists: PRO'S and CON'S. Write down the facts you learn and place them in the list where you think it belongs, pro or con. The Lord has used this simple exercise MANY times to 'lift the fog', to help me see clearly His will. Don't get jumpy and don't get discouraged! The Lord will eventually show you, if He hasn't already! But a very helpful step in the process of decision making is the next step, THINK AHEAD!

Ok, you're facing a decision! You've prayed about it, and you're willing to do whatever the Lord shows you. You have gathered as many facts as you can, listing them as 'pro's' and 'con's'. You still aren't quite sure.

Try the next step:

THINK AHEAD!

Ask God to help you carefully think about what will happen, good or bad, if you choose a particular option. This is very important. You did that when you came to Christ; I'm sure it crossed your mind what your future would be like if you accepted or rejected Christ. Do the same as you make other decisions! The Lord will use this step to help lead you.

When you graduate and take your first job, you will be deluged with credit card applications. A couple of years ago, I received one advertising 2.8% interest, which caught my interest! You know the rest...2.8% for 6 months THEN 18.5%!!! Wow, thanks a lot! If I had taken the card without looking ahead, then it really would not have been a wise decision!

THINK AHEAD!! As well as you can, think about what future results will come from your present decision.

Again, list the pro's and con's as you think ahead. Write them down.

Thinking ahead will help you make decisions in everyday stuff. It will also help you when you have to decide between right and wrong. About 15 years ago, I was facing a decision about whether I was going to do something wrong, something I knew was wrong, but I wanted to do it! Wanting to do something wrong is called temptation. This temptation didn't just go away, I struggled with it for several weeks. I prayed, read my Bible, still struggled. The way the Lord eventually helped me resist this temptation was to simply think ahead. I sat down one afternoon and thought of everything that would probably happen if I chose to do wrong. I was amazed at the potential for heartache. My point is, the Lord helped me make the right decision when I took the time to think ahead.

Young people, if you follow these steps: pray, think and think ahead, the Lord will give you the inner peace and external guidance to help you make the right choice.

So now, you're ready for the last step.

DECIDE

When I say decide, I mean decide with confidence. Since the Lord has led you to this point, decide to walk on and stay on the road He has led you!

Good Morning!! How Are My College Buddies?

Here's few thoughts:

1. The road the Lord wants you on sometimes gets 'bumpy'. Walking in God's will doesn't make us immune from struggles. So don't automatically 'bail out' when life gets difficult.
2. Thank the Lord for His perfect plan for your life. This decision you have just made is a part of His good and perfect will for you.
3. Eventually you will see the fact that the Lord did lead you to the best choice! And that will help you depend upon Him more in future decisions.

College Buddies, nothing in this article is truly profound or brilliant. But I hope that you will go through these steps as you face your next decision:

PRAY THINK THINK AHEAD DECIDE

And then you will see the truth in this Bible verse:

"As for God, his way is perfect."
Psalm 18:30

Love You!!   Praying for You!!   Proud of You!!   Bro. Post
✶✶✶✶✶✶✶✶✶✶✶✶✶✶✶✶✶✶✶✶✶✶

"Breakable!! - Handle With Care"

Biblical Principles About How We Treat Other Christians
Rev. LaVon Post

Introduction

College Buddies, about once a year I write a long article about a subject that I feel is very important in our Christian lives. There are some areas that I cannot cover adequately in the short devotionals so I write a longer article, hoping it will be helpful.

You are part of a wonderful family!! It is God's family and I hope you feel welcome and joyful to be a part of your Father's family!! But when you think about it, every family has different members and there needs to be some principles about how these family members treat each other! If not, then the family can dissolve into bitterness and anger and vindictiveness.

Thankfully, our Father has given us some wonderful principles in the Bible concerning how we treat each other!! These words, from the Bible, can set us free to enjoy our brothers and sisters in Christ!! They can be a huge blessing to us and we can be a huge blessing to them!!

When we use these principles, it can be a beautiful experience. Watch a group of Christians who obey these principles and you will see an incredible witness for Christ. Deep spiritual affection, sincere compliments, happiness over another's joys, tender concern for another's burdens - these are some of the characteristics of Christians who treat each other Biblically.

However, no one can hurt you as deeply as a family member! When we ignore these Biblical principles on how to treat each other, then our behavior to each other can become very hurtful and spiritually destructive. Actually, sometimes Christians' behavior to others can be appalling and disgusting. Think about this. In my 30 years as a pastor, I have never seen a Christian hurt deeply by the criticism of an unbeliever. Oh, they may not have liked the criticism, but they were not deeply hurt. Sadly, I have counseled many times a Christian who was hurt deeply by the words or actions of another Christian - I've seen many weep, all were wounded, a few quit living for the Lord. Now we know why God gave us clear instructions on how to treat another family member: love them, enjoy them, but always remember:

Breakable! Handle With Care!!

Chapter 1: What a Family!!

Fast forward and imagine with me a family gathering...in heaven. Everyone's there, the Father and all of his children. Each child in the family is treated as a special dignitary. And they are special!! They receive a place of honor there, living with a Father who adores them and pampers them. Whenever they walk around heaven, angels are incredulous and amazed - after all, these are the very children of God

Good Morning!! How Are My College Buddies?

the Father......the ones for whom Jesus the Son died a brutal death on the cross.

No, we won't have any problem at all honoring and respecting and loving each other, once we get to heaven and realize fully how special we are!!

The tough part is recognizing that truth now!! How well do you recognize the 'specialness' of that Christian coworker, that Christian family member, that Christian neighbor.

I believe that this is the key to changing our attitude to other Christians...to realize how dearly they are loved by our Father.

When I was in seminary, the couple next door had an adorable 1 year old daughter. The couple absolutely adored their daughter and this little girl had won the hearts of all the seminary couples there. One day, the mom asked me if I would baby sit her for 2 hours, her regular baby sitter had cancelled. Sure, I thought, no problem. Problem is, I had never taken care of a toddler in my life. (What a joke!) I was extremely careful, even nervous. I watched her constantly to make sure she was ok. I pampered her, if she pointed at candy...yeah, I gave it to her. :-) This child was totally pampered and protected carefully for those 2 hours! The reason? I knew how much her mom and dad adored her!

We should have the same attitudes toward all Christians. Why should I sin by speaking evil of the son/daughter of a king?! Why would I be foolish enough to harm, by words or actions, the adored child of a king?! AND, if I DO mistreat a child of the

King...what does that say about MY feelings toward that King?!

Here's what the Bible says about this subject...... let's apply it to every Christian we know:

> "But you are a chosen people, a royal priesthood, a holy nation, a people belonging to God, that you may declare the praises of him who has called you out of darkness into his wonderful light." I Peter 2:9

Wow, what a family!! Where I live, you can upset people quickly by speaking evil or 'badmouthing' someone's child! It's like, "You don't belong to our family, stop talking about our family!" When it sinks in how special all of God's children are in HIS eyes, some changes start occurring in our hearts. We start learning how to keep our mouth shut - we refuse to highlight other's faults. We start learning to open our mouths - we frequently praise and compliment our family members. More about this later.

Chapter 2: True Equality...Get It?

All of God's children are loved equally...forgiven equally...cherished equally... and valued equally!

Treat Them That Way!

In God's family, there are no 'super saints' - children of His who are more important......or loved more. What a disgusting thought!! How insulting it is to our Father to imply that HE plays favorites with

His kids.......come on, surely you do not believe that He would do that?!

This truth of the equality of God's children is a precious and liberating truth in the Bible. But you know, we've ignored this truth and for centuries, we have established a spiritual 'caste' system and we have become experts at 'ranking' the saints!! Pathetic. Here are some of the ways that we implement our 'caste' system today:

POSITION IMPORTANCE: If someone's a minister, or a missionary, or a SS teacher........ you catch my drift. We put them on a pedestal and think that they are more important than other Christians!!

POSSESSION IMPORTANCE: We subconsciously give more respect to wealthy Christians. It's easy to do because we live in a culture of greed. But to assume that a Christian is more important because they own more? Ridiculous. (Actually, the ones I respect are the ones who own less, who struggle to pay the bills...and they still honor the Lord with their money. These are true inspirations to me.)

APPEARANCE IMPORTANCE: Yep, we do this also. We give preference to Christians who have physical beauty.......notice how many beauty pageant winners or athletes are asked to give testimonies in church.

POWER IMPORTANCE: To those in a position of power, we almost always show preference to them. So, if a person is a Christian congressman, does that position elevate his importance in God's eyes? Of course not.

Good Morning!! How Are My College Buddies?

NOTICE: This 'caste' system of giving preference to certain Christians, is EXACTLY what our American culture does. I believe that this is an example of 'worldliness' - allowing the culture that we live in to shape our attitudes, to squeeze us into their mold, not God's.

Ok, let's look at what the Bible teaches us: All of God's children are EQUAL: Equally Forgiven...... Equally Cherished by God.........Equally Valued in God's eyes!!

If I start treating Christians differently, because I place different values on them, if I use my 'caste system' to rate them......then I am an immature, worldly Christian.

College Buddies, we have to be careful here because the 'caste system' is so sneaky. Take two Christians who are caught in a sin.......one has sinned with inner greed or covetousness. The other Christian has stumbled in an outward, obvious sin of adultery. Then both of them repent and want to return to the Lord. Now which Christian will get hammered more? Shunned more? Which one will be received back more easily by other Christians? See my point? We are forgiven equally by God but it seems that we use a 'caste system' in offering forgiveness: we will forgive you as long as you don't do anything really bad! I bet a lot of churches would forgive quickly the covetous but place the adulterer on 'spiritual probation!' Sad, but it happens all the time.

We must remember that we are equally loved in God's eyes because of our position: WE ARE, VERY

SIMPLY, THE SONS AND DAUGHTERS OF THE GREATEST KING THAT THERE IS!!

We get into trouble when we rate people by profession: A minister is no greater in God's eyes than any other Christian, neither is missionary etc. God is not impressed by what we do......He is impressed by WHO we are – His precious, forgiven and adored kids.

Chapter 3: "No Way You Got a Problem Alone!"

One of the saddest things you will ever see is another Christian with a severe problem and that Christian is having to carry that burden alone. No way is this supposed to happen! Yet sadly, it happens all the time. God's plan is for a Christian never to carry a burden alone...His plan is for other Christians to help carry most of the load for that suffering Christian.

Think about what it's like to carry a burden alone. First, there are the concerns about the problem...worries about how it will work out. Just this process of constantly mulling over the problem is exhausting. Then there are 'panic times' - times in which the Christian imagines the worst scenario. Suppose there is no encouragement from another, no one there to help us to trust in God- now the believer's faith gets strained and weaker. When the suffering Christian doesn't have another Christian praying for them - often the burden is so heavy that the burdened Christian despairs. Think about the above scenario.......sadly, that is just what some of

Good Morning!! How Are My College Buddies?

your Christian brothers and sisters are enduring at this very moment.

Here's what the Bible says to all of us:

"Continue to bear one another's burdens and so fulfill the law of Christ."

Here is God's plan for all us: If you have a burden, it automatically becomes my burden! You are no longer in this trial alone, I and other Christians are right beside you, trusting God to deliver you.

I cannot tell you how important this ministry is!! It is a huge blessing to the suffering Christian!!

Don't ignore them, give them your COMPASSION: We see Jesus showing this....... His heart was often stirred with compassion. My favorite time is when He healed a leper - a man with a horrible, dreaded disease. Now the man had asked Jesus to heal him, he knew that if Jesus was willing, he would be healed. I love Jesus' response. The Bible says He was moved with compassion, He said "I am willing" to the leper. However, He did one other thing before He healed him. He actually reached out and TOUCHED the leper...Jesus placed His hand upon the revolting, odious skin of that man. Then He healed him.

Why would Jesus do that? I believe the touch of Jesus was how He showed His compassion. He actually identified with the man's problem. It certainly wasn't necessary for Him to touch the man, but He did.

Good Morning!! How Are My College Buddies?

How well do we reach out and 'touch' people with severe problems? It's always easier to try to love them 'long distance' - to try to share God's love far enough away that we do not feel burdened. This rarely works. God wants our actions and words to convince the suffering Christian that their 'alone' days are over...we are now right beside them in their suffering.

EXPECTANT FAITH: After you have shared God's `compassion with them, tell them that you are praying and expecting God to work in their lives. This so crucial because some Christians' trials are so severe that they have a hard time even believing God anymore! You believe God for them - use your faith to trust God for them!

Actually there is a clear example of this in the Bible. Remember the 4 men who ripped a hole in the roof? They had a friend who had been paralyzed for years and years. These 4 men believed Jesus would heal their friend, so they picked up the man on his mat, climbed to the top of a roof, tore a hole in it and lowered their friend down, directly in front of Jesus.

What the Bible says next is thrilling to me. It says that when Jesus saw their faith - the faith of the men on the roof - that He healed their friend. Think about that. It never mentions the faith of the paralyzed man, it mentions the faith of the 4 men who believed God on behalf of their friend!

Start doing that today, use your expectant faith to pray for a blessing for a Christian who is struggling. Their faith may be battered...use your faith to believe for them.

TENDER GENTLENESS: Here's the third gift you can give them, a gentle empathy that assures them that you really care about their suffering. It's amazing how helpful this is to the burdened Christian!! No longer I feel alone, there is actually another person who CARES that I am hurting!! I use to wonder why suffering Christians treasure this gentle empathy so much - after all, I may have gentle compassion, but I can't solve their problems. I think I now know the answer. When a Christian is hurting they long to know that God cares about them, that He still loves them. However, they can't see God, but they can see you. When you offer them God's compassion, you actually become a visual aid for them - you are becoming like Jesus to them!! Their faith is restored, they now believe God loves them and cares for them. Why? Because God has used you to love and care for them.

If all we offer them is Christian clichés, or just offer Bible verses......that does little good. What we should offer them is our heart...that allows them to open their heart...then we can share God's encouragement from the Bible. The results can be amazing!!

I do want to mention that if you will carry other Christian's burdens, it will be a HUGE joy and blessing to you. You will go to sleep at night thanking God for allowing you to be used in this beautiful ministry.

Got a problem in your life? It is really not yours, it belongs to all of us!! Know someone who has a problem? Guess what, it is your problem also!!

Let's ask God to help us joyfully bear each other's burdens.

Chapter 4: God's Talk or Street Talk?

The easiest way to see my mature faith is to listen to my words. The easiest way to see my immature, childish faith is to listen to my words. My words are a perfect mirror to my soul, my words show my sincere or immature faith.

Is this true? Actually, James states it even more strongly:

> "If any among you seem to be religious, but bridles not his tongue, this man's religion is worthless."

Wow, that's pretty blunt. There are two reasons why the Lord uses such strong language in describing the use of our tongue.

The first is the devastating damage that we can do - unbelievable harm and damage to others!!

The second reason is the unbelievable good that we can do for others, using the words that we say.

HERE'S A 'NO-NO' LIST OF WRONG WAYS TO SPEAK:

Profanity: Using God's name or sacred words in a baseless way.

Sacrilege: Taking the holy things about God and ridiculing them or debasing them. (Watch out for some jokes here, they may be funny, but some of them are definitely a sacrilege.)

Judging: Making assumptions about another's character.

Insinuation: Saying things in a way that implies the other person is guilty or inferior. 'Guilt trips'!!

Condescension: Saying things in a way that implies that the other person doesn't measure up to you, that they are inferior in this area that you are discussing, so you must enlighten them!! This is so insulting, but watch how often this happens among Christians! (Especially in sharing blessings with others. :-)

Gossip: Hearing something, assuming it is true, (boneheaded to do this! :-), then passing on what we have heard along to others. This can be so hurtful and so destructive!!

Slander: Here where many Christians have been deeply wounded. This involves telling others something that impugns, or throws mud on, the character of another. This may be done purposely, (lying slander), or involuntary, (passing along something that we think is true.) Slander is slander, it doesn't matter whether I'm lying or whether I think I am telling the truth! God will help me to keep my mouth shut. This is what I call 'Street Talk' - a vicious habit that does horrible harm. This is how Jesus was crucified - they had to make up a reason to crucify Him - so they just believed the 'Street Talk' about Him!

I could list some more, but these are enough. I hope you can catch a sense of how harmful our words can be!! David once prayed that the Lord would place a guard over his tongue, to protect him from sinning.

This is why I named this article, "Breakable! Handle With Care!"

The wonderful truth is that God can use our words to be a tremendous blessing!! Our words can act as spiritual medicine, to go to a person's heart and give encouragement and help to them.

Here is a list of wonderful ways to use our words:

Praise & Thanksgiving: Imagine how this thrills our Father's heart, to hear His kids use their words to praise Him and thank Him!! In your prayers, start telling your Father how wonderful He is and how awesome are His works!

Encouragement: Imagine someone drowning in tough trials. You then go to them and gently tell them you are praying and that God will help them. What a beautiful way to use your words!!

Affirmation: This is when you sincerely compliment a person, you point out things about them that you respect, areas in which they excel. This is a WONDERFUL ministry!! It 'lifts' people and helps them excel even more. Remember this: When the Apostle Paul wrote to the NT church, he started his letter with sincere compliments!! Let's use our words to do the same.

Witness: Obviously, God can use our words to tell others about His saving grace.

Singing: This is an incredible ministry. Our Music Minister has a beautiful voice. When she sings, often before I preach, the Holy Spirit prepares my heart, He encourages me through her ministry. Can you sing? Use that talent for the Lord!

Teaching: Some parts of the Bible aren't easily understood, we need teachers to make it clear to us.

Of course this is an incomplete list, but hopefully we can see the tremendous opportunities we have for the Lord to use our speech!! Let's dedicate our words to God and expect Him to use them for good, not for evil.

5. Agape Attitudes

In conclusion, there are certain 'love attitudes' that God wants us to always have in our hearts, controlling our actions and our words toward other Christians. These attitudes come from God Himself and He can fill us with these 'agape attitudes.'

Agape Love: This love is God's love. It basically means that we long and seek the best for others. We deeply want the very best for them in life and we know only God can give them the very best. It is a tender, sensitive love, this love causes us to look for ways to help others. This love makes the thought of harming someone in any way very repugnant to us! We ask God for ways to help others, we ask God to help us NEVER harm anyone.

Tenderheartedness, Compassion: This attitude allows us to actually feel part of the misery and suffering of others. We then are able to pray and help them more effectively.

Preference: This is the attitude of "You First." When we have this attitude, the needs and concerns of others take higher priority than your own needs. I know some Christians today that exhibit this beautiful quality. If I share a personal problem with them, it doesn't matter that they have worse problems, they will take my problem and help me carry it.

Forgiveness: The ability to put aside an offense and forgive from the heart. The easiest way to do this is to take time and remember how much God has forgiven us - then we can offer the same to others.

Kindness: Jesus showed gentleness and kindness. Kindness is like oil on a rusty hinge...kindness makes all of my relationships with others more rewarding and enjoyable.

College Buddies, when we allow God to fill us with these 'agape attitudes', then we truly treat other Christians in a way that honors our Father in Heaven.

Many of you, in English Literature, have read 'Ode To A Grecian Urn.' Suppose your professor had the exact urn that inspired John Keats to write this poem. Now the prof wants YOU to deliver the urn to a downtown museum.

How would you handle the urn? Would you jump in your car and toss it in the back seat? Would you carry this priceless urn carelessly under your arm? Of course not.

You would remember the tremendous VALUE of the urn and treat it accordingly. You would guard it, protect it, cherish it.

When it comes to value, you will never meet anyone more valuable to God than when you look at another Christian! Treat them accordingly, guard them, protect them, cherish them.

When we treat each other this way, filled with 'agape attitudes', then we truly understand the words of Jesus:

"By this shall everyone know that you are my disciples, if you have love one for another."

THE END

"On The Days That End in Why?"

A Strong God for Tough Times
Rev. LaVon Post

College Buddies, this article is about how God helps us in our rough times, on the days when it seems like your world has been turned upside down. One common experience of all Christians is that God occasionally allows us to go through tough times, days in which the circumstances are frightening and we are tempted to despair. These are the days that end in "Why?" College Buddies, the issue is not whether we will have tough times, the issue is when. This purpose of this article is help us think about the stages of a trial, from the frightening beginning to God's solution.

The reason I am writing this article is because many of you have written me recently and I have been amazed at the difficult trials that many of you are enduring at this present time. I have also been amazed at the current trials of people to whom I am their pastor. I hope this article is encouraging and that it gives you a renewed confidence in your Heavenly Father.

I. SOME WRONG REACTIONS TO TOUGH TIMES

   A. "God is punishing me, that's why this happened."

   Congratulations, you've just discovered the favorite lie of Satan. If your Enemy can convince you that this is true, then despair, disillusionment and desertion always follows.

   Think about how illogical this is!! If God wanted to punish me for my failures, then my life would be a constant trial!! For the rest of my life I would have a miserable time! Why? Because, I fail God DAILY! Not because I want to fail, but because I am still a flawed person until I get to heaven. On the very best days of my Christian life, I will, at times, still fail God in the way I speak, in the way I think and in the way I act. God would not have to look very far until He could find plenty of reasons to make my life miserable! College Buddies, we'll see later in the article the Biblical reasons for tough times, but please, please refuse to believe this!

B. "The only way that I can survive tough times is if my faith is strong enough."

Sounds ok, right? Not really. College Buddies, the issue is not how strong your faith is, the issue is how strong your God is! There are times in which I have seen excellent Christians in difficult times - their faith has taken a battering - they are worn out physically, emotionally devastated and spiritually in despair. Do they still have faith in God? Yes, but that faith is very weak. Then God moves in this situation and delivers them. Now if you talk them later, they will not talk about how strong their faith was in the trial - they will talk about how wonderful their Father was in the trial! Remember the poem about footsteps in the sand? These Christians will talk about how God carried them when they could not take another step. We'll think about this more later in this article.

C. "I will not survive this."

Yes you will, God will see to it. There is no such thing as a 'last straw' that breaks your back. You see, God's reputation is at stake in your life. Remember Job? Satan would have loved it if Job had not survived! But God helped Job and sustained him through some very fierce trials...and He will do the same for you. Now it's perfectly normal to have spiritual 'down times' in which you don't think you will survive!! David wrote beautiful psalms about these bleak times. But God won't leave you in these times, He has beautiful ways of encouraging you when we're down, and giving you hope in a storm. We'll see some of the ways He does this later.

I started this article with these wrong reactions to tough times because I have been amazed at the damage these wrong attitudes can cause!! As a pastor, I have heard these three wrong attitudes spoken to me many times. Please remember that the Enemy is the author of these lies and He would love for you to buy into them.

Satan has three goals for any Christian enduring tough times. First, he wants you to DESPAIR - to believe that you have no future and that God cannot or will not help you. Then he wants you to be DISILLUSIONED - that means he wants you to think that God has let you down and the Christian life is futile. Lastly, he wants you to DESERT God, for you to leave the Lord and no longer live for Him. And these three lies are his number one tool, you will hear them over and over again. So please, College Buddies, be forewarned.

Now let's look at God's tender help to us in the three stages of a trial.

STAGE ONE: BEWILDERMENT AND CONFUSION, FEAR AND PANIC

About 15 years ago, I received a phone call regarding a family in our church. The purpose of the call was to ask me to find this family and deliver to them some horrible, devastating news. I found the family enjoying a beautiful Saturday together, working on a house that they had just bought. They were laughing and enjoying their day together. If you would have been there with me, you would seen a clear picture of the first stage of a trial. As I gently told them the news, these four emotions overwhelmed them:

BEWILDERMENT CONFUSION FEAR PANIC

College Buddies, these initial feelings are NORMAL. These feelings come in different degrees, but they do come at the beginning of a trial. Notice how David describes his feelings when he was in a severe trial:

> "Be gracious to me, O Lord, for I am languishing; O Lord, heal me, for my bones are shaking with terror. My soul also is struck with terror ....I am weary with my moaning; every night I flood my bed with tears; I drench my couch with weeping." Psalm 42

Wow, King David was a man of faith and a very honest man!! He was hurting and afraid and panicky and he admitted that in his prayer to God.

There are good reasons why the first part of a trial is so tough. First, we often have little warning, we feel 'blind sided' - we're shaken badly and that leads to fear and panic. We feel highly vulnerable. Then our panic fuels our imagination - we catch ourselves imagining future scenarios, and all of them end in disaster! Then the Enemy starts whispering to us with those three lies. We don't sleep, at least not as well, and we don't eat as well.......Does any of this sound familiar?! :-)

If this does sound familiar, then you are a normal Christian - you're not inferior, you're not lost....... you are just normal, you're enduring what all Christians endure.

God is very gentle and kind to us in this first stage of a trial. He doesn't scold us and berate us for these feelings, He is waiting until we turn to Him. When we do turn to Him, then He starts the process of restoring our battered faith. Notice this beautiful verse:

> "I waited patiently for the Lord, he inclined to me and heard my cry. He drew me up out of the pit of tumult, out of the miry clay, and set my feet upon a rock, making my steps secure." Psalm 40:1-2

Notice two things about these verses: 1. The word 'inclined' is a graphic Hebrew word. It means to bend over and listen to the whisper of someone. It is a beautiful image of God's fatherly love to His child who is too weak to even speak. 2. Notice that David says that GOD lifted him up! That is our confidence, that God will work and release us from the misery of a trial.

What is God doing in our soul during the first stage of a trial? He is getting us to the point where we cry out to Him and trust HIM. When we do this, even though our feelings are ragged and our faith is battered, then He starts to work.

College Buddies, this is why I have recommended to you many times that you take a piece of paper and write out your problem. Put the date on it. "Dear God, I trust you about this problem. I believe you have the power to solve this in your perfect way. I now trust you." Sign it and place it in your Bible and leave it there until God answers.

If you are shaken and afraid, that's ok, you can still trust and commit. When you do commit this trial to the Lord, then the Lord brings you to the second stage of a trial.

STAGE TWO: SPIRITUAL PROGRESS IN THE MIDDLE OF THE TRIAL

When we commit our trial to the Lord, and ask Him to help us, it would SO nice if the Lord solved our problem immediately! However, the Lord rarely does that. There is almost always an interval between the time we commit the problem to Him and the time that He answers. This interval is actually the time in which we really grow, in the days in which we are still trusting God, even though the problem is not any better, or may even be worse!

If God solved our problem instantaneously, would we really need faith? Of course not. It is our faith in the MIDDLE of the fiery test that honors the Lord. It is this faith that gives us comfort in the miserable present, that God will create a better future.

This faith always settles us down and gives us peace. I do not mean that we don't have times of fear and dread, we do. What I do mean is that God can give us peace and confidence during the majority of the time. And this is incredible to experience and to watch others experience.

"And the peace of God, WHICH PASSES ALL UNDERSTANDING, will guard your hearts and minds in Christ Jesus." Philippians 4:7

This is the first blessing that God gives you in the middle of a trial: PEACE.

But the Lord doesn't stop there, He always gives you another blessing: PROGRESS. He actually enables us to function and make progress in all areas of our lives, even though we are carrying the burden of tough times. He enables us to get out of bed, get dressed, go to work or class, assume our duties, perform them and make progress. This in itself is a wonderful witness for Christ! Why? Because now you are showing others, BY YOUR ACTIONS, that you actually believe that God will work, that He will solve the problem. Remember the ten lepers that Jesus healed in the Bible? Jesus told them to first go show themselves to the priest. Why? I believe that

Good Morning!! How Are My College Buddies?

Jesus was waiting until they turned to walk toward the temple, THEN He healed them. Jesus wanted them to show by their actions that they believed that He would solve their problem.

About 7 years ago, a wonderful minister came and preached a series at the church where I was the pastor. This minister is an excellent preacher. (I took lots of notes! :-) He preached noon and evening services, he visited the sick, he spent time encouraging us. On the day before he was to leave, he told me that when he got back home in Louisiana, he would immediately have surgery for cancer. I was stunned, but I really shouldn't have been. You see, God was giving this man PEACE and helping him make PROGRESS. The Lord will do the same for you and me.

However, this does not mean that we will not have spiritually 'down times', times in which our faith gets a little ragged. This is perfectly normal! In the middle of a trial, all of us have occasions when we struggle. The great thing is that we can be spiritually proactive, we can actually stop ourselves and refocus our faith in God. It is VERY important to know this and to practice this! Notice these two scriptures about King David, how he refocused his faith:

> "David was in danger, because all the people spoke of stoning him, because all the people were bitter (at him). But David ENCOURAGED HIMSELF in the Lord his God." I Sam. 30:6

David writes: "Why are you cast down, O my soul, and why are you disquieted (shook up!) within me? Hope in God; for I shall again praise Him, my help and my God." Psalm 42:11

Wow, I love David's honesty!! He was so real, I can relate to him. "Ok, I am having a rough time. Everything has gone south in a hand basket! I don't see any way that this can work out. AND I am really shook up and scared!! (Even a little ticked off!) But right now, I am turning this over to God and I believe that He will work this out so that in the future, I will praise Him for solving this mess!"

This is proactive faith. This is faith that helps you sleep at night. This is faith that gives you hope in a storm.

College Buddies, when we are in a trial, the first stage is always CONFUSION and FEAR. That's ok, when you commit it to the Lord, then you enter the second stage of PEACE and PROGRESS. Eventually the Lord takes us to the third stage.

STAGE THREE: DELIVERANCE FROM THE TRIAL

This is always on God's timetable. He knows how long to allow us to stay in the heat of the problem, He also knows the perfect time to relieve the pressure. Some Christians believe that God will solve every problem immediately, if we have enough faith. They say that if we still have the problem, then it's because we don't have enough faith. This is one of the cruelest things I have ever heard, this false idea causes struggling Christians to sink even further in despair. (I won't say anything else about this, this causes my blood pressure to rise! :-)

The truth is that God knows each of His children perfectly - He knows the exact amount of time to allow us to struggle and He knows the perfect time to deliver us. He is a kind, gentle, patient and loving parent, and He is deeply in love with His kids.

But He also knows that we can only learn some things in the fire of a trial. Here are some of things He teaches us.

1. He IS in control and He DOES have the power to protect us.
2. He uses us, in a trial, to 'preach' great sermons to other people – your example becomes a tremendous encouragement to others who are struggling.
3. He makes our heart more tender and compassionate - afterwards we are better prepared to comfort others.
4. He makes us more like Christ through this process. It is a lot like a silversmith, who takes the silver and places it in intense heat. During this time of heat, the impurities in the silver is burned away. The silversmith knows when the process is successful - when the silversmith can see his own reflection in the silver.
5. And the Lord WILL turn down the heat! He will ease the trouble, solve the problem, restore happiness again. The result is that you will feel a deep sense of gratitude to your Father.

Good Morning!! How Are My College Buddies?

One thing to remember: In the Bible, when God solved someone's problems, He either did it all at once, or in stages or increments. Again, He chooses the best way to do this, the way that honors Him.

College Buddies, I hope these simple thoughts are helpful. I love each of you very much and I want God's best for each of you. Because of this, I want to remind you that you will have occasional rough times in life – not because you are a poor Christian, but because you are a good Christian.

Your Father won't let you down, He's right beside you in the dreary days and the long nights. He will see to it that you are protected and that you grow in these miserable times. Please ask your Father to give you peace and to help you make progress - In The Days That End in "Why?"

Love You!!   Praying for You!!   Proud of You!!   Bro. Post

LaVergne, TN USA
30 June 2010
187940LV00001B/1/P